Theologia Prima

Theologia Prima

What Is Liturgical Theology?

Second Edition

David W. Fagerberg

Hillenbrand Books®

Chicago / Mundelein, Illinois

Theologia Prima: What Is Liturgical Theology? Second Edition
© 2004 Archdiocese of Chicago: Liturgy Training Publications,
3949 South Racine Avenue, Chicago, IL 60609; 800-933-1800;
fax: 800-933-7094; email: orders@ltp.org. Website: www.ltp.org.
All rights reserved.

Hillenbrand Books® is an imprint of Liturgy Training Publications (LTP)
and the Liturgical Institute/University of St. Mary of the Lake. The
Hillenbrand Series is focused on contemporary theological thought concerning the liturgy of the Catholic Church. Further information about
Hillenbrand Books® is available from LTP or from www.usml.edu/liturgical
institute.org; phone: 847-837-4542. University of St. Mary of the Lake
/Mundelein Seminary, 1000 East Maple, Mundelein, IL 60060.

This book was edited by Kevin Thornton. Anna Manhart and Larry Cope
designed the series. Larry Cope designed the cover. Jim Melody-Pizzato was
the production artist and coordinator.

The index was compiled by Mary Laur. The cover photo is by Image Club
Graphics, Inc.

Printed in the United States of America

Library of Congress Control Number: 2012941960

ISBN: 978-1-59525-039-1

23 22 21 20 19   4 5 6 7 8

HTPP

To Sharon Balcom
and "the doctrinaires" at the Church of the Nativity
who taught me Catholic liturgical theology

Contents

Preface

This is a second edition of my 1992 book, *What Is Liturgical Theology? A Study in Methodology*. It is both gratifying and discomforting to revisit expressions and categories more than ten years old. At the time it was being written, it was being thought. Now the understanding of liturgical theology I was then trying to attain is with me constantly, conditioning all my theological reading and thinking. Returning to first efforts feels a little like listening to a tape recording of your voice from adolescence. I have not changed my mind, but my voice has changed. The way I understand and explain liturgical theology has continued to unfold. This presented a problem in how aggressive to be in editing this second edition. On the one hand, there was the temptation to change the book to reflect all the new sources and images and authors that have visited me since then; on the other hand, there was a risk of putting new wine in old wineskins. Were I to clutter the text with too many additional thoughts, then the original work would not only lose its identity, but the chapters might lose their coherence.

The solution I have struck upon is to confine completely new material to completely new chapters. The first and last chapters were written for this second edition. The former reflects an element of liturgical theology I had overlooked the first time, and the latter is less a conclusion than it is an invitation to the reader to begin considering the consequences of liturgical theology. As for the material in between, no paragraph has been left untouched, but the changes I have made were more in appearance and form than in content. The material has been divided into chapters differently, in an attempt to be friendlier to a course syllabus, and it has been shortened a bit overall. I have kept a shortened introduction to the work of Prenter, Vajta, Brunner, and Wainwright for illustrative purposes, but not in the detail of the first edition. I hope these changes have made this second edition more direct and forthright, and of interest to a greater audience, because I am persuaded that this understanding of liturgical theology has consequences beyond the academy for both theology and liturgy.

Liturgical theology is normative for the larger theological enterprise because it is the trysting place where the sources of theology function precisely as sources. Liturgical theology is furthermore normative for liturgical renewal because such efforts should arise out of the tradition of the Church and not our individual preferences. The subject matter of theology is God, humanity, and creation, and the vortex in which these three existentially entangle is liturgy.

My working definition of liturgical theology continues to be owed to Alexander Schmemann, Aidan Kavanagh, and Robert Taft. I take the term to mean the theological work of the liturgical assembly, not the work done by an academic upon liturgical material. It may seem easier to approach the idea as theology considered in the light of liturgy, or liturgy considered in the light of theology, but I consider this approach misleading because it leaves the impression that there are two subjects (liturgy and theology) instead of one subject (liturgical theology). The simple aim of this book remains the same: to gain some clarity in understanding about the shape and deployment of the term "liturgical theology" by proposing a distinction between it and other ways theologians treat worship. Rather than saying liturgical theology occurs wherever theology places liturgy upon its list of discussion topics, or wherever piety leaves the church to enter the scholar's study, I propose two defining attributes of liturgical theology: it is *theologia prima* and it is found in the structure of the rite, in its *lex orandi*. It recognizes that the liturgical community does genuine theology, although admittedly of a primary and not secondary kind, and it recognizes that the law of prayer establishes the Church's law of belief. Liturgical theology is the faith of the Church in ritual motion, as Kavanagh was fond of saying; a genuine theology, but one manifested and preserved in the rite as *lex orandi* even before it is parsed systematically.

The new tone running throughout the present edition comes from my increasing conviction that in order for us to grasp this, the modern concept of liturgy must be enlarged and the scope of theology increased. From having observed how the first edition was received, I have increased my focus in this edition upon the impact that the synthetic whole (liturgical theology) must have on our understanding of the parts (liturgy and theology). In other words, I do not think liturgy dilutes theology; I think liturgical theology dilates our understanding of both liturgy and theology. The result is a concept of liturgy and theology that I think is closer to what the early Church possessed, and which we would do well to recover. In attempting that recovery, I have become conscious of the importance of an element that went relatively unnoticed in the first edition. I refer to asceticism.

As an example of the kind of seeds planted by mentors while their students are unaware, only to blossom later, I find these words from Kavanagh at the very outset of his book *On Liturgical Theology:*

> Far from being something esoteric to Christianity, asceticism is native to the Gospel and is required of all. Specifically monastic asceticism was generated, it seems, in that same process by which living the Gospel began to take on ecclesial form in the earliest Jewish-Christian churches. . . . One must therefore take the continuing fact of organized asceticism in Christian life as a given which provides access to whole dimensions of Christian perception and being. The existence, furthermore, of specifically monastic asceticism is a theological datum which lies close to the very nerve center of Christian origins and growth. One cannot study Christianity without taking monasticism into account. One cannot live as a Christian without practicing the Gospel asceticism which monasticism is meant to exemplify and support. A Christian need not be a monk or nun, but every monk and nun is a crucial sort of Christian. . . .

At the time of the first edition I was still discovering asceticism's place, but now I consider it of crucial importance if we are to understand how Mrs. Murphy (Kavanagh's famed practitioner of liturgical theology) can be called a liturgical theologian. A fuller articulation of liturgical asceticism will have to wait for a forthcoming work, but I have given it greater representation in this revision.

Christianity involves liturgy, theology, and asceticism the way a pancake involves flour, milk, and eggs: They are ingredients to the end result. Leave one out and you don't have exactly the same thing anymore. Liturgy is a substantially theological enterprise; asceticism is a product of and prerequisite for Christian liturgy; liturgy and theology integrate by ascetical means. I do not see myself trying to coordinate two dyads (liturgical theology and liturgical asceticism), but I see myself trying to understand how the terms in one triad (liturgy-theology-asceticism) relate to each other. The horizontal base line of the triangle is liturgy. "Seek the reason why God created," Maximus the Confessor counseled, "for that is knowledge." This wisdom is possessed by the liturgical theologian, and liturgical asceticism is the price of its possession.

It is almost worth the effort of writing a book for the opportunity to publicly acknowledge the graces one has received along the way; it is certainly worth the effort of revising one. That revision has been done at the University of St. Mary of the Lake/Mundelein Seminary, and I am grateful for the friendships forged during the creation of the Liturgical Institute there, especially for the support given by the rector, Father John Canary, and academic dean, Father John Lodge. I am indebted to my friend, Monsignor Francis Mannion, for extending the invitation to come to the Liturgical Institute. I owe John Cavadini thanks for a critical read of the first chapter, and am honored to be joining him, and all my new colleagues, at the University of Notre Dame. Kevin Thornton oversees the Hillenbrand imprint of books at Liturgy Training Publications for the Liturgical Institute, and his commitment to this project brought it about. His editorial suggestions also helped keep me focused on the forest for the trees. And, finally, if I am speaking of graces received, I must name Elizabeth again, with whom I have now been 30 years in sacrament. Plato thought the shadows cast by the fire in the cave was an inferior kind of knowledge compared to what could be seen in clear, abstract light. I have had fun dragging these ideas once more into an abstract light, but Plato was wrong: The knowledge there is nothing as compared to the things that I have seen by the light of the hearth fire in the domestic church.

Part I

What Is Liturgical Theology?

Chapter 1

Deepening the Grammar of Liturgy

The need to deepen the grammar by which we speak about liturgy is readily evident from certain attitudes exhibited toward liturgy. Aidan Kavanagh commented on having seen an advertisement for a summer course called "Creative Worship" in which participants were to be taught how to "creatively use liturgy, liturgical robes, banners and stoles." Even if this course is no longer on the books, it reveals an attitude that can still be found easily enough, and Kavanagh's response remains fully applicable: "The relationship of embroidery to the driving of a diesel locomotive seems easier to demonstrate than the connection between stoles and proclaiming the Gospel. Something here seems to have been enthusiastically trivialized."[1] This work seeks to join the opposition to that trivialization. It seeks to understand Alexander Schmemann when he calls liturgy the *locus theologicus par excellence*,[2] and Kavanagh when he calls liturgy the place where the church transacts its faith in God under the condition of God's real presence in both church and world,[3] and Robert Taft when he calls liturgy nothing less than the ongoing saving work of God's Only-begotten Son.[4] The tradition once connected liturgy, theology, and asceticism easily and naturally and necessarily, and that is the tradition I am trying to understand. I do not want to dilute theology with liturgy, I want to dilate our grammar of liturgy until our Christian doctrine and our Christian life find their rightful home there.

I borrow the metaphor of grammar from Ludwig Wittgenstein, a linguistic philosopher for whom the analysis of language was the way into a concept. He once remarked, almost casually, that "theology is a grammar."[5] I take this to mean that it is one thing to know theological words, and another thing to know how to use words theologically. Wittgenstein thought it was wrong to think of words possessing meanings in themselves, and preferred to say that people mean by using words. We use words to mean with. By our words we express meaning. Therefore a word's meaning is found in how it is used, in its grammar, in how it plays in what Wittgenstein called a "language game."[6] To know the meaning of a word is not just to know its ostensive definition from the dictionary; it requires knowing how to play with the word in its language game. Wittgenstein illustrated his point by observing how different it is to know the name of a chess piece (say, a knight or a queen) from being able to move it effectively on the board during a game.

It is possible to speak meaningfully, therefore, even if one is not a professional grammarian. One can use a grammar even if one cannot describe a grammar. Paul Holmer notes that when we acquire mastery of a language "we do not speak the grammar itself but we say everything else in accord with the rules we have already learned. The more skilled we become in writing or speaking, the more does our knowledge of grammar inform everything we say and write."[7] The reason one can use words intelligibly and intelligently even if one cannot parse the sentence is because grammar is first of all a tool to use, and second, a subject to examine. Grammar books are for specialists who reflect on or study the nature of language, but the grammar itself is for anyone who wishes to say something. People use grammar tacitly: They look through the grammar at the subject at hand.[8] The subject matter of a grammar book is grammar, but the subject matter of a grammatical sentence can be anything. The professional grammarian may be of regular help to the speaker, but the speaker has a priority over the grammarian that should not be denied.

Similarly, it is possible to be an intelligent theologian even if one is not an academic theologian. The academic theologian may be of regular help to the liturgical community, but there is a priority here, too, that should not be denied. It is possible to speak theologically even if one does not have that specialized knowledge about how the deposit of faith has been parsed systematically or historically. Liturgy creates a Christian grammar in the people of God who live through the encounter with the paschal mystery, and then have something to say. But what they have to say is usually about God, and not about ritual! They may therefore be said to speak theologically, even if they have not made theology their topic of conversation. So Holmer concludes, "If theology is like a grammar, and certainly it is, then it follows that learning theology is not an end in itself. . . . [Theology] is the declaration of the essence of Christianity, . . . [its] aim is not that we repeat the words. Theology must also be absorbed, and when it is, the hearer is supposed to become Godly."[9]

Liturgical theology may therefore be called faith's grammar in action—a genuine theology, but one manifested and preserved in the community's *lex orandi* (law of prayer) even before it is parsed into *lex credendi* (law of belief). It is discovered in the structure of the liturgy, which shapes the lives of liturgists. Kavanagh was fond of calling liturgy the faith of the Church in motion. "This means that the liturgy of a church is nothing other than that church's faith in motion on certain definite and crucial levels. . . . Thus a church's worship does not merely reflect or express its repertoire of faith. It transacts the church's faith in God under the condition of God's real presence in both church and world."[10] In my language game, the structure of the liturgical *lex orandi* I call liturgical theology, and the process of shaping lives I call liturgical asceticism. The liturgy doesn't just make the thinker think doxologically, or theologize prayerfully; it forms a believer whose life is theological.

There was a time in Christian tradition when liturgy interpenetrated both theology and asceticism. Absorbing theology to the point of becoming Godly was an ascetical capacitation for liturgical theology. Yves Congar's historical survey of the word *theologia* reflects this evolution within the context of asceticism. Although the term had its roots in the Greek philosophers (Plato used it to point out the educational value of mythology, and Aristotle identified it with metaphysics because the divine is present in all being), Congar observes that Christians narrowed *theologia* to mean knowledge of divine things, beginning with Clement of Alexandria who called it a science of divinity, and Origen, for whom the term meant a doctrine about God—which for Christians meant teachings about Christ. By the time of Eusebius of Caesarea, *theologia* had been so associated with the Savior that when Christians applied the term to the pagan gods they had to qualify it as "false theology." Christians used *theologia* to refer to Sacred Scripture itself because it contained true theology (Dionysius recognized a mystical theology, too[11]). Athanasius could use the term simply to refer to the doctrine of the Trinity. Even so, these Christian theologians worked from a concept of God's transcendence that was even greater than that of the Neoplatonic philosophers. God cannot be explained, and God cannot be known, but by his will God has become participable. That is why *theologia* took on special meaning with the monks and mystical writers. Congar therefore concludes that for the fathers, theology meant

> a knowledge of God which is either the highest form of the gnosis or of that illumination of the soul by the Holy Spirit which is more than an effect since it is the very substance of its divinization or godlike transformation. For Evagrius Pontikus, followed by Maximus Confessor and others, *theologia* is the third and the most elevated of the degrees of life. In short, it is that perfect knowledge of God which is identified with the summit of prayer.[12]

Climbing to the summit of prayer is an arduous business. Reaching this liturgical zenith requires a disciplined training, which is just what the word *askesis* means. The root of the word *asceticism* implied a training designed to produce a specific character or pattern of behavior. Used of an athlete, it referred to the training one underwent in order to accomplish a goal. Evagrius of Pontus went to the deserts of Egypt in the fourth century to train with these athletic monks, and he systematized their discoveries. Evagrius spoke of three stages: first, an initial ordering of basic passions *(praktike);* second, a contemplation of nature *(theoria physike)* whereby the world is known as it truly is by reflecting on scripture's revelation; and third, contemplation of the Holy Trinity—which is synonymous with *theologia* itself. Within this context, theology is less the fruit of a graduate program at university, and rather the fruit of a rightly-ordered existence. But while the ascetical capacity for theology may have been brought to perfection in the sands of the desert, it is born in the waters of the font. As Kavanagh says, "Ascetics blaze the trail all must follow, but they do not walk it alone."[13]

This book will speak about liturgical theology, but in order to apprehend the term adequately our ideas of liturgy and theology and asceticism must be adjusted. This first chapter explores their interconnection. It discovers that liturgy is the place of communion with God; that asceticism is the imitation of Christ by a liturgist; and that the end of liturgical asceticism is sharing God's life, rightly called *theologia.* Being a theologian means being able to use the grammar learned in liturgy to speak about God. Even more, it means speaking of God. Yet even more, it means speaking with God. That's why Evagrius of Pontus calls prayer theology ("If you are a theologian you truly pray. If you truly pray you are a theologian"[14]), and why I think liturgical theology involves liturgical asceticism. Before there were universities with theology faculties, it was possible to learn and to use this theological grammar.

Asceticism was especially integrated with theology as a liturgical consequence in Eastern Christianity. In saying this, I do not imply it is absent in the West. The scholastics knew that theology was not like other human sciences. In Congar's words, they understood theology as "an extension of faith, which is a certain communication and a certain sharing of God's knowledge." Theology's object is not only the knowledge of a generic divine subject, but also "a certain *constructio ipsius subjecti,* namely, the construction of God in us, or rather the construction of Christ in us."[15] But with the relocation of theology to the university auditorium, the harmonization of liturgy, theology, and asceticism might have become less recognizable in the West, and there may be benefit in tuning our ears to voices from the East. Tomas Spidlik's digest of Eastern spirituality notes that the Eastern Fathers "understood the practice of theology only as a personal communion with *Theos,* the Father, through the *Logos,* Christ, in the Holy Spirit—an experience lived in a state of prayer."[16] Theology was as much a practice as a cognition. Asceticism is the path to prayer; prayer in the Spirit is the Christian liturgical life in practice; this gives rise to perfect knowledge, which is the path to theology. Commenting on Maximus the Confessor, Georges Berthold defines theology as "direct communion with God in pure prayer, and 'to theologize' is to pray in spirit and in truth."[17]

To make sense of such remarks will require a different grammar of liturgy—a deeper grammar, one in which the word *liturgical* is more than just an emotional adjective. The liturgy is participation by the body of Christ in the activity of the Trinity; the Church's ritual activity is itself theological; and asceticism is the capacitation of the baptized for that participation. I do not seek to *add* liturgy to asceticism or theology; rather I seek to enlarge our understanding of liturgy by discovering its very theological and ascetical dimensions. Although the phrase "liturgical theology" contains two words, only one thing is being named. The two words together reference an organically single phenomenon, and both words are necessary for a full understanding. The task is not to glue together two heterogeneous realities, resulting in either a theological appraisal of liturgy or a doxological appraisal of theology; the task is to name the ritualized response by the body of Christ to the activity of the Trinity. This response is itself, in its ritual form, theological.

Liturgical theology is theology that is liturgically embodied. The phrase is a complex name (in the philosophical sense of being multiple) of a simple reality (in the philosophical sense of being one indivisible thing). Put colorfully, liturgical theology is not yellow liturgy marbles mixed with blue theology marbles to make a jar full of yellow and blue marbles: Liturgical theology is green marbles. Or, to use a more dignified example, liturgical theology is simple in the way a human being is simple. The scholastics said form and matter make one substance, so that a human being, although both soul and body, is one substantial being, not two. Liturgical theology is simple in the same way a human being is simple. It is no more appropriate to speak of bridging liturgy with theology or asceticism than it is appropriate to speak of bridging soul and body, when the human being cannot be understood apart from soul or apart from body. Liturgy and asceticism and *theologia* cannot be understood apart from each other. This means liturgy is not ritual cliché in need of theological additives and supplemental spiritualities. But so long as liturgy is misperceived in this manner, the widespread mistake will continue to spread even more widely that liturgical renewal has more to do with relocating furniture in the sanctuary than with reallocating hearts to God. Liturgical asceticism capacitates the liturgist. Christian asceticism is a substantially liturgical activity.

Enlarging Our Terms

One way to enlarge our grammar of liturgy might be to change our use of the word *liturgist*. I do not use it in either of two conventional ways. Ordinarily, a liturgist is thought to be either the person who might want to read (or even write) a book like this one, or else the person who remembers to order the branches for Palm Sunday. That is, the person we ordinarily call "liturgist" is the one who conducts classes, or conducts choirs. But this does overlook one very significant person. When a verb is turned into a noun, the subject is usually the one who commits the action: A wrestler is one who wrestles, a builder is one who builds, and a plumber is one who plumbs. So also, I would like to primarily call by the name "liturgist" the one who commits liturgy, and only secondarily the one who studies it or directs it.

If, as will be made clear below, liturgy names an action, then we ought to be directed to the ones who do that action. Liturgists make up the Church, and the Church is made up of liturgists, and the word *liturgist* can be used as virtually synonymous with *baptized* or with *laity* to name the members of the mystical body of Christ.

The roots of this viewpoint are in the doctrine of creation. It is a doctrine that places man and woman, as microcosm, at the interface between the spiritual realm and the material realm. Louis Bouyer pictures it in this way:

> The tradition of the Fathers has never admitted the existence of a material world apart from a larger creation, from a spiritual universe. To speak more precisely, for them the world, a whole and a unity, is inseparably matter and spirit. . . . Across this continuous chain of creation, in which the triune fellowship of the divine persons has, as it were, extended and propagated itself, moves the ebb and flow of the creating *Agape* and of the created *eucharistia*. Descending further and further towards the final limits of the abyss of nothingness, the creating love of God reveals its full power in the response it evokes, in the joy of gratitude in which, from the very dawn of their existence creatures freely return to him who has given them all. Thus this immense choir of which we have spoken, basing ourselves on the Fathers, finally seems like an infinitely generous heart, beating with an unceasing diastole and systole, first diffusing the divine glory in paternal love, then continually gathering it up again to its immutable source in filial love.[18]

Man and woman were created as rational liturgists of the material world and placed at the apex of the systolic action in order to translate the praise of mute matter into speech and symbol. I am interested in rediscovering an understanding of this cosmological priesthood by seeing Christ's priesthood as the eschatological recapitulation of Adam and Eve's dignity. The fall was the forfeiture of our liturgical career. The economy of God, climaxing in Christ's paschal mystery, was the means to restore it.

Therefore, this cosmological priesthood in the structure of the world should not be confused with either the Church's common priesthood of the laity, or the Church's ministerial priesthood of the ordained. The latter two are for the healing of the first. The common priesthood of the laity is directed toward the cure of this now corrupted structure of the world, and the ministerial priesthood is at the service of the common priesthood to equip them for their lay apostolate. The *Catechism of the Catholic Church* seems to be describing the liturgical job description of the baptized when it says, "The whole community of believers is, as such, priestly since the faithful exercise their baptismal priesthood through their participation, each according to his own vocation, in Christ's mission as priest, prophet, and king."[19] In order to equip and capacitate this common priesthood of his body, Christ instituted the ministerial priesthood, which is "directed at the unfolding of the baptismal grace of all Christians. The ministerial priesthood is a *means* by which Christ unceasingly builds up and leads his Church."[20] The clergy alone is not Church, with lay spectators; and the laity alone is not Church, with hired ordained leaders. Therefore, "though they differ from one another in essence and not only in degree, the common priesthood of the faithful and the ministerial or hierarchical priesthood are nonetheless interrelated: each of them in its own special way is a participation in the one priesthood of Christ."[21]

Liturgical theology is derivative from the liturgists' encounter with God. Liturgical theology materializes upon the encounter with the Holy One, not upon the secondary analysis at the desk. God shapes the community in liturgical encounter, and the community makes theological adjustment to this encounter, which settles into ritual form. Only then can the analyst begin dusting the ritual for God's fingerprints.

These methodological assertions affect the arena where we can expect liturgy to operate, as well as the density of our concept of liturgy. Two uses of the term *liturgical* must be accounted for, and I shall suggest one be called thin, the other thick. Paul Holmer has said, "Liturgy is not an expression of how people see things; rather it proposes, instead, how God sees all people."[22] I propose that liturgy in its thin sense is an expression of how we see God; liturgy in its thick sense is an expression of how God sees us. Temple decorum and ritual protocol is liturgy only in its thin sense; in its thick sense, liturgy is theological and ascetical. Both senses are true and necessary, and one way of constructing the question would be to ask how thick liturgy is expressed in its ritual form (thin). I take this thicker meaning, residing behind the rubrics, to be what Alexander Schmemann means when he identifies the proper object of liturgical theology:

To find the Ordo behind the "rubrics," regulations and rules—to find the unchanging principle, the living norm or "logos" of worship as a whole, within what is accidental and temporary: this is the primary task which faces those who regard liturgical theology not as the collecting of accidental and arbitrary explanations of services but as the systematic study of the *lex orandi* of the Church. This is nothing but the search for or identification of that element of the *Typicon* which is presupposed by its whole content, rather than contained by it. . . .[23]

A problem arises, however, when we limit ourselves to speaking only about the thin sense. In that case, it's hard to imagine liturgical theology meaning anything more than devotional affectation, and "it's hard to imagine liturgical asceticism meaning anything more than the songbooks monks used. Liturgy is more than rubric, like music is more than score. Just as the word *music* can name either the notes or the act of making music, so the word *liturgy* (thin) can name the ritual score or a supernatural dynamic (thick).

The Church can modify the liturgy, but only in its thin sense. In its thick sense, it is liturgy that creates the Church: a theological corporation, Kavanagh said,[24] and practitioners of asceticism. It is my overarching objective to keep this thicker liturgical grammar before the face of liturgical studies curricula. Failing this, liturgy is relegated in divinity schools to practical "how to" courses for ecclesiastics who get a thrill out of rubrical tidiness, and in the academy at large it is relegated to departments of history or anthropology or comparative ritual, if it is studied at all. Sometimes it is treated as a branch of spirituality, i.e., the doxological titillation of the otherwise stolid theological mind. Sometimes it is handled as a branch of history, and as historians might treat the creeds or papal documents they might likewise investigate an obscure medieval psalter. Sometimes it is subsumed under a branch of systematics, usually sacramentology, but also under various "theologies of . . ." worship, prayer, doxology, and so forth. And finally, and increasingly in vogue, liturgy is made into a branch of ritual studies that attempts an uncritical report of the worship protocols practiced by any given community. These branches of academic study are inadequate to fully comprehend liturgy because, as Taft bluntly says, "Liturgy, therefore, is theology. It is not history or cultural anthropology or archeology or literary criticism or esthetics or philology or pastoral care."[25]

Liturgy (whose grammar we are trying to discover in its amplitude) had a larger meaning when Christians borrowed it in the first place. *Leitourgia* was "the usual designation for a service performed by an individual for the state (often free of charge)."[26] "In classical Greek, liturgy *(leitourgia)* had a secular meaning; it denoted a work *(ergon)* undertaken on behalf of the people *(laos)*. Public projects undertaken by an individual for the good of the community in such areas as education, entertainment or defense would be *leitourgia*."[27] The word became especially appropriate to name religious cult, that complex of actions that surrounded public services done in the name of the city, "because they were linked to its most vital interests. In a culture permeated by religious values (as most of the traditional cultures were), 'liturgy' thus understood was predicated first and foremost of actions expressing the city's relations to the world of divine powers on which it acknowledged itself to be dependent."[28] The mark of liturgy was its reference to the organized community. A work, then, done by an individual or a group was a liturgy on behalf of the larger community to which he, she, or they belonged. As Schmemann puts it:

> It meant an action by which a group of people become something corporately which they had not been as a mere collection of individuals—a whole greater than the sum of its parts. It meant also a function or "ministry" of a man or of a group on behalf of and in the interest of the whole community. Thus the *leitourgia* of ancient Israel was the corporate work of a chosen few to prepare the world for the coming of the Messiah. . . . Thus the Church itself is a *leitourgia*, a ministry, a calling to act in this world after the fashion of Christ, to bear testimony to him and His kingdom.[29]

Liturgy was an act of largesse; it required magnanimity; it was not a domestic act for one's kith and kin, but a public act for the community in which one dwelled.

That means there is something wrong with thinking liturgy is the work of the clergy on behalf of the laity (clericalism), or with thinking that liturgy is not valid unless everyone has a share in the work of the ministerial priesthood (laicism). In fact, liturgy is the work of Christ on behalf of the vital interests of the clan to which he belongs: the family of Adam and Eve. Christ is the premier liturgist, head of a body animated by the Holy Spirit, and so it is Christ's work that the Church performs—which is to say the thick liturgy done by the Church must always and only be Christ's liturgy, never its own. The sacramental power of baptism creates the people of God *(laos)* and commissions them to perform Christ's work *(ergon)*. That's where liturgists come from: They are regenerated. Christ is the firstborn of many little liturgists who perpetuate a Christic, kenotic, salutary, sacerdotal, prophetic, and royal work.

The liturgy is therefore both our product and not our work at all. It is why the presiding celebrant is said to be an *alter Christus.* Romano Guardini saw the difference between the eucharistic memorial and other types of memorial in the fact that Jesus did not say, "On a certain day of the year you are to come together and share a meal in friendship. . . ." Such an act would issue from the humanly possible, Guardini says, and only the event it was celebrating would be divine.

> Christ spoke differently. His "do these things" implies "things I have just done"; yet what He did surpasses human possibility. It is an act of God springing as incomprehensibly from His love and omnipotence as the acts of Creation or the Incarnation. And such an act He entrusts to men! He does not say: "Pray God to do thus," but simply "do." Thus he places in human hands an act which can be fulfilled only by the divine . . . God determined, proclaimed, and instituted; man is to execute the act. When he does so, God makes of it something of which He alone is capable.[30]

Cultic Antinomy

The fact that the Church finally adopted the word *leitourgia* to name her cult "indicates her special understanding of worship, which is indeed a revolutionary one. If Christian worship is *leitourgia,* it cannot be simply reduced to, or expressed in terms of, 'cult.' The ancient world knew a plethora of cultic religions or 'cults'. . . . But the Christian cult is *leitourgia,* and this means that it is *functional* in its essence, has a goal to achieve which transcends the categories of cult as such."[31] Schmemann identifies this peculiar characteristic of the Christian cult by calling it antinomous. In an antinomy a contradiction is felt between two principles that seem equally necessary and reasonable. An antinomy integrates contradictory aspects into one total truth. In the words of the Russian theologian-philosopher, Pavel Florensky, that something is antinomous means "both the one and the other are true, but each in its own way. Reconciliation and unity are higher than rationality."[32] The thesis and the antithesis together form the expression of the whole truth. At the heart of the liturgy there is an antinomy between our cultic expression of Christianity and the radical abolishment of cult, as Schmemann says. "The Christian *leitourgia* is not a 'cult' if by this term we mean a sacred action, or rite, performed in order to establish 'contact' between the community and God. . . ."[33] We celebrate a supercultic reality in cultic form.

This accounts for the defection by primitive Christians from classic religious jargon, no doubt making themselves enigmatic to their neighbors. Christians were charged with atheism. For one thing, notes Josef Jungmann, they did not call their cultic leaders by the name *iereus:*

> Among the pagans and even in the Old Covenant, the *iereus* was someone who himself, in his own name or at the command of the community, acted as mediator with the deity. Such a possibility does not exist in the new Covenant. For there is only one mediator between God and man, Jesus Christ, and all others are merely His instruments, able to act not in their own name but only in His. The term *iereus,* was therefore applicable only to Christ and to the whole communion of the faithful, the holy Church, in so far as it joined to Christ.[34]

Congar makes the same observation. "If it pertained to a *iereus,* whether in Judaism or paganism, to immolate a victim in offering and so to be a 'sacrificer,' then in Christianity there was only one deserving that name, Christ. . . . The ministers of the eucharist were not acting as 'sacrificers' because, in celebrating that efficacious memorial as the Lord had given his Apostles power and commandment to do, they were simply making Christ's one sacrifice actual and present to the faithful."[35] Taft says the apostle Paul never once used "cultic nomenclature (liturgy, sacrifice, priest, offering) for anything but a life of self-giving, lived after the pattern of Christ. When he does speak of what we call liturgy, . . . he makes it clear that its purpose is to contribute to this 'liturgy of life'. . . ."[36]

So on the one hand, liturgy directs its participants to a goal different from the cultic goal of attaining contact with God. Everything that religious cult foreshadowed has had its fulfillment in Christ. He is the new temple and the new sacrifice, as well as the new altar, priest, king, prophet, Torah, Sabbath, and tabernacle. Everything we use in Christian liturgy has passed through the hypostatic union. The goal of liturgy, in Schmemann's words, is "the *Church* as the manifestation and presence of the 'new *aeon*' of the Kingdom of God."[37] Christ did not found another religion; he founded a new age, the age of the Church, which is populated by a new race of people in unity with himself. This is his body, the *totus Christus*. On the other hand, liturgy uses many of the same forms religious cult uses to accomplish this end. Liturgy celebrates the supercultic end of temples, priests, and sacrifices by means of liturgical temples, liturgical priests, and liturgical sacrifices. I suppose this to be an instance of grace perfecting nature, and again I say, all cultic matter must pass through the hypostatic union in order to be serviceable to Christian liturgy. The liturgy is antinomous because what cult cannot contain is contained in liturgical cult, just as what heaven and earth could not contain was contained in the womb of the Theotokos.[38]

Liturgy is not a species in the genus of religious ritual. That's why the thick sense of liturgy is only partially grasped by studying its thin cult. For example, liturgical time is not merely religious festival, but it is celebration of the cosmic eighth day; liturgical space is not a history of sacred architecture, but it is standing on the ground of Mt. Tabor when we stand before the altar; liturgical assembly is only partially understood by a sociology of religion because it is the body of Christ; liturgical hymn is not music with a certain piety, but it is the angels' Trisagion passed through human vocal chords. Liturgy is the paschal mystery sacramentalized in ritual time, space, assembly, and the arts, like God was incarnated in the flesh. The stage of Christian liturgy is cosmic. In his study on liturgy in the book of Revelation, Erik Peterson measures the scope of the Christian liturgy when he says, "[This] is not the liturgy of a human religious society, connected with a particular temple, but worship which pervades the whole universe and in which sun, moon, and all the stars take part. . . . The Church is no purely human religious society. The angels and saints in heaven belong to her as well. Seen in this light, the Church's worship is no merely human occasion. The angels and the entire universe take part in it."[39]

In short—and here I come closer to the grammar I seek—liturgy is not the religion of Christians; liturgy is the religion of Christ perpetuated in Christians. The religion Jesus enacted in the flesh before the Father is continued in the Church, liturgically. "The Church . . . has a part too in the religion of Christ towards His Father in order to continue upon earth the homage of praise that Christ in His Sacred Humanity offered to His Father."[40] There is therefore no altar in the Church as the pagans knew it, but there is the *hagia trapezia* (holy table), which presents Christ, who is the altar of God. There is no sacrifice as cults knew it, but there is the Eucharist, which is the body of Christ, in which sacrifice the Church liturgically participates. There is no temple as religious impulse builds, but the assembly becomes a living temple and the building thereby becomes sacred place. Christ is the intermediator between heaven and earth, between thick liturgy and its ritual form. Liturgy is not our religious expression, but God's theology. And when this divine grammar is imprinted upon liturgists, then they are on their way to becoming a theologian. But the imprinting is an ascetical process. Every liturgist is called to be a theologian (even if not of the academic variety) and every liturgist is called to be an ascetic (even if not of the monastic variety).[41]

This is not a denunciation of ritual in Christianity. In just a moment I shall agree with Jean Corbon that "the liturgy cannot be lived at each moment . . . unless it is celebrated at certain moments."[42] But Christ did not come that we may have ritual and have it abundantly. "His followers were aware that he came not to invent or overhaul a liturgical system but to redeem a world."[43] Christianity is a religion, and liturgy is a ritual, in the way that Jesus was a man: fully, but not only. G. K. Chesterton said it is true to call a peacock's tail blue — there is blue in it. It is true in the same way to call liturgy a ritual — there is ritual in the work done by the people of God. But it is imprecise, and would be misleading, to use the terms *liturgy* and *ritual* interchangeably, as people sometimes do when they call any repetitive, organized, and ruled event a liturgy. Ritual form alone, without a divine content, does not make a liturgy. The liturgy uses cultic ritual to do something more than cult can ritualize. Therein lies the antinomy.

Liturgical antinomy is parallel to, because based upon, the incarnation. As in the latter, so in the former the illimitable is circumscribed, and the eternal resides in time, and the incorporeal is spatially located. The incarnation is the paradox of God present in the flesh, and the liturgy is the paradox of He who cannot be contained in thought or space or time or matter, presenting Himself to us in doctrine and temple and feast day and sacrament. Liturgy is icon, and "a place of meeting or joining *[sum-bole]* of different realities."[44] Apophatic theology is required to see the reality behind the reality, the prototype behind the icon, the divine action within the human ritual. Andrew Louth has made this clear in his study of Maximus the Confessor's commentary on the Divine Liturgy. Apophatic theology "is the realization in the Christian soul of what is accomplished and celebrated in the Church's liturgy, . . ." which means the eucharistic liturgy is

> a corporate, ecclesial encounter with God that draws each participant towards the attainment of the reality that it sets forth, and that attainment involves passing beyond everything we can conceive or understand, the rejection of everything that is simply *about* God, for the sake of an encounter in love with God Himself, an encounter in which we become transparent to God, and are deified.[45]

The eucharistic liturgy is an encounter to be experienced *(pathein)*, but not information to be learned *(mathein)*.[46] "But it is not an encounter that is open to anyone on any terms: it is an encounter that demands faith and ascetic struggle. . . . it is a way open to any baptized Christian, and indeed a way required if we are to remain faithful to our baptism, but it is a way of human, or personal, transformation that is costly."[47]

The locus of liturgy is the Church, but the location of the Church is in the world, so the liturgist's calling is to rule in right relationship (righteously) over material creation and contribute its splendor to the great cosmic *sobornost,* which is the gathering of heaven and earth, angel and human, round the throne of God. The principal meaning of the existence of the world is to build the kingdom of God, says Leonid Ouspensky, and the principal meaning of the Church in that world "is the work of drawing this world into the fullness of the revelation—its salvation."[48] The Church is not in the world like a marble is in a lump of bread dough. The Church is a piece of the dough, removed, leavened, and returned to raise the whole loaf. It is why Schmemann speaks of liturgy as a journey of leaving the world for the sake of the world. It is why Kavanagh was fond of saying that liturgy is the Church doing the world the way the world was meant to be done. The ultimate object of liturgy is not itself (that would be liturgical egotism), but the world. The liturgical community does not gather to do something irrelevant to the world; it is the heart of the world above the altar, beating without sin's arrhythmia.

Georges Florovsky said, "the doctrine of the Church itself is but an 'extended Christology,' the doctrine of the 'total Christ,' *totus Christus, caput et corpus.*"[49] Liturgical theology is ecclesiological self-analysis. The *Catechism of the Catholic Church* affirms that "Christ and his Church thus together make up the 'whole Christ'." It affirms this with Augustine ("Let us rejoice then and give thanks that we have become not only Christians, but Christ himself. Do you understand and grasp, brethren, God's grace towards us? Marvel and rejoice: We have become Christ. For if he is the head, we are the members; he and we together are the whole man . . .") and with Gregory the Great ("Our redeemer has shown himself to be one person with the holy Church whom he has taken to himself") and with Thomas Aquinas ("Head and members form as it were one and the same mystical person").[50] Liturgy is the manifestation of the new creation, which is the God-Man perpetuated temporally, personally, sacramentally, and socially until the Lord of the Church returns as Lord of the World (Pantocrator). Liturgy is not one cult among others to be inserted into the deck of religious practices in the human hand; it is the manifestation of a new creation and a new race. *Church* is the noun form of the verb *liturgy*, like *Christian* is the noun form of the verbs *faith, hope,* and *charity*. The job description of a liturgist is someone who strives for this life of Christ, and who, to the measure he or she attains it, is witness to the world of its final destiny. Here we have visited liturgical asceticism again.

Liturgical ritual cannot be isolated from our Christian life because liturgy ritualizes identity. According to Taft, "the purpose of all Christian liturgy is to express in a ritual moment that which should be the basic stance of every moment of our lives,"[51] and this lived liturgy is always what the apostle Paul seems to have had in mind.

> To express this spiritual identity, Paul uses several compound verbs that begin with the preposition *syn* (with): I suffer with Christ, am crucified with Christ, die with Christ, am buried with Christ, am raised and live with Christ, am carried off to heaven and sit at the right hand of the Father with Christ. . . . This seems to be what Christian liturgy is for St. Paul. Never once does he use cultic nomenclature (liturgy, sacrifice, priest, offering) for anything but a life of self-giving, lived after the pattern of Christ. When he does speak of what we call liturgy . . . he makes it clear that its purpose is to contribute to this "liturgy of life," literally to edify, to build up the Body of Christ into that new temple and liturgy and priesthood in which sanctuary and offerer and offered are one.[52]

The world's future is to become the temple of God, and the human future is to become participants in the eschatological liturgy. The world exists to be transfigured into the kingdom, as John of the eagle eye witnessed in his apocalyptic vision where the heavenly Jerusalem in its entirety had become God's dwelling place (Revelation 21:1–2). The present creation is the heavenly Jerusalem in potency, and God is at work in unseen ways to bring it to its omega. Kavanagh used to say that God works on both sides of the Church-world equation, and he writes, "Christian theology cannot talk of God, any more than Einstein could talk of energy, without including the 'mass' of the world squared by the constant of God's eternal will to save in Christ."[53] This creation is oriented to its fulfillment and transfiguration, and our eternal beatitude will consist of being perfect liturgists, as Macarios of Egypt states.

> The soul that has not yet acquired this citizenship in heaven and is not yet conscious of the heart's sanctification should be full of sorrow and should implore Christ fervently. . . . [The soul will then go forward,] receiving unutterable gifts and advancing from glory to glory and from peace to greater peace. Finally, when it has attained the full measure of the Christian life, it will be ranged among the *perfect liturgists* and faultless ministers of Christ in his eternal Kingdom.[54]

Now the human creature is invited by the Creator to serve as priest of material creation. Liturgy is the Son's energy possessing those baptized into him, enabling them to do before the Father, by divine breath, the very work which he himself does before the Father. Liturgy, then, is to enter into the Trinity, and liturgy began at the moment that this potency was tendered humankind, which Jean Corbon describes.

> The mystery that had been wrapped in silence through everlasting ages, and then had been concealed in creation, now journeyed with human beings and entrusted itself patiently to our fathers in the faith during the time of the promises. Its coming in the fullness of time was made known in the kenosis of the incarnate Word until it became event in the hour of Jesus' cross and resurrection. At that point the liturgy streamed forth.[55]

To see by the light of this mystery (to see God's revelation, ourselves, the world) is liturgical theology, and to be capacitated for this eternal vocation is liturgical asceticism. Schmemann complains that liturgical study has moldered into rubricism on the one hand, and historical studies on the other. Liturgy has been disconnected from both theology and life. For that reason he wishes for liturgical theology to be seen "as a slow and patient bringing together of that which was for too long a time and because of many factors broken and isolated—liturgy, theology and piety, their reintegration within one fundamental vision."[56] To reintegrate these factors would not consist of combining disparate things (like gluing a stick to a stone); it would be an act of reuniting things that were made for each other and should never have been separated in the first place (like healing a fractured bone). Reuniting, as opposed to combining, means that things which appear to be separate are in fact related by their nature, their ground, and their end. Under the thick definition of liturgy that we are seeking, liturgy is the locus for both Christian theology and Christian asceticism.

LITURGICAL *ASKESIS* IN THE CHRISTIAN NARRATIVE

The objective of this initial chapter has been to deepen the grammar by which we speak about liturgy itself, and to do so in order to prepare us to speak specifically about liturgical theology in the chapters that follow. Since I intend to follow the lead of Schmemann in developing a connection between liturgy and theology that could be called organic, my definition of liturgical theology raises a wide range of questions about the vocation of liturgists. Before trying to locate liturgical theology on the larger map in the next chapter, it would be helpful to speak directly about this liturgical vocation. This is, in other words, a clearer elucidation of liturgical asceticism.

There are general definitions of asceticism from which liturgical asceticism must be distinguished. The term *askein,* from which *askesis* comes, meant "to work." Asceticism thus came to mean discipline and training, especially the sort that an athlete undergoes, as John McGuckin explains:

> The word "asceticism" derives from the Greek term for physical exercise, such as athletic practice. The idea of training the soul to virtue by disciplining the body is fundamental to monastic theory. Here, Christian monasticism provided a distinct and original anthropology. In many Greco-Roman theories the purpose of "philosophic" asceticism was to purify the soul of the body's influence. . . . In its purest form the Christian concept of ascesis seeks not the liberation of the soul from the body but the integration of the person, spiritually and materially. Ascesis was thus a manner of disciplining the body and training the mind by

prayers, vigils and fasting, until the whole person was attuned to his or her best ability to hear and obey the voice of God.[57]

Asceticism therefore involves the idea of self-sacrifice and self-discipline. Since there are a large number of reasons for which one might submit to a discipline, I have no objection to a large number of uses for the word *asceticism*. When an athlete is placed under discipline in order to train for a prize, it is athletic asceticism; when a person disciplines excessive consumption of goods for the sake of distributive justice it might be called moral asceticism; when a person refrains from those same goods during wartime, it may be called patriotic asceticism; when a child learns to discipline wants and outbursts of frustration, that self-discipline may also be said to have an ascetical quality about it. In this way, different types of asceticism could be identified by different formal causes. Paul Evdokimov admits this range of meaning, too:

> The word "ascesis" comes from the Greek *askesis* and means exercise, effort, exploit. One can speak of the athletic ascesis when it seeks to render the body supple, obedient, resistant to every obstacle. The ascesis of scientists and doctors shows their magnificent abnegation that sometimes costs them their lives. Monastic tradition has given to this term a very precise meaning; it designates the interior combat necessary in order that the spiritual acquire a mastery over the material.[58]

It is easy to imagine religious causes of asceticism, too. Religious asceticism would be a disciplined endeavor to find God. The existence of pre-Christian and extra-Christian asceticism is a phenomenological fact (just like the existence of pre-Christian and extra-Christian religion is a phenomenological fact). But I shall maintain that liturgical asceticism is different from both moral asceticism and religious asceticism, and distinguish them not so much by the practices employed, but by the cause and end to which they are employed. That is exactly why two words (*liturgical* and *asceticism*) are required to name the single, simple reality *liturgical asceticism*. It is a theological category, not a moral, civic, religious, or athletic one. Evdokimov states it succinctly: "An athlete exercises his body; an ascetic, his flesh."[59]

Christianity shares many religious practices with the whole of humanity. This is a corollary of believing that grace perfects nature, and there is no alarm in this admission: It is, in fact, a sign of the solidarity and compatibility of Christianity with human nature. Perhaps no one understood this better than G. K. Chesterton, whose writings often contained an apology for the rather pagan quality of certain Catholic acts. For example, when critics of Catholicism complained that "ritual feasts, processions or dances are really of pagan origin," Chesterton replied, "they might as well say that our legs are of pagan origin. Nobody ever disputed that humanity was human before it was Christian; and no Church manufactured the legs with which men walked or danced, either in a pilgrimage or a ballet."[60] Neither do I deny that fasting, vigils, and solitude were practiced by religious persons before they were practiced by Christians. The Church did not create asceticism, and I do not deny that there were ascetics before there were Christians. In fact, liturgical asceticism does possess this religious dimension, meaning by "religion" what Archimandrite Boniface Luykx meant when he called it "making a path for God to come to you by."[61] There is a religious aspect to liturgical asceticism. After all, Christian ascetics who make a profession are called "religious" (priest, lay, religious).

However, Chesterton also pointed out modernity's tendency to overlook content when noticing similar forms, a tendency which he said led ethical societies and parliaments of religion to conclude that "the religions of the earth differ in rites and forms, but they are the same in what they teach." Chesterton contradicts this. "It is false; it is the opposite of the fact. The religions of the earth do not greatly differ in rites and forms; they do greatly differ in what they teach. . . . They agree in machinery; almost every great religion on earth works with the same external methods, with priests, scriptures, altars, sworn brotherhoods, special feasts. They agree in the mode of teaching; what they differ about is the thing to be taught."[62] Similarly, I will suppose that liturgical asceticism and religious asceticism agree in their machinery: They will use the same external methods of fasting and celibacy. But liturgical asceticism will differ from religious asceticism in its *arche* and *telos* (origin and end, principle and purpose). Not all asceticism is liturgical, any more than all worship is Christian; but liturgical asceticism does exist, as does liturgical worship. Jeremy Driscoll affirms this in Evagrius who recorded the understanding of the Desert Fathers: "Evagrius himself is witness . . . to how at base this monastic heritage has a distinctive Christian face which distinguishes it from all other traditions of spiritual exercises, from other cultural manifestations of monasticism. This distinctive face, again, is the face of the incarnate Lord who is with the monk in every stage of his exercises. . . ."[63] Every mystery of the Church—its sacraments, its laws, its hierarchy, its exercises, its ministry—exists for the sole purpose of being a means to participate in the mystery of Christ. Therein lies the difference between Christian asceticism and other religious asceticism. What makes it *liturgical* asceticism is the fact that it is a means of participating in Christ. There is a natural virtue of moral discipline that might lead a person to make ascetical experiments in goodness or justice or humility before Almighty God, but I am speaking of a discipline that is required to become a liturgist in Christ's body. Asceticism is requisite to being a liturgist and to becoming a liturgical theologian.

All this is presented to help explain the kind of theology a liturgical theologian does. Liturgy is not just ritual; it is a way of living and a way of thinking, expressed ritually. I will try to make this point by nesting asceticism and theology within the fundamental liturgical mysteries of creation, sin, salvation, and deification. Our liturgical life is our synergistic participation in the economy of God, as the Almighty gathers up history to bring it to eschatological perfection.

I will turn to the Christian East (particularly the fourth-century hymnographer, Ephrem) in order to speak of asceticism as a vocation that includes the liturgist, and not only the monk. I will do so for a reason John Paul II understood when he wrote: "In the East, monasticism was not seen merely as a separate condition, proper to a precise category of Christians, but rather as a reference point for all the baptized, according to the gifts offered to each by the Lord; it was presented as a symbolic synthesis of Christianity."[64]

From the beginning, God intended to share divine life with man and woman, and the incarnation is simply the flowering of the paradisal seed God planted. Jesus is called the "final Adam" because he is, finally, what Adam and Eve were meant to be. Jesus is the *eschatos Adam*. The life *anthropos*[65] simultaneously leads in the visible and invisible worlds is the anthropological potential for the incarnation. The incarnation is neither an afterthought by God, nor a simple case of damage control, for the Father had Christ before his eyes when Adam and Eve were made.

> God sculpted the human person while looking at his Wisdom, the celestial humanity of Christ. . . . In the thinking of the fathers, above the potential abyss of the Fall, God sculpted the human face while looking at the humanity of Christ in the depths of his Wisdom. . . . Christ did not become

incarnate in a foreign and utterly alien element, but he found in man his own heavenly and archetypical image, for God created man while looking at the heavenly humanity of the Word of God (1 Corinthians 15:47–49), preexistent in the Wisdom of God.[66]

From the moment God created, the economy was under way that would lead to the moment when God would appear in the midst of his ecstatic product, material creation. Jesus is the ground of God's hierarchies.

Human being is unique among other ways of being in the world, and in at least three ways. First, *anthropos* is microcosmic because in men and women can be found everything that is in the entire cosmos. *Anthropos* is made of matter and spirit. Gregory Nazianzus said God produced a being "endowed with both natures, the visible and invisible. . . . Thus, in some way a new universe was born, small and great at one and the same time. God set this hybrid worshipper on earth to contemplate the visible world, and to be initiated into the invisible; to reign over earth's creatures, and to obey orders from on high."[67] No other creature is enrolled as simultaneous citizen in both realms.

Second, this microcosmic capacity enables *anthropos* to be royal priest, ruling over matter in the image of God. In Schmemann's words:

All rational, spiritual and other qualities of man, distinguishing him from other creatures, have their focus and ultimate fulfillment in this capacity to bless God, to know, so to speak, the meaning of the thirst and hunger that constitutes his life. *"Homo sapiens," "homo faber"* . . . yes, but, first of all, *"homo adorans."* The first, the basic definition of man is that he is *the priest.* He stands in the center of the world and unifies it in his act of blessing God, of both receiving the world from God and offering it to God—and by filling the world with this eucharist, he transforms his life, the one that he receives from the world, into life in God, into communion with Him. The world was created as the "matter," the material of one all-embracing eucharist, and man was created as the priest of this cosmic sacrament.[68]

Men and women were created with the capacity to recognize the *logoi*[69] of material things (reflected in the biblical story of Adam naming the animals; he called things as they are). There is a world to be celebrated. The angels know it, but cannot experience it sensually; the animals experience it, but cannot know it spiritually. Only man and woman praise God for a world taken in through the senses and wondered at by the intellect. At the incarnation, the Word will not assume an angelic nature, or an animal nature, but rather a human nature, because of this microcosmic and priestly potential. Gregory asks,

> Do you realize how much your Creator has honored you above all creatures? He did not make the heavens in his image, nor the moon, the sun, the beauty of the stars, nor anything else which you can see in the created universe. You alone are made in the likeness of that nature . . . you alone are a similitude of eternal beauty, a receptacle of happiness. . . . Nothing in all creation can equal your grandeur. All the heavens fit into the palm of God's hand. And though He is so great that He can grasp all creation in His palm, you can wholly embrace Him; He dwells within you, nor is He cramped as he pervades your entire being.[70]

The third way *anthropos* is unique is because this is given as potential that is not actualized without our cooperation. In order to be a liturgical temple in whom God is not cramped, *anthropos* must act. Other beings are finished as soon as they are made. There is nothing else to add to a dog to make it finally canine, a cow does not progressively grow more bovine, and a cat is sufficiently feline as a kitten. But men and women are made *homo viator:* a being-on-the-way. *Anthropos* is a verb (a human *being*) until he or she becomes a noun (saint).

Ephrem says God created *anthropos* this way in order that men and women would enjoy the potential to contribute to their own reality. Human nature was made with the capacity to participate freely and willingly in a process of growing into the likeness of God. Created in the image of God, a human person also lives by relationship, and this provides for maximum individuality. God planned beings who could attain maximum personality:

> For this is the Good One, who could have forced us to please Him,
> without any trouble to Himself; but instead He toiled by every means
> so that we might act pleasingly to Him of our free will,
>   that we might depict our beauty
> with the colours that our own free will had gathered;
> whereas, if He had adorned us, then we would have resembled
> a portrait that someone else had painted, adorning it with his own colours.[71]

We were created for immortal happiness—and I do not mean by the modifier how long the happiness will last, but from whom it must come. Only the Immortal One can satisfy us, and communion is the ordered end for men and women. The liturgical posture of *homo adorans* is even more basic to *anthropos* than *homo erectus*, and happiness will elude us until we stand aright in our vocation as liturgical beings.

Happiness does elude us, because we have recanted our vocation as *homo adorans*. As a result, we have not only wronged ourselves, but we no longer "do" the material world the way it was meant to be done. God's response was, characteristically, merciful: God expelled us from the environs of the Tree of Life lest we be eternally disfigured. Do not think we were expelled from paradise because God was jealous of divinity and would not share it with *anthropos*. The Christian narrative is not the myth of Prometheus. The expulsion was on account of man and woman's untimely grasping at that for which they were not prepared. The sin was not that man and woman took something which God never intended them to have; the sin was that the serpent convinced them to take it prematurely. Thus, Ephrem says,

> He deceived the husbandman
> so that he plucked prematurely
> the fruit which gives forth its sweetness
> only in due season
> —a fruit that, out of season,
> proves bitter to him who plucks it.[72]

God would have given Adam and Eve the knowledge they sought after preparing them for it, but when grasped precipitately the knowledge impaired their created capacity for liturgical priesthood. A double knowledge was hidden in the tree: knowledge of God's glory and of our lowliness:

> But when Adam boldly ran
>   and ate of its fruit
> this double knowledge
>   straightway flew toward him,
> tore away and removed
>   both veils from his eyes:
> he beheld the Glory of the Holy of Holies
>   and trembled;
> he beheld, too, his own shame and blushed,
>   groaning and lamenting
> because the twofold knowledge he had gained
>   had proved for him a torment.

> Whoever has eaten
>   of that fruit
> either sees and is filled with delight,
>   or he sees and groans out.[73]

If *anthropos* had eaten the tree's fruit as God gave it—in love—then men and women would have seen everything with a knowledge that is delighted by the sight of God's glory and by the sight of their humility (just as Dante describes souls in heaven). But when *anthropos* ate the tree's fruit as the tempter gave it—in jealousy—then the sight of God's glory and our humility filled men and women with envy (just as Dante describes souls in hell). Through time, sin's cataracts have obscured *anthropos'* liturgical vision.

Because of our fallen state, we no longer see the world as material sacrifice for the glory of God, or as sacramental means for communion with God. Man and woman no longer fulfill their vocation as *homo adorans* because they are plunged into a sea of forgetfulness. Makarios of Egypt says the prelapsarian soul was to have progressed and attained full adulthood, just as a newborn child, who is the image of a full-grown adult, must progress and grow up.

> But through the fall [*anthropos'* soul] was plunged into a sea of forgetful-ness, into an abyss of delusion, and dwelt within the gates of hell. As if separated from God by a great distance, it could not draw near its Creator and recognize him properly. But first through the prophets God called it back, and drew it to knowledge of Himself. Finally, through his own advent on earth, He dispelled the forgetfulness, the delusion; then, break-ing through the gates of hell, He entered the deluded soul, giving himself to it as a model. By means of this model the soul can grow to maturity and attain the perfection of the Spirit.[74]

Since that cataclysm, material things have held so much potential to make us amnesiac that the ascetical tradition warns us to discipline the body, warns about material things, and even warns about the danger of these things recurring in memory and imagination. We have lost our equilibrium. The fall affected our nature in such a way that we have grown accustomed to the unnatural state of forgetting the sacra-mental dimension of good, material things. In Schmemann's words, "the 'original' sin is not primarily that man has 'disobeyed' God; the sin is that he ceased to be hungry for God and God alone. . . . The only real fall of man is his noneucharistic life in a noneucharistic world."[75] The microcosm that God had created—a spirit in matter—should have spiritualized the material universe in which it was placed. Instead, man and woman abdicated their office in the cosmic liturgy. This causes Evdokimov to lament, "There are no more singers for the cosmic liturgy because the Taboric light has no longer been seeded in the opacity of our bodies, and the glory of God has lost its place in a nature put to another and illegitimate use."[76] Although the fall took place on a spiritual level, it affected matter, which is why this asceticism must be done to the body, through the body, by the body, for the body. "By what rule or manner can I bind this body of mine?" asks John Climacus. "He is my helper and my enemy, my assistant and my opponent, a protector and a traitor. . . . If I strike him down I have nothing left by which to acquire virtues."[77]

Asceticism is necessary in order to think straight—about ourselves (anthropology), the world (cosmology), and God (theology). The place where we can think straight is the place where we stand straight. At the opening of the anaphora in the Divine Liturgy of St. John Chrysostom, the deacon bids the Church, "Let us stand aright; let us stand with fear; let us attend, that we may offer the Holy Oblation in peace." There is nothing wrong with matter, but matter has been wronged by us. By turning away from the Creator, *anthropos* does not use matter eucharistically or receive matter sacramentally. We have wounded creation, and by our fault matter does not fulfill its end any more. Ephrem describes the reaction of the sun to human idolatry:

The sun bellowed out in silence to the Lord against his worshippers.
It was a suffering for him, the servant, that instead of his Lord
    he was worshipped.
Behold the creation is joyful that the Creator is worshipped. . . .
Since fools honored the sun, they diminished him in his honor.
Now that they know he is a servant, by his course he worships his Lord.
All the servants are glad to be counted servants.
Blessed is he who set the natures in order!
We have done perverse things that we should be servants to servants. . . .
Since fools honored the sun, they diminished him in his honor.
Now that they know he is a servant, by his course he worships his Lord.
All the servants are glad to be counted servants.
Blessed is he who set the natures in order!
We have done perverse things that we should be servants to servants. . . .[78]

That is why creation groans in travail, waiting for the redemption of
anthropos. Asceticism is required of the liturgist so that earth may be
healed; asceticism is required of the theologian in order to see the
matter clearly.

In *The Lion, the Witch and the Wardrobe,* C. S. Lewis describes
the effect which eating enchanted food could have upon a son of
Adam.[79] A little boy named Edmund and his siblings had stumbled
into Narnia and threatened the reign of the white witch, so she gave
to Edmund a candy upon which an enchantment had been placed.
Its first effect was "anyone who had once tasted it would want more
and more of it, and would even, if they were allowed, go on eating it
till they had killed themselves."[80] Second, when Edmund sat down to
supper, he did not enjoy the meal because, Lewis observes, "There's
nothing that spoils the taste of good ordinary food half so much as
the memory of bad magic food."[81] The Christian doctrine of original
sin claims that each human being is born with a spoiled appetite, and
that humanity was expelled from paradise before we killed ourselves
eternally, and that the memory of this bad magic food has spoiled
the taste of this good ordinary earth. Asceticism is the weaning of
our appetites from magic food, but it does not make us less human, it
makes us finally human. Man and woman were plunged into a sea of
forgetfulness by the delectability of the world, and the first reaction
of God was mercy: They were expelled from the garden until they got
their appetites under control. But this was not the last action of God.

The way to rectify the being of a microcosmic hybrid who had
come under the trance of the corporeal is for God himself to become
corporeal flesh. Satan warped our spirits so that creation would work
an opposite effect upon an unrighteous being. We are idolatrously
blinded by the heavenly luminaries, impoverished by the avarice that the
goods of creation create in an unrighteous heart, and alienated from
God by the very book of nature that was created to disclose God. The
only countervail would be an incarnate inversion. In Ephrem's words,

> The All-Knowing saw that we worshipped creatures.
> He put on a created body to catch us by our habit,
> to draw us by a created body toward the Creator.
> Blessed is He Who contrived to draw us to Him.
> The evil one knew how to harm us; with the luminaries he blinded us.
> With possessions he maimed us, by gold he made us poor.

With graven images he made us a heart of stone.
Blessed is He who came to soften it![82]

If the sinner will no longer look through matter to God, then God will himself become matter to be looked at. It is a principle of iconography that the faculty of sight is the most active of the senses, reaching out to seize and take in the object apprehended. We become what we look at. God became human so that we might see him and be made divine. Irenaeus says, "The Word was made flesh . . . that all that exists could see . . . its King, and also that the paternal light might meet with and rest upon the flesh of our Lord, and come to us from his resplendent flesh, and that thus man might attain to immortality, having been invested with the paternal light."[83] The incarnation is crucial to our justification.

When Satan burgled Eden, he took the most valuable possession and imprisoned it in a stronghold he thought was secure. The evil one thought he could hide *anthropos* from God by shame and accusation and death. He took Adam to a place he thought was out of God's reach, but he was mistaken.

Adam was heedless
as guardian of Paradise,
for the crafty thief
stealthily entered;
leaving aside the fruit
—which most men would covet—
he stole instead
the Garden's inhabitant!
Adam's Lord came out to seek him;
He entered Sheol and found him there,
then led and brought him out
to set him once more in Paradise.[84]

When the man and the woman hid themselves from the presence of the Lord God among the trees of the garden, the Lord God called, saying, "Where are you?" (Genesis 3:9). The cry, "Adam, Eve, where are you?" sounded in the garden that first time. Then angels went to the corners of the universe shouting the question, not only because they were bid by their Lord to do so, but also because they missed the humans' voices in the celestial choir. The king sent inquisitors with the question through the long corridors of history—Abraham, Moses,

Elijah, Isaiah—but neither could find Adam and Eve. Finally, the Lord put on flesh, so that he could die, so that he could look in the last, last place. And there, in Sheol, he found them: deaf, mute, ashamed, dead. And the Lord brought out the man and woman and led them once more to paradise. This dogma is written in icon, too.

Whereas Christ overcame the passions; whereas struggling against the passions increases the share we have in Christ's life; whereas our renewed humanity is an icon of Christ, who is the icon of the invisible God; and whereas the work of this renewed humanity is to perpetuate Christ's own *ergeia* in the world, therefore the discipline practiced by Christ's mystical body ought to be called liturgical asceticism. Liturgical asceticism was not possible until after the incarnation any more than iconography—and for the same reason. The uniqueness of liturgical asceticism derives from the uniqueness of the hypostatic union. And since liturgy is living by grace this hypostatic union that was natural in Christ, the new reality into which a Christian is baptized brings with it a discipline to make Christ's image visible in our faces. It begins with death. It is sacramental, spiritual, pre-biological death, made efficacious by mysterious union with Christ's own death. Evdokimov states, "If philosophy brings knowledge of death, Christian ascesis offers the art of going beyond it and thus anticipating the resurrection."[85] Liturgical asceticism corroborates the death of Christ in our own bodies by taming those passions that accompany life-in-the-body so that we may notarize with our hope that death has not been victorious. Instead, death, when grasped in a radical act of faith, has been made a portal to the new age. The pall has become a white baptismal garment, which is our swaddling cloth.

That is why liturgical life begins in the font. The asceticism, which is made possible by the theological virtues infused by baptism (faith, hope, and charity), is the discipline that increases the measure by which the Christian can participate in the liturgical life this sacrament initiates. Baptism drops the spirit of the Holy One into our veins, but there is no fire where there is not matter to burn; liturgical asceticism makes us combustible. In his foreword to *Unseen Warfare*, Nicodemus of the Holy Mountain describes the book's ascetical subject matter in this way: "It teaches not the art of visible and sensory warfare, and speaks not about visible, bodily foes but about the unseen and inner struggle, which every Christian undertakes from the moment of his baptism, when he makes a vow to God to fight for Him, to the glory of His divine name, even unto death."[86] If it is remembered that the word *sacramentum* once meant the vow taken by a soldier upon enlistment in the army, then it will be understood that liturgical asceticism is the fulfillment of every Christian's baptismal *sacramentum*. If it is remembered that baptism creates the people of God, named by the word *laos*, then it will be understood that this life is the *ergeia* of the *laos*.

Liturgical asceticism is not born out of hatred of the world, and it is not an exercise of our religious faculty alone. Christian liturgical asceticism is born in the waters of the font where the liturgist-in-formation is immersed into the blood of a suffering Christ. Evdokimov sees the cross "planted at the threshold of the new life — *vita nova* — and the water of baptism receives the sacramental value of the blood of Christ. From then on, ascesis teaches participation in the 'health' of the Savior, but this entails a victory over death and therefore a preliminary purification."[87] This labor is incumbent on every Christian who has passed through what Gregory of Nyssa calls the mystical sea.

> Those who pass through the mystical water in baptism must put to death in the water the whole phalanx of evil — such as covetousness, unbridled desire, rapacious thinking, the passion of conceit and arrogance, wild impulse, wrath, anger, malice, envy, and all such things. Since the passions naturally pursue our nature, we must put to death in the water both the base movements of the mind and the acts which issue from them. . . . If someone should still serve them, even if he should happen to have passed through the water, according to my thinking he has not at all touched the mystical water whose function is to destroy evil tyrants.[88]

Therefore, liturgical asceticism is for every baptized Christian. It is not confined to the Desert Fathers and Mothers, but they blazed the trail and it is to them that generations have turned when seeking creative recovery and interpretation of this spirituality.

Paul Evdokimov describes the kingdom of God in this way: "It is in the offering of the heart to God that the Spirit manifests itself and introduces the human being into the eternal circulation of love between the Father and the Son, and this is the 'Kingdom.' "[89] I suggest that this is the only adequate definition of liturgy. Liturgy is living in that eternal circulation of love within the Trinity. For us to love God, our appetites must be put into control: *ordo amoris*. In the liturgy

God presents Himself to be loved, and by loving we know Him, and knowing the Trinity is what Athanasius simply called "theology." It is liturgical theology, practiced by liturgists in the ascetical discipline of *theologia prima.*

---

1. Aidan Kavanagh, *On Liturgical Theology* (New York: Pueblo Press, 1984) 47.

2. Alexander Schmemann, "Liturgical Theology, Theology of Liturgy, and Liturgical Reform," in *Liturgy and Tradition: Theological Reflections of Alexander Schmemann,* ed. Thomas Fisch (Crestwood, NY: St. Vladimir's Seminary Press, 1990) 40.

3. Aidan Kavanagh, *On Liturgical Theology,* 8.

4. Robert Taft, "The Liturgy in the Life of the Church," *Logos: A Journal of Eastern Christian Studies,* vol. 40 (1999) 187. See also "What Does Liturgy Do? Toward a Soteriology of Liturgical Celebration: Some Theses," *Beyond East and West: Problems in Liturgical Understanding, 2nd ed.* (Rome: Pontifical Oriental Institute, 1997).

5. "*Essence* is expressed by grammar. . . . Grammar tells what kind of object anything is (Theology as grammar)." *Philosophical Investigations* (New York: The Macmillan Company, 1958) paragraphs 371–73

6. This is as true of the spoken word as the written word. Wittgenstein's example of the former is a worker who utters the sound "Board!" and one time is distinguishing boards from planks from beams for his assistant's education, and the next time calls out this sound in order to command his assistant to bring him the board. An example of the latter can be recognized from a time I found the inscription *pix* written in the margins in my own hand, but could not remember whether I was abbreviating the word *picture* or was referring to the ninth page by roman numerals.

7. Paul Holmer, *The Grammar of Faith* (New York: Harper & Row, 1978) 17. Holmer was a philosopher at the University of Minnesota and at Yale, and used this Wittgensteinian approach to consider the grammar of theology, and the grammar of a life, ala Kierkegaard.

8. The benefits of Michael Polanyi's work on the tacit dimension of knowing may also be brought to bear here. He says that "people know more than they can say." See *Personal Knowledge: Towards a Post-Critical Philosophy* (University of Chicago Press, 1958); *The Tacit Dimension* (Doubleday & Company, 1966); and two collections of essays and lectures: *Meaning* (University of Chicago Press, 1975, ed. Harry Prosch) and *Knowing and Being* (University of Chicago Press, 1969, ed. Marjorie Greene).

9. Paul Holmer, *The Grammar of Faith,* 19.

10. Aidan Kavanagh, *On Liturgical Theology*, 8.

11. A superb integration of apophatic theology and Christian liturgy is accomplished by Alexander Golitzin's masterful thesis on Dionysius: *Et Introibo Ad Altare Dei: The Mystagogy of Dionysius Areopagita, with Special Reference to its Predecessors in the Eastern Christian Tradition* (Thessaloniki: George Dedousis's Publishing Co., 1994). When I speak of dilating our concept of *leitourgia*, it would be to the size of the Ecclesiastical Hierarchies as Golitzin describes them.

12. Yves Congar, *A History of Theology* (New York: Doubleday & Company, Inc., 1968) 31.

13. Aidan Kavanagh, "Eastern Influences on the Rule of Saint Benedict," *Monasticism and the Arts,* ed. Timothy Verdon (Syracuse: Syracuse University Press, 1984) 56.

14. Evagrius, *The Praktikos & Chapters on Prayer* (Kalamazoo: Cistercian Publications, 1981) 65.

15. Yves Congar, 261–62.

16. Thomas Spidlik, *The Spirituality of the Christian East* (Kalamazoo: Cistercian Press, 1986) 1.

17. George Berthold, *Maximus Confessor: Selected Writings* (New York: Paulist Press, 1985) 92.

18. Louis Bouyer, *The Meaning of the Monastic Life* (London: Burns & Oates, 1955) 28–29.

19. *Catechism of the Catholic Church*, 1546.

20. *Catechism of the Catholic Church*, 1547. The Catechism here affirms teachings that both preceded its publication and followed it. *Lumen gentium* affirms that, "The baptized, by regeneration and the anointing of the Holy Spirit, are consecrated as a spiritual house and a holy priesthood, in order that through all those works which are those of the Christian man they may offer spiritual sacrifices and proclaim the power of Him who has called them out of darkness into His marvelous light" (LG, 10). The ways mentioned by which the common priesthood is exercised include persevering in prayer and praise, presenting oneself as a living sacrifice, joining in the offering of the Eucharist, receiving the sacraments, witnessing in holy life, and living in self-denial and active charity. The 1997 Instruction, *On Certain Questions Regarding The Collaboration Of The Non-Ordained Faithful In The Sacred Ministry Of Priest*, underscores that the difference between common priesthood and ministerial priesthood "is not found in the priesthood of Christ, which remains forever one and indivisible, nor in the sanctity to which all of the faithful are called. . . . This diversity exists at the mode of participation in the priesthood of Christ. . . ." (#1). The ministerial priesthood is rooted

in the Apostolic Succession, vested with *potestas sacra,* and consists of the faculty and responsibility of acting in the person of Christ the Head and Shepherd. It renders its ministers servants of Christ and of the Church. The reason for the diversity of members and functions is for the building up of the Church. For that reason, "Christ gives to [ordained] priests, in the Spirit, a particular gift so that they can help the People of God to exercise faithfully the common priesthood which it has received" (#1).

21. *Lumen gentium,* 10.

22. Paul Holmer, "About Liturgy and Its Logic," *Worship* 50:18–28.

23. Alexander Schmemann, *Introduction to Liturgical Theology* (Crestwood, NY: St. Vladimir's Seminary Press, 1975) 31.

24. Aidan Kavanagh, "Response: Primary Theology and Liturgical Act," *Worship* 57. See also Paul McPartlan, *The Eucharist Makes the Church: Henri de Lubac and John Zizioulas in Dialogue* (Edinburgh, T & T Clark, 1993) for a survey of what de Lubac rediscovered in patrology, and what Zizioulas has made all the stronger.

25. Robert Taft, "Liturgy as Theology," *Worship* 56:2 (March 1982) 115.

26. Arndt & Gingrich, *A Greek–English Lexicon of the New Testament and Other Early Christian Literature* (Chicago: University of Chicago Press, 1957) 472.

27. Lawrence Madden, "Liturgy," *The New Dictionary of Sacramental Worship,* ed. Peter Fink, (Collegeville: Liturgical Press, 1990) 740.

28. I. H. Dalmais, "The Liturgy as a Celebration," in *The Church at Prayer, vol. I: Principles of the Liturgy,* ed. A. G. Martimort (Collegeville: Liturgical Press, 1987) 233.

29. Alexander Schmemann, *For the Life of the World* (Crestwood, NY: St. Vladimir's Seminary Press, 1976) 25.

30. Romano Guardini, *Meditations Before Mass* (Manchester, NH: Sophia Institute Press, 1993) 71.

31. Alexander Schmemann, "Theology and Eucharist," in Fisch, 79.

32. Pavel Florensky, *The Pillar and Ground of the Truth* (Princeton University Press, 1997) 118.

33. Alexander Schmemann, "Theology and Liturgical Tradition," in Fisch, 40.

34. Josef Jungmann, *The Early Liturgy* (South Bend: University of Notre Dame Press, 1959) 18. See also Jungmann's *Liturgical Worship* (NY: Frederick Pustet Co., 1941) where he discusses this again. His main point is that all priesthood comes from Christ. That is why he notes that the titles *iereus* or *sacerdos* "were given only to Christ, to Christ principally and then secondarily (as we shall presently declare more in detail) also to the faithful as a whole" (32). But this is not to the detriment of the ordained priesthood. "In the mind of holy Scripture the priestly dignity and honor belongs first and exclusively to Christ the Lord, to the personal Christ. In the second place it belongs to the whole Christ, which is the totality of those who compose His Mystical Body and therefore share His life and also His priestly dignity. . . . Only after that does the question come up who within the community of the faithful has a special share in the priestly function of Christ, who properly speaking is the organ through whom the community performs those acts for which a special power is necessary. . . . From this point of view the priesthood of the faithful is seen in its proper light, in the light that takes from it every dangerous and exaggerated tendency. To be sure, this teaching has in the past been abused, particularly by the reformers of the sixteenth century. The universal priesthood, which in the Middle Ages lay in obscurity, they acclaimed so enthusiastically as to declare any special priesthood superfluous, and hence they threw overboard the sacrament of ordination" (39). Jungmann does go on to register his opinion that an adequate definition of the common priesthood must take the priesthood of Christ as its starting point, and not make the ordained priesthood its starting point, because the method of contrast could fail to arrive at a positive meaning. But what Jungmann hopes for seems to be exactly what *Lumen gentium* delivers: The common priesthood of the faithful and the ministerial priesthood are interrelated, but each is a participation in the one priesthood of Christ in its own special way.

35. Yves Congar, *Lay People in the Church* (Westminster: The Newman Press, 1865) 149–50.

36. Robert Taft, "Toward a Theology of the Christian Feast," *Beyond East & West, Problems in Liturgical Understanding* (Washington, DC: The Pastoral Press, 1984) 5.

37. Alexander Schmemann, "Theology and Eucharist," in Fisch, 79.

38. "O undefiled One, all the ranks of the angels have been struck by the mystery of your awesome birthgiving. How is the One who gathered the whole world together with his hand now held in your arms as an infant? How is the pre-eternal One to receive a beginning in time? How is He who feeds every living being with his ineffable goodness now nourished with milk? Therefore, they glorify you with praise, for you are truly the Theotokos." The Sunday Office, Resurrectional Tones, *The Office of Matins,* compiled and adapted by the Sisters of the Order of St. Basil the Great (Uniontown, PA, 1989) 84.

39. Erik Peterson, *The Angels and the Liturgy* (NY: Herder & Herder, 1964) 22, 50.

40. Abbot Columba Marmion, *Life of the Soul,* (London & Edinburgh: Sands & Co., and St. Louis: B. Herder Book Co., 1931) 284.

41. I hope someday to make one more application of liturgical theology under this form: Every liturgist is a priest, even if not of the ordained, clerical variety. The membership of the Church consists of theologians, religious, and priests, but these are special expressions, for the sake of ministry, of a common liturgical identity.

42. Jean Corbon, *The Wellspring of Worship* (New York: Paulist Press, 1988) 79.

43. Aidan Kavanagh, *Elements of Rite* (New York: Pueblo Press, 1982) 6.

44. Alexander Golitzin, *Et Introibo Ad Altare Dei,* 219.

45. Andrew Louth, "Apophatic Theology and the Liturgy in St. Maximos the Confessor," in *Criterion: The Divinity School of the University of Chicago* (vol. 36:3, Autumn 1997) 6. Also printed in *Wisdom of the Byzantine Church* (Department of Religious Studies, University of Missouri, 1998.

46. _____, *Denys the Areopagite* (Geoffrey Chapman, 1989) 25. Symeon the New Theologian's teacher, named Symeon the Elder, also told him: "Gain God for yourself and you will have no need of books." Liturgical theology is *pathein.*

47. _____, "Apophatic Theology and the Liturgy in St. Maximos the Confessor," 5.

48. Leonid Ouspensky, "The Meaning and Language of Icons," in Ouspensky & Lossky, *The Meaning of Icons* (Crestwood, NY: St. Vladimir's Seminary Press, 1983) 28.

49. Georges Florovsky, "The Ever-Virgin Mother," in *The Mother of God, a Symposium,* ed. E. L. Mascall (Westminster: Dacre Press, 1959) 52.

50. *Catechism of the Catholic Church,* 795.

51. Robert Taft, "Sunday in the Byzantine Tradition" in *Beyond East and West: Problems in Liturgical Understanding* (Rome: Pontifical Oriental Institute, 1997) 52.

52. _____, "Toward a Theology of the Christian Feast," *Beyond East & West,* 5.

53. Aidan Kavanagh, *On Liturgical Theology,* 4.

54. Macarios of Egypt, *The Philokalia,* vol. 3 (London: Faber & Faber, 1986) 334. Emphasis added.

55. Jean Corbon, *Wellspring of Worship,* 77.

56. Alexander Schmemann, "Liturgical Theology, Theology of Liturgy, and Liturgical Reform," 46.

57. John McGuckin, "Monasticism," in *The Blackwell Dictionary of Eastern Christianity* (Oxford: Blackwell, 1999) 321.

58. Paul Evdokimov, *The Struggle with God*, (New Jersey: Paulist Press, 1966) 135. Reprinted as Ages of the Spiritual Life (Crestwood, NY: St. Vladimir's Press, 1998). Peter Phan treats of asceticism in the thought of Evdokimov in chapter 10 of his dissertation, *Culture and Eschatology: The Iconographical Vision of Paul Evdokimov* (New York: Peter Lang, 1985).

59. _____ , *The Struggle with God*, 101.

60. G. K. Chesterton, "The Superstition of Divorce," *What's Wrong with the World*, in *The Collected Works* vol. IV, (San Francisco: Ignatius Press, 1987) 264.

61. Personal conversation at Holy Transfiguration monastery, California.

62. G. K. Chesterton, *Orthodoxy, The Collected Works*, vol. 1 (San Francisco: Ignatius Press, 1986) 333.

63. Jeremy Driscoll, *The "Ad Monachos" of Evagrius Ponticus* (Rome: Pontificio Ateneo S. Anselmo, 1991) 380.

64. John Paul II, *Orientale Lumen*, 9.

65. There are times when I don't want to refer to humanity as a race, or to individual beings in that race, or to the attribute "human." There are times when I want to refer to the singular entity "man." Gregory of Nyssa noted that "To say that there are 'many human beings' is a common abuse of language. Granted there is a plurality of those who share in the same human nature . . . but in all of them, humanity is one." But in our day, people have narrowed the use of "man," assigning it other connotations. This leads me to use the Greek word for man, male and female.

66. Paul Evdokimov, *Art of the Icon*, 47, 191, 206.

67. Cited in Olivier Clement, *The Roots of Christian Mysticism* (New York: New York City Press, 1996) 77.

68. Alexander Schmemann, *For the Life of the World* (Crestwood, NY: St. Vladimir's Seminary Press, 1973) 15.

69. *Logos* is the Greek word for *word, reason, rationality, order, intelligibility.* The second person of the Trinity was called the Logos, and through him all things were made; therefore creation is reasonable, rational, ordered, and can be spoken about intelligently. Created things possess *logoi* (plural of Logos).

70. Gregory of Nyssa, *From Glory to Glory: Texts from Gregory of Nyssa's Mystical Writings*, Selected and Introduced by Jean Danielou, trans. Herbert Musurillo, (Crestwood, NY: St. Vladimir's Seminary Press, 1979) 162.

71. Ephrem, *Hymns on Faith*, cited in Sebastian Brock, *The Luminous Eye: The Spiritual World Vision of St. Ephrem the Syrian* (Kalamazoo: Cistercian Publications, 1985) 61.

72. Ephrem, *Hymns on Paradise* (Crestwood, NY: St. Vladimir's Seminary Press, 1990) 161.

73. _____, 93.

74. Saint Symeon Metaphrastis: Paraphrase of the Homilies of Saint Makarios of Egypt in *The Philokalia,* ed. Palmer, Sherrard, Ware, vol. 3 (Boston: Faber & Faber, 1986) 306.

75. Alexander Schmemann, *For the Life of the World,* 18.

76. Paul Evdokimov, *Art of the Icon,* 76.

77. John Climacus, *The Ladder of Divine Ascent,* (New York: Paulist, 1982) 185–56.

78. Ephrem, *Hymns on the Nativity,* in *Ephrem the Syrian: Hymns* (New York: Paulist Press, Classics of Western Spirituality, 1989), 180–81.

79. A lengthier use of Turkish Delight as an illustration can be found in Fagerberg, "Liturgy, Christian Asceticism, and Turkish Delight," *New Theology Review,* vol. 9:4, November 1996, 93–101.

80. C. S. Lewis, *The Lion, the Witch and the Wardrobe,* (London: William Collins Sons & Co., 1982) 38.

81. _____ .

82. Ephrem, *Hymns on the Nativity,* 180–81.

83. Irenaeus, *Against the Heretics* IV.xx.2.

84. Saint Ephrem the Syrian, *Hymns on Paradise,* 135.

85. Paul Evdokimov, *The Struggle with God,* 174.

86. *Unseen Warfare, Being the Spiritual Combat and Path to Paradise of Lorenzo Scupoli,* ed. Nicodemus of the Holy Mountain, rev. Theophan the Recluse (Crestwood, NY: St. Vladimir's Seminary Press, 1987) 71.

87. Paul Evdokimov, *The Struggle with God,* 158.

88. Gregory of Nyssa, *The Life of Moses* (New York: Paulist Press, 1978) 84–85.

89. Paul Evdokimov, "Saint Seraphim of Sarov," *The Ecumenical Review,* 15 (April 1963) 273.

Chapter 2

Where Does Liturgical Theology Belong?

A taxonomy classifies by dividing into ordered groups or categories, arranged by natural relationships. Liturgical theology has been treated with confusion because it is not immediately evident where it belongs in the current theological taxonomy. Is it a special type of theology? If so, then among theologies organized around the principles of history, systematics, morals, the Bible, and philosophy, there would be a theology organized around the principle of liturgy. Or is it a special approach to liturgy? If so, then among theologies controlled by the special interests of literary criticism, social ritual, or comparative studies of religion, there would be a theology controlled by special interests in liturgy. Where does liturgical theology belong? The simple aim of this book is to create a place for liturgical theology on the scholar's grid, and to gain some clarity about the shape and scope and deployment of the term. The tendency to treat liturgy as devoid of theological content makes this book necessary. Otherwise it will be the case, as it often enough is, that anything concerning worship or liturgy or doxology or sacrament is indiscriminately called liturgical theology. I am proposing a more careful application of the title.

The thesis explored here says that to uncover liturgical theology one must begin with the structure of the liturgical rite. However, the subject matter under consideration is not ritual, but it is the Church's corporate theological adjustment to encounter with the Father through Christ in the Holy Spirit.

This adjustment to God-wrought change is no less critical and reflective an act of theology than any other of the secondary sort. Unlike these, however, it is *proletarian* in the sense that it is not done by academic elites;

it is *communitarian* in the sense that it is not undertaken by the scholar alone in his study; and it is *quotidian* in the sense that it is not accomplished occasionally but regularly throughout the daily, weekly, and yearly round of the assembly's life of public liturgical worship.[1]

To uncover liturgical theology one must begin with the proletarian, quotidian, and communitarian liturgical theology of the rite.

This is not a starting point with which academic theology is accustomed. Theology done on the second order usually establishes a theology of worship first, and then searches for texts or rubrics to support the theory. Second order theology decides what theological principles need investigation, and then glances about to see whether they can be demonstrated by liturgical evidence or communicated through liturgical practice. Such scholarship may exhibit adroitness in rubric, history, or theory, but it is a case of the tail wagging the dog. The starting point for liturgical theology must be real liturgies, and they do not exist in the abstract. Actual liturgies exist. This was the point behind the analogy of grammar in chapter one. *Lex orandi* relates to *lex credendi* the way speech relates to grammar: first there are people talking, and then there are grammarians who analyze it. Second order analysis attempts to uncover the structure and basic laws of language, but it does not write these laws nor establish these structures. Kavanagh states,

> Philologists do not set the laws which permit language. They study its acts as formalized in words. Editors do not create language. They arrange its acts as formalized in words. Philosophers do not originate language. They formulate intelligibility tests to clarify and bring greater precision to the implications of its acts as formalized in concepts and words. All three of these honorable activities represent not first but second order enterprises.[2]

People mean with language, i.e., they transact their business with reality by language, and then philologists analyze the structure of something already in place. Similarly, people mean with gesture and icon and symbol, and then the meaning can be subjected to analysis. Liturgical theology is what transpires in the first half. This can then be written down, but the task of writing down a liturgical theology depends upon looking at the theology a liturgical community has transacted. Regrettably, this is not often the normal procedure, as Taft notes.

In the history of liturgical explanation . . . there has been a contrary shift from structure to symbolic interpretation. Most medieval liturgical commentators attended only to meaning, and their interpretations often did violence to structure. In the Reformation period structure was bent to serve theology. *Legem credendi statuat lex supplicandi* was turned around, and theology determined rather than interpreted liturgical text and form. . . . In my own work I attempt to reverse this process, insisting with the structuralists on the importance of imminent analysis of the structure before relating it to other disciplines such as history, sociology—or even theology. These disciplines are essential for explaining the hows and the whys, but prior structural analysis is necessary to recover the what.[3]

Liturgical theology must begin with liturgies, and it must begin with the meaning of the whole rite, not merely with texts and rubrics. Liturgical theology does not search for a symbolic interpretation of liturgy, but for its meaning, and the meaning of a liturgy resides in its structure. Structures reveal "how the object works," Taft claims, and even though liturgical theology utilizes historical research significantly, "the purpose of this history is not to recover the past (which is impossible), much less to imitate it (which would be fatuous), but to *understand liturgy* which, because it has a history, can only be understood in motion, just as the only way to understand a top is to spin it."[4]

The definition of liturgical theology being proposed therefore rests upon two crucial affirmations about the theology done by the liturgical community: 1) it is genuine theology, although it is *theologia prima* and not *theologia secunda,* 2) and it is *lex orandi.*

Regarding the first point, it must be said that academic theology is a species within the genus theology, but it is not the whole genus. It is true that the theological outcome of a liturgy is quite different in form and purpose from the theological outcome of an academic study, but I deny that theology is only really done when one crosses the threshold out of liturgy into the academy. The liturgical rite is the ontological condition for what is itself a genuine theology, albeit of a different kind: It is primary theology and not secondary theology. It can be translated into secondary theology for certain purposes, but it is not necessary to do so in order to have real theology instead of the mere rudiments of theology. Regarding the second point, a premier role for liturgical theology is established because as *lex orandi* the liturgy is where human words about God are grounded in the Word of God. Liturgical theology is normative for the larger theological enterprise because it alone, of all the activities that make up the family of theological games, is the place where the sources of theology function precisely as sources.

Any theological effort involves a quest for meaning *(logos)*. But in this case, the quest does not occur inside the scholar's mind; it is a meaning sought by the liturgical community. This is why Kavanagh calls their adjustment a genuinely theological effort. He discerns three logical moments in the liturgical event. First, the assembly encounters the Holy One; second, by consequence of this encounter the assembly is changed; third, the assembly must adjust to this change, and this act he calls theological.

> "Theology" is not the very first result of an assembly's being brought by the liturgical experience to the edge of chaos. Rather, it seems that what results in the first instance from such an experience is deep change in the very lives of those who participate in the liturgical act. And deep change will affect their next liturgical act, however slightly. . . . It is the *adjustment* which is theological in all this. I hold that it is theology being born, theology in the first instance. It is what tradition has called *theologia prima.*[5]

The scholar seeks to understand what the liturgical community understood. Liturgy itself is a stab at intelligibility, a search for understanding and meaning. Theology does not take place over there in the world of reason and intellect, beyond liturgical ceremony which is only an indulgence in pious feeling. Liturgy is itself theological for reason of being a meaningful understanding of such questions as why God created, the destiny of *anthropos,* how spirit and matter interpenetrate, the cosmological presuppositions of the kingdom of God in our midst and its eschatological consequences. Granted, because of its subject matter *(theos)* this stab at meaning is unlike any other that the human being makes. The subject matter of theology is God, humanity, and creation, and the vortex in which these three existentially entangle is liturgy. I take this to be why Schmemann calls liturgy "the ontological condition of theology, of the proper understanding of *kerygma,* of the Word of God, because it is in the Church, of which the *leitourgia* is the expression and the life, that the sources of theology are functioning precisely as sources."[6] If the subject matter of liturgical theology were human ceremony instead of God, it would be self-delusional to call it theology; it would be anthropology, not theology. Worse, it would be ritual narcissism. But liturgy is, in fact, theological precisely because here is where God's revelation occurs steadfastly.

When a dichotomy is imposed between theology and liturgy, then liturgy doesn't even appear on the theological map. It is off the taxonomical page. It is as if theology exists for academicians, while liturgy exists for pure-hearted (but simple-minded) believers. This prejudice supposes a two-step procedure from the believer's faith-expression (liturgy) to the academic's rational reflection (theology). The working definition of liturgical theology I am uncovering challenges the supposition that theology only exists in the second phase.

A Contrast of Approaches

In this chapter I will trace the boundaries of liturgical theology from the outside, so to speak, by describing two approaches that are different from liturgical theology. I call them a) theology *of* worship, and b) theology *from* worship.[7] Then in chapter three I can turn to the pioneering contribution made by Alexander Schmemann in defining c) liturgical theology, before going on to a more complete definition in chapters four and five, and giving two examples of liturgical theology in chapters six and seven.

It is important to state emphatically at the outset that defending liturgical theology as genuine theology does not correlatively mean discrediting other theological talk about worship. To say that liturgy is *theologia prima* does not imply that *theologia secunda* is meaningless or mistaken or improper or useless. Theological treatments of worship have their own *raison d'être* and value. Another of Wittgenstein's observations is helpful at this point. He considers how manifold are the activities that fall under the title "games." There are board games, card games, ball games, and Olympic games, and they are all appropriately called games even though some are playful and some are serious, some require equipment and some do not, some are competitive while some are just for fun, and some are played in teams, some in pairs, and there is even the game of solitaire. It is perfectly meaningful to call them games even though they are different. Saying that poker is different from football does not mean that one is a game while the other is not. In a similar fashion, when I say that liturgical theology is different from other theological treatments of worship, I am not saying that one is theology and the others are not. It is not my intention to devalue these other theologies; it is only my hope to establish liturgy's value in the eyes of theologians. I do also make the additional claim that liturgical theology is foundational to the taxonomy in a unique way.

One way to identify liturgical theology's unique quality is to think in terms of overcoming a dichotomy that has pitted liturgy against theology. It is difficult, indeed, to overcome a division as deeply entrenched in our minds as the one that opposes ritual and academics, spirituality and reason, liturgy and ascetics, theology of the rite and theology in the library. Perhaps a couple of analogies would help. The first comes from J. Huizinga, a historian of medieval culture, who argues in his book *Homo Ludens* that play is the basis of civilization. The play-factor, as he calls it, is active in the cultural process, producing fundamental forms of social life (ritual, poetry, music and dancing, philosophy, warfare, conventions of noble living). He concludes, then, by asserting that "civilization is, in its earliest phases, played. It does not come *from* play like a babe detaching itself from the womb: it arises *in* and *as* play, and never leaves it."[8] Analogously, liturgical theology is, in its fundamental phase, liturgical. It does not come from liturgy, like a babe detaching itself from the womb: This theology arises in and as liturgy, and never leaves it. Kavanagh uses remarkably similar language when he speaks about the identity-causing quality of language. "In this sense a human community does not merely use a language; it *is* the language it speaks. Similarly, a Christian church does not merely use a liturgy; it *is* the liturgy by which it worships."[9] Theology which is liturgical arises in the liturgical structures and does not detach from them; liturgy is theology in action, it is not merely a rubrical resource for the allegedly real theologians to rummage through.

The second analogy comes from Gabriel Marcel, a philosopher who concerns himself with the dichotomy between self and body implicit in our language. Even when trying to unite the two poles by saying "I have a body," a self is still posited on the one hand, and a body on the other. Marcel suggests that some advance is made by altering the expression to "I am a body," but this shift from a possessive metaphor to an ontological metaphor still supposes an "I" and a "body." Finally, he recommends "I am bodily."[10] His suggestion can parallel my efforts to distinguish liturgical theology from the two other approaches. Like the first of Marcel's formulas, what I have called theology of worship supposes that "worship has a theology," but it must be uncovered and explained by a theologian. It imagines that a theologian, already possessing an idea of what worship is, can train his attention upon a liturgy and discern the theology *of* worship that resides there. Like the second of Marcel's formulas, what I have called theology *from* worship supposes that "worship is theological." It imagines that theology benefits from taking into account Christianity's worshipful expression, but an academic theologian must organize the existential rudiments into a theological product. And it supposes that the person who is translating liturgy into theology must occasionally correct the liturgy in the process. Marcel's third formula expresses my understanding of liturgical theology. "I am bodily" means that the way I am, is bodily. "Liturgical theology" means that the way this theology is, is liturgically. This is *theologia prima* in liturgical form. Liturgical action is theological. This is already real theology even though it is performed communally by people who do not speak the language of the scholar's guild. In the Church's *lex orandi* theology happens, and that makes it the ontological basis for the Church's expression of herself in *lex credendi*.

The differences in method and consequence between these three approaches can be made clearer by a lengthier description of the two approaches I think should not be confused with liturgical theology. Two examples will be utilized in each case: Regin Prenter and Vilmos Vajta for the approach I am calling theology of worship, and Peter Brunner and Geoffrey Wainwright for the approach I am calling theology from worship. My concern at all times will be methodological, not critical. I do not want to ask whether these theologies are correct, but I want to ask how their approach differs from liturgical theology.

THEOLOGY OF WORSHIP

The subject matter in this approach is worship, and if liturgy is treated at all, it is used to illustrate the subject under discussion. Liturgical rite *per se* is immaterial to the approach. It is as if theology is a telescope trained upon a subject under investigation, a subject that could have been christology, or the existence of God, or miracles, but it happens in this case to be worship.

Regin Prenter is a Lutheran who would call himself a dogmatician under a special definition of dogma that reflects his concerns. Although the original use of the word was in the plural (dogmas) to denote the doctrinal definitions of the Church councils, he prefers to use it in the singular (dogma) to mean "the basic insight into the essential content of the Christian message, an insight which is immediately given in and with faith in the truth of the message, but which cannot be directly equated with faith, inasmuch as the faith which contains the insight is itself more than the insight."[11] It is incumbent on the theologian to lay the foundations of an authoritative point of departure, and Prenter's is the Trinity as reflected in the Nicene Creed. The theologian does not begin with history, philosophy, or anthropology of religion; he or she begins with the God of revelation. Therefore, there is no relationship with the Father "outside of that congregation where the Holy Spirit reveals the hidden essence of God the Father by uniting his people with him through Jesus Christ the Son, the king of God's people. We underscore here the expression 'living relationship.' "[12]

We already begin to see the significance of worship in Prenter's dogmatics. It is in worship that Jesus functions as Lord, the Bible functions as scripture, and theology functions as dogma. "We reject, further, all possibilities of finding the right relationship to the living Christ outside that congregation where the Holy Spirit reveals who Jesus Christ is by gathering for God the Father a worshiping people in the Son who is this people's king."[13] What Christ accomplishes for us as Savior (atonement) is worked out in our lives through worship (renewal). Prenter is concerned with a theology of worship because he proposes to begin with the central dogma of the Church, which is God at work in the life of renewal. He offers a tidy schema to speak about this life of renewal, which brings us directly into the heart of worship. Its origin is baptism, its growth is sanctification that comes about through the proclaimed Gospel, its goal is the Eucharist, the community of the renewal is the Church, and the fruit of the renewal is eschatological glorification. What was initiated in baptism, and struggles forward as sanctification, finds its fruition at the Lord's Table.

This context in turn conditions a theology of sacrifice and of the real presence of Christ. Perfect, sacrificial, giving up of oneself cannot be accomplished by any member of fallen humanity, but it was accomplished by the New Adam, Jesus. Prenter is thus able to distinguish sacrificial life in Christ from works-righteous sacrifice. Our sacrifice is not heroism, self-willed, or self-chosen, because the place and time of our sacrifice is not biographically but sacramentally determined. This reflects directly upon a theology of real presence. Prenter's position demands that the Lord's Supper is "the constant presence in the church of the sacrifice of Calvary. In fact it must be said that in the Lord's Supper we bring not only communion elements and prayers as a sacrificial gift, but the memorial *(anamnesis)* of [Christ's] one sacrifice, which is the only gift of love we can bring."[14] In evangelical theology, these ideas have remained in the background because of sixteenth-century polemics against the medieval doctrine of the Mass, but since Prenter's goal is to explicate the Christian dogma (singular), he presents his theology of sacrifice and presence not as partisan Lutheranism, but as the Lutheran confessional perspective upon a single dogma of the Eucharist which he thinks should be commonly shared.

Prenter's theology of worship is dressed out to serve his larger project. He wants to establish a normative point of departure (the saving act of God), which is foundational to the faith (dogma in the singular), and what he says about worship is said in light of this dogmatic project. His subject matter is not the liturgy; it is the life of regenerated humanity. But since that life originates at baptism, and sustained by the proclaimed word, and fulfilled at the Eucharist, he is led to consider Christian worship. This is a theology of worship.

Vilmos Vajta's book also provides an example of this approach, although in this case it is not his own theology of worship; rather, it is Luther's. Vajta believes that most treatments of Luther have assumed that the reformer had minimal (or marginal) interest in worship. Vajta sets out to correct this mistake. Though one must admit that "from a merely historical viewpoint, [Luther's] liturgical output may indeed appear meager and inadequate,"[15] Vajta maintains there is actually a deep, inner connection between Luther's theology as a whole and Luther's theology of worship. Far from being tangential to Luther's agenda, worship can be understood to be of central concern to his theology. Luther could not avoid coming to grips with the Mass because his theological convictions led to a complete reorientation of the worship service, and the intent of Vajta's study is "to link Luther's theology of worship with his teaching on creation, the atonement, the church, and justification. If proof of this connection can be established—and we mean to furnish it—it follows that Luther's theology of worship points to the very center of his whole thought."[16]

One could hardly ask for a better manifesto of the approach I call theology of worship. In Vajta's viewpoint, because worship and doctrine develop in "mutual dependence," Luther's reforms of the practices of worship depend upon his theology of worship. The latter explains the former. Overlooking this accounts for why most scholars begin backward, in Vajta's opinion. "Their liturgical interest begins where it should end, viz. at the question of liturgical forms. Often they pay scant attention to the theology which underlies these forms. . . ."[17] Vajta's book means to correct this sequence, by beginning with an outline of Luther's theology of worship before turning to its consequence on the liturgical forms.

One can easily see the twin north stars that guided Luther's theology: grace and faith. Since Luther's theology is built upon the conviction that faith is summoned forth by grace, so also must be Luther's theology of worship. This applies to all people, and all worship. "Worship is inherent in the created nature of man. As man must form a concept of God, so he must worship. Faith breathes worship. Fallen man has not only a false faith and a false confidence in idols, but also false worship. . . . Man is not free to choose his cult."[18] Nevertheless, worship cannot be invented according to our own tastes, because God cannot be had except where His self-revelation occurs. Vajta seeks to demonstrate that the reformer's insistence on justification by faith is not irrelevant to his theology of worship. Rather, this doctrine is the foundation for the reforms Luther proposed to liturgical cult. This sets the stage for Luther's distinction between *beneficium* and *sacrificium,* which Vajta says is general wherever Luther refers to worship.[19] The Lord's Supper is God's beneficent gift to us, not our sacrificial gift to God. This "Copernican revolution" that Luther exercised upon the Mass is only the practical application of his theological insights. When Luther critiqued ceremony, it was doctrine that was at issue. "He considered the Words of Institution not a law concerning outward ceremonies, but the 'gospel in a nutshell'. . . . These convictions guided both his criticism and his reform of the mass."[20] Luther's critique of the Mass stems not from reactionary objection to external form, nor from simplistic objection to abuses surrounding the private Mass, but rather from the fundamental distinction between righteousness as God's gift as opposed to righteousness as God's justice, which humans must fulfill.

Vajta now turns to look at Christian worship itself in a twofold light. Luther's theology of grace and faith is the paradigm for Vajta's division of the material into two parts: worship as the work of God, and worship as the work of faith. The work of God in Christian worship consists of proclamation of the Word, the presence of Christ in the

Lord's Supper, and the office of the ministry. The Gospel originally "was not a book but a sermon, and the church is not a *Federhaus* (quill house), but a *Mundhaus* (mouth house)"; the sermon is "Christ's continued advent."[21] The presence of Christ in the Lord's Supper is distinct because although God is omnipresent, here God is present-for-us uniquely. And this leads Luther to locate ministry within a theology of worship. Because the Word is a message, it must be preached and requires messengers; because the sacrament is a gift, it must be received and so requires administrators. Therefore Luther thought the office of minister was indispensable, even as he also thought Rome had caused confusion by equating function with a rank.

Having established the priority of God's work in worship, Vajta can turn to what Luther says about worship as the work of faith. Vajta admits his study would be incomplete if it did not include the threefold work of faith, namely, worship, the priestly sacrifice of believers, and the relationship between freedom and order. Worship, like faith, is not our work, but God's; therefore, worship's highest state is found where faith has been formed by the Word of God. Faith cannot be without worship, and faith constitutes the highest form of worship. This is all the more true of sacrifice. "The point of reference for the idea of sacrifice in Luther's theology is the priesthood of all believers. Sacrifice is an element of faith. Luther never forgot this fact, even in his most violent polemics against the Roman perversion of sacrifice. But as sacrifice is a function of faith, it cannot be without faith."[22] For Luther, the concept of sacrifice is primarily an expression of the total claim of faith, and so true sacrificial worship consists of spiritual praise, and prayer done obediently (because obedience is the mark of faith), and material offerings that provide for the needs of the poor.

Vajta holds true to his promise, and brings us to the ceremonies of the Church only after a theology of worship has been established. He only asks what liturgical forms have to do with worship at the end of his study. On this subject, he says, Luther takes a paradoxical stand. On the one hand, Luther sounds the bell of liberty, extending our freedom from the Law to include liturgical laws, too; on the other hand, this should not be mistaken as liberty for an anti-ceremonial, spiritualized version of the Mass. So both Rome and the extreme Protestant reformers miss the mark. "Whatever the pope had commanded for salvation, [the Enthusiasts] meant to prohibit. They failed to see that man is justified neither by the performance nor by the neglect of certain rites. They tyrannized the conscience of men as much as the pope and were as slow to grant freedom in the use of liturgical forms."[23] Vajta concludes that Luther's program of liturgical reform was a congruent consequence of his theology of worship.

Observations on Prenter and Vajta

The purpose of briefly outlining these two authors has not been to evaluate what they say, but to examine what they cover. My concern at the moment is methodological, not critical. I want to use them to point out how a theology of worship differs from liturgical theology. Toward that end, notice that both authors were able to theologize about worship without particular comment upon the details of liturgical practice or structure. The theology has been abstracted from the enactment in order to speak about the theme of worship, even if corrections deriving from this theology led to an occasional remark about liturgical practice. The subject matter in Prenter and Vajta was worship, and Kavanagh makes the intriguing suggestion that this *modus operandi* is not just accidental to some theologians; it has become endemic to the later Western tradition.

> I tried to be candid about the difficulties we moderns have when we try to attain so holistic a notion of liturgy and rite. Our minds, it seems, were significantly altered on such matters by various factors which built up a critical mass during and after the Renaissance of the fifteenth and sixteenth centuries in the West. What emerged from this period of immense stress was a rather novel form of endeavor known as "worship" rather than "liturgy" in its previously understood sense. The result was that Western Christianity as a whole, and the various Protestant churches in particular, embarked upon a hitherto unknown way of dealing with the Word of God in its written, incarnate, and ecclesial manifestations. This way was, due to the nature of the new "worship," increasingly shorn of the witness of the rite as I have tried to describe it. . . . Secondary theological influence increased greatly, primary theology receded.[24]

Theology of worship generalizes about elements of worship, like one generalizes about "the American" or "the college student" without examining particular cases. Thus it speaks generally about prayer in worship without discriminating between the opening prayer, the prayer over the gifts, the eucharistic prayer, the prayer after communion, the intercessory prayer of the Church, and final blessing prayer. Thus it speaks generally about the blessing at communion without attending to the structural elements of the canon: thanksgiving, epiclesis, institution narrative, anamnesis, intercession. The way a theology of worship speaks abstractly about worship is reminiscent of the way theology manuals once spoke about real presence and transubstantiation without mentioning the ritual action of Eucharist.[25] Taft said that liturgies can only be understood in motion because they have a history, just as tops are only understood if they are spinning. But a theology of worship tends to halt the top's revolution in order to get a clearer picture. Its method is to freeze the motion for the sake of an abstraction. The dilemma, however, is that the object of study is changed when it is stopped.

The method of liturgical theology differs from a theology of worship because the former does not seek to generalize. Liturgical theology seeks to observe the rite in motion, to notice detail, and the convenience of sameness does not blind it to structurally unique components. The subject matter of liturgical theology is not worship in general, but the theological meaning which derives from the symphony of structures called rite. Taft insists that particular structures must be dealt with because it has been his "constant observation that liturgies do not grow evenly, like living organisms. Rather, their individual structures possess a life of their own."[26] The meaning of a liturgical action is revealed not merely by its textual content; it is also revealed by the structure in which the text resides. This structure is discerned when it is in action.

I can appreciate the effort Prenter and Vajta have made to include worship among the topics relevant to theology. For a variety of reasons, theology has sometimes treated worship with less seriousness than these two authors would prefer. What I am at pains to point out, however, is that their approach still takes the attitude that worship "has a theology." Prenter calls academic theology the "reflective unfolding of the content of the theology of the liturgy apart from the worship of the Church, whereas the theology of the liturgy is the unreflected, living manifestation in the worship of the church of that truth analyzed by academic theology."[27] The division remains in place: Liturgy is one thing and theology another. Liturgy has a theology that can be excised for examination in the academy. Is this division not implied by the fact that although Prenter goes to lengths to use the term *dogma* (singular) to mean the faith which is manifested in the worship of the Church, his purpose is to analyze the insight, not the liturgy? Is it not implied by the fact that when Vajta criticizes those whose liturgical interest begins where it should end (namely, at the question of liturgical forms), his real purpose is the systematic presentation of the theology of worship which lies under those forms?

There is an additional, unanswered question implicit in both our authors. They want to determine what makes a true theology of worship. In both, a polemic is going on. In both, the theological plumb line for worship is the Lutheran agenda of justification that gives special attention to God's prevenient action in word and sacrament. I am not now disputing whether this is a good plumb line, I am only pointing out that this seems to be the reason why certain parts of the worship service receive preponderant treatment. Both authors accented the parts of worship pertinent to their polemic. But liturgy doesn't function well as this kind of resource, as Kavanagh illustrates.

> The liturgy is neither structured nor does it operate in such a way as to provide doctrinal conclusions. These are distilled from the liturgy by theologians according to the general principle that data are not *given* but must be consciously *taken*. Doctrinal conclusions are lifted from the liturgical engagement of Christians by theologians whose consciousness at the time of the lifting ineluctably affects what is lifted. This means that doctrinal conclusions are selective and may well tell one more about the theologian, and about the state of theological discourse at the time the conclusions are taken, than about the liturgy itself.[28]

When a theology of the liturgy gets determined in advance of the liturgical experience, then the Catholic tradition is threaded through that needle's narrow eye. Unfortunately, not all of it fits and some truths are lost.

Such an approach does not understand liturgy's *lex orandi* as normative. Liturgy is treated as the expression of a theology of worship, which came first and was determined by the perspective advocated. Faith is assent to doctrine, and that doctrine can, in turn, be expressed in various styles according to the liturgical taste of a community. This expression, thought to be confused and untheological, needs occasional correction by clear-headed theologians. This is precisely Vajta's conclusion in an article entitled "Creation and Worship." He writes that "Liturgy is, accordingly, the dogma of the Church viewed in a special dimension—the dimension of prayer."[29] He thinks this is proven by history. "Dogma was the unconscious background of the beginning of worship in the early Church. There was an interrelationship between dogma and liturgy, and one can hardly give priority to one or the other link."[30] This unconscious background expresses itself in both dogmatic formula and liturgical form, and that's why the

> dogmatic developments of each age have influenced the liturgical form. This is as true for the early Church as for medieval scholasticism, for the Reformation, for the age of orthodoxy or Pietism, or for modern theological developments.
>
> The point for our ecumenical discussions on worship can be drawn from the insights in the laws of liturgical development. It could read like this: *the confessional differences in the interpretation of the dogma of the Church are also reflected in different liturgical forms* [Vajta's emphasis].[31]

Like Prenter, whose article "Theology and Liturgy" Vajta cites at this point, the latter theologian also desires to reunify dogmatics and liturgy. Vajta thinks dogmatics is too often done without consideration of the dimension of liturgy, and when this occurs he says it becomes excessively intellectual and scholastic. Liturgy would open up new aspects of dogmatic statements that "are more than intellectual exercises but are instead existential in nature. Certainly a *liturgical theology* is a legitimate claim on the work of the basic consideration on the foundation of the Church in God's acts revealed and worshipped" [Vajta's emphasis].[32] Employing such a method would not only increase the sum total of material of interest to dogmatics, it would also definitely contribute to a more complete understanding of the dogma itself. The distinctive mark of Vajta's so-called "liturgical theology" will be that it expresses the theology of worship in an existential mode. He thinks it good to occasionally leave theology in this mode, appreciating its worship dimensions, because abstracted theology by itself is in danger of becoming cerebral and scholarly. However, a doctrinal backbone of liturgy must be provided by the secondary theologian who alone is in a position to critique liturgy's form and practice. This is why although Vajta considers liturgiology (the study of liturgy) important as a discipline, it "cannot be regarded as theological discipline without a consideration of the creative force of all liturgical development in dogma itself."[33] Without a dogmatic dimension, liturgiology will have nothing to offer theological evaluation.

It is in this context that Vajta invokes the theological principle *"lex credendi – lex orandi"* [sic]. "As long as this principle includes only the setting of an interrelationship between liturgy and faith, one cannot object to it. Nevertheless, a critical remark is necessary, especially on the interpretation that development in worship sets a rule for the Christian faith. When men worship God, developments can take place where the critical norm of the divine revelation is called upon to bring about a correction."[34] Since even liturgical areas are not immune to the effects of sin, liturgy, too, stands in need of the corrective norm of revelation which is enunciated by dogma. He mentions Roman Catholic Marian dogma as proof of the failure which ensues if the law of worship sets the law of belief. Here he thinks a custom of prayer established something in isolation from the roots of divine revelation. The law of prayer set up a dogma that must be rejected when examined by revelatory norms enunciated by theologians. Thus he concludes, "It is important . . . that the interrelationship between dogma and worship is clearly viewed without giving preference to one or the other factor."[35] The interrelationship seems to be mutually transitive: Dogma must correct worship's expression of theology when it is faulty, and worship opens up an existential dimension to theology. For Vajta the critical norm is expressed in dogma. Secondary theology, not liturgy as *theologia prima*, provides the theological norms.

Vajta's concerns are valid only so long as liturgy is conceived in its thin sense. If worship is a group expression of our piety, then *lex orandi* would mean nothing more than taking a poll. But this is precisely where liturgical theology parts company with this approach. Liturgical theology does not think of liturgy as an existential expression of theological dictums. Liturgy in its thick sense is a transaction in the divine mystery that issues in *theologia prima*. Liturgy is not for the purpose of expressing a theological thought; it is for the purpose of deifying liturgists (ascetically) who can speak theologically about themselves and the world.

THEOLOGY FROM WORSHIP

To repeat an earlier metaphor, theology of worship was like a telescope that trained itself upon an object in the sky called worship. The lens was ground by academic theologians, according to their specifications, in order to focus upon the object elected for study. The second approach we now turn to, theology from worship, looks at liturgy a little more closely. Liturgy receives the closer attention a miner would use when panning for gold. The academic theologian stirs the sand with his finger looking for a theology that can be derived from the Church's doxological expression. Liturgy is the mine from which to quarry this data. To distinguish this second approach (theology from worship) from the first (theology of worship), and to differentiate liturgical theology from both of them, it will again prove helpful to make a brief review of two concrete examples: in this case, Peter Brunner and Geoffrey Wainwright. I will remind the reader once more that this is not for the purpose of evaluating their content, but for the purpose of observing how the relationship between theology and liturgy is treated.

Peter Brunner is a German Lutheran theologian, and author of *Worship in the Name of Jesus*.[36] This work searches for a definition of worship adequate to its proper spiritual application. "Our task must now be formulated thus: What happens in those assemblies of Christians by virtue of divine institution and as certified by the divine Word, and what must, in consequence, be done in such assemblies by us today? With this question we have formulated our task as a dogmatic one in the strictest sense of the word."[37] This is a dogmatic task, it would seem, because one must know the revelation of God in order to explain what takes place in the Christian assembly, as well as to find a guide for what should be done. Since liturgy is assumed not to be theological, this is in the purview of dogmatics. And the service is what dogmatics gives to the Church. Dogmatic theology provides a canon that permits one to evaluate worship and render prescriptive judgments about the choices a community makes. The worshiping community (both congregation and clergy) should be informed about the content of revelation in order to arrive at a proper pneumatic application of worship, and this is what makes a correct doctrine of worship so important.

Brunner's approach in part one of his book sounds much like a theology of worship, our first approach, when he describes how dogmatic theology serves the Word of God. Through his theological telescope he has sighted worship in three corners of the dogmatic heavens: in God's universal plan of salvation, in the anthropological place of worship, and in the cosmological place of worship. First, worship manifests the right relationship between God and human beings because "Man cannot be God's image without the immediate, adoring word of acknowledgement, of gratitude, of glorification addressed to the Creator,"[38] and sin consists of failing to worship, because this cuts asunder the bond of love between Creator and creature. Second, God's plan of salvation is the process whereby true worship was restored to man and woman. God's personal and gracious presence began anew with Abraham, and we may see Israel, Jesus, and the Church as an interrelated and connected whole, leading humankind to the true worship that Pentecost allows. And, third, worship is part of dogmatics' cosmological concern. The worship of the angels, Church, and all earthly creatures are bound together around the same focal point: the One seated on the throne and the crucified and exalted Jesus at His right hand.

However, in part two of his book there is an attention to detail that indicates a different methodology, and for which reason I offer it as an example of the second approach, theology from worship. In part two, Bruner looks more closely at his Lutheran worship service and derives a theology from it. He starts with two pillars of worship: God's sacramental gesture whereby the human race is reached by God's Word, and humanity's sacrificial gesture which is its response through prayer, confession, and glorification. The task he has assigned himself is that of discovering what divine institution desires in assemblies of Christians, and he discovers it by observing what happens in the downward gesture of grace and the upward gesture of prayer. But Brunner assigns himself a further task now. He wishes also to determine the proper *usus* of worship, as the reformers called it. We will never know what proper use to make of worship without a correct doctrine of worship. Once this use is established, then pragmatic questions concerning the form and materialization of worship could be answered. "The Reformation has demonstrated impressively that far-reaching dogmatic decisions are involved in the manner in which we appraise the form of worship and especially in the concrete form in which we conduct worship. Consequently, there must be a doctrine of the form of worship."[39]

Brunner seeks to find a theology in the worship service, which could yield ecumenical benefit if properly articulated. Therefore he does not attend to those concrete acts that provide order and form to a service, because "no divisions in Christendom dare arise over the question of form of worship within this wide area."[40] These are liturgical matters and not dogmatic ones, after all, and at this level there are only guidelines, not commands for uniformity anyway. Instead he attends to a theological nucleus that could be recognized in worship by all Christians. It is threefold: worship is first, an assembly in the name of Jesus; second, the place where the Gospel's proclamation is heard; and finally, where the command "Do this in remembrance of me" is obeyed. The actual form of worship is a free, Spirit-wrought conjunction of these three commanded elements. This permits a unity that is not uniform, and an outlook that may be friendly to ecumenism. "If any form of worship may lay claim to ecumenical character, it is the one in which the following basic order is observed: after an introductory invocation, God's Word is presented to the congregation by the reading of Scripture and by the sermon; the congregation submits its petitions to God; it collects the thank offerings; and amid thanksgiving it celebrates the Lord's Supper."[41] This is a basic theology that can be mined from the practice of Christian assemblies who have followed the divine institution.

This theology from worship is even applicable in arbitrating how the Church should pray at the sacrament of holy communion. Since his own Lutheran tradition had once scaled back the use of a eucharistic prayer, his guidelines may seem surprising. He affirms that in accord with Christ's example, the Church should not only pronounce the words of institution but pray in words of grateful, anamnetic praise; the words of institution should project prominently in their special function; a consecratory prayer is possible and appropriate preceding Christ's words; it is appropriate to join the spoken anamnesis to the words of institution; petition for the salutary reception of the gifts should not be left to the priest as individual but expressed in the liturgical We; the congregation may pray for the perfection of the body of Christ; and this action of blessing begins with the preface and is best concluded with the Lord's Prayer. That is a concrete example of how a dogmatician decides liturgy's content, based upon the theology which Brunner can glean from its historical expression.

Geoffrey Wainwright also provides an example of theology from worship. This can be inferred in the very subtitle of his book *Doxology*, which reads, *The Praise of God in Worship, Doctrine and Life: A Systematic Theology*.[42] Wainwright hopes to offer the reader a systematic theology that will take seriously the presence of doxology in worship, doctrine, and life. He calls this a "liturgical way of doing theology" because he finds it essential to weave the thread of worship into the fabric of the Church's life and thought. Persuading systematic theology to be cognizant of the Church's liturgy has long been Wainwright's goal, as evidenced by his book nine years previous to this one, entitled *Eucharist and Eschatology*. Wainwright wrote then that "the eucharist should figure among the interests of all the various disciplines of Christian theology: our understanding of the eucharist should be aided by all the theological disciplines as they apply themselves to its study from their own particular angle, and (in the reverse direction) the eucharistic phenomenon itself should help to shape the total outlook of the various theological disciplines."[43] Now Wainwright repeats this assertion in *Doxology* more broadly and explicitly.

In most systematic theologies, the current flows only one way, namely from systematics to liturgy. Wainwright would have the current flow also in the reverse direction, so that the eucharistic phenomenon itself would shape theology's total outlook.

> My conviction is that the relations between doctrine and worship are deeper rooted and further reaching than many theologians and liturgists have appeared to recognize in their writings. In recent years there has indeed been a growing awareness of the links between worship and doctrine, but writers have still usually stopped short after a paragraph or two on the subject. Certainly I know of no complete systematic theology deliberately composed with these links in mind.[44]

A systematic theology written from a liturgical perspective would certainly bring liturgy and theology into closer conversation—at least a closer conversation than they had enjoyed before Wainwright's two influential books. I applaud that accomplishment. But there are differences between the approach Wainwright urges on the individual theologian, and the corporate quality of liturgical theology.

Wainwright argues that a liturgical way of doing theology happens when theology is shaped and colored by the Christian vision of reality. And just where is this vision found with greatest force and clarity? In worship. Although theology is an intellectual activity, "the sources and resources of theology are richer than the human intellect. . . . Insofar as the theologian is a believer, his thinking cannot be disengaged from his faith. . . . His intellect is at the service of his existential vision and commitment."[45] The specific task of the

theologian lies in the realm of doctrine, which is a coherent intellectual expression of the Christian vision, but the vision being expressed
coherently and intellectually has roots in life and experience. "Worship
is the place in which that vision comes to a sharp focus, a concentrated
expression, and it is here that the vision has often been found to
be at its most appealing. The theologian's thinking therefore properly
draws on the worship of the Christian community and is in duty
bound to contribute to it." [46] When struggling to make a systematic
expression of the Christian vision, one must go to where the vision
is found. While Brunner accented the theological structure he thought
he found in the liturgy, Wainwright concentrates on the existential
(doxological) experience in which the theologian, as believer, participates. In that way, Wainwright goes further in recognizing liturgy as
foundational, since the vision with which the theologian should work
is found in worship. Worship is the "point of concentration at which
the whole of the Christian life comes to ritual focus." [47] This does not
deny theology's guardianship role, however. The theologian should
examine the liturgy from the angle of doctrine "both in order to learn
from it and in order to propose to the worshiping community any
corrections or improvements which he judges necessary." [48]

We can find examples of how systematic theology is shaped
and colored by Christian worship in each of the three parts of the
book. In the first part, Wainwright considers the components of the
Christian vision (image of God, Christ, Spirit, and Church). Our
human capacities in the image of God are revealed when Jesus acts as
the paradigm of our worship, and the Holy Spirit leads the Church
to transformation. In the second part, Wainwright considers the
traditional means by which the Christian vision has been transmitted
(scripture, creeds/hymns, *lex orandi,* and *lex credendi*). Scripture is
best understood where it functions as a sacred book, which is in the
context of liturgical confessions and hymns that occur in "first-order
language." The value of this language to *lex credendi* comes from
its ability to celebrate paradox richly. In the third part, Wainwright
considers contextual questions today (ecumenism, revision, culture,
ethics). The fruits of establishing a relationship between worship
and theology have borne fruit in the ecumenical field, where Wainwright's
work has contributed significantly by placing worship practices within
a larger frame of scripture, tradition, and common doctrine. How
to make Christian teachings relevant to the surrounding culture can

be seen in a new light when worship interfaces both with culture and with our ethical obligations.

Wainwright says at one point, "It might almost have been possible to entitle the whole book *Lex orandi, lex credendi.*"[49] This is because in systematic theology, the current almost always flows from doctrine to worship; Wainwright's agenda could be said to persuade his readers that it is equally possible to also reverse the flow. "The linguistic ambiguity of the Latin tag corresponds to a material interplay, which in fact takes place between worship and doctrine in Christian practice: Worship influences doctrine, and doctrine, worship. Much of the present book is taken up with explorations of that interplay."[50] So at the same time worship is providing theology with its comprehensive vision, theology is exercising a guardianship over worship. Where else would one turn if popular devotion took "an aberrant turn?" What else would one do if worship itself needed to be evaluated? How else could one decide which divergent group has taken the right course? Wainwright proposes four questions to mark out the kind of doctrinal authority that can be imputed to worship: one wants to know when the worship practice arose, what was its relation to other instances of doctrinal authority, whether all cases are equally authoritative, and what was its role in the development of doctrine? To take a few examples of mutual influence, consider how the liturgical creed shaped christology, or baptismal practice shaped Trinitarian doctrine, and more recent Marian dogma has been shaped by popular devotion. "In all three cases, worship practice was in advance of doctrinal decision. Yet it is also clear . . . that magisterial influence has been brought to bear on the liturgy for the sake of establishing a developing or developed doctrine—sometimes before, sometimes after formal definition."[51]

Wainwright's emphasis throughout his work seems to be that both theology and liturgy are necessary; neither is dispensable; and if the former corrects the latter, the latter is source for the former. A structural shift occurs when moving from doxology to doctrine, but if the believer making worship and the theologian making doctrine are cognizant of this category shift, then the poetic language of liturgy can be reconciled with the prosaic language of theology. Liturgy is a contributing source to systematic theology because in worship the Christian vision comes into sharp focus, but it is theology's task to make coherent, intellectual expression of this vision, and, when necessary, recommend corrections to the worshiping community.

Observations on Brunner and Wainwright

Brunner proposes a doctrine that explains what worship assemblies do, and Wainwright proposes a systematic theology written from a liturgical perspective. I have offered them as samples of theologies from worship because when constructing this theology they both find it important to look closely at worship. That seems to be why Brunner includes an outline of what the congregation does when it assembles in Jesus' name, and why Wainwright repeatedly directs the theologian to that place of concentrated expression as he struggles to express that vision theologically. To this end, it was necessary for both authors to examine the words and actions of the Christian assembly in more detail than did either Prenter or Vajta in their theology of worship. Having done so, they also feel they are in the position to offer theological critique if worship deviates from a theological norm.

A theology can be read off worship because worship is an expression of Christian dogma (Brunner) or the Christian vision (Wainwright). The way in which we attain a doctrine of worship, says Brunner, is by looking at the activity of worship; Wainwright feels his agenda is distinct among other theologies of worship because he has recognized the influence worship has upon the imagination of theologians. Both are concerned with the theology that results when worship is treated as a source, and by this treatment they have nudged *lex orandi* and *lex credendi* closer together. The theologian does not merely look at the subject of worship (theology of worship), the theologian looks at worship practices to see what theology can be derived from them (theology from worship). Out of the doxological activity of this community the theologian derives the faith-identity and makes it theologically explicit. This theology, when adequately articulated, in turn guides and protects worship, which is understood to be a further task for theology. In this approach, the tide of influence flows in both directions. Brunner examines the worship event, true, but affirms at the outset that what dogma teaches to the worshiping assembly will be determinant for the proper *usus* of worship. Wainwright argues that worship shapes and colors the theologian, true, but claims a critical and architectonic role for theology. Theology from worship

offers help and guidance to worship practice. Is *lex orandi* the foundation for *lex credendi,* or is *lex credendi* the foundation for *lex orandi?* The
answer given here is Yes. Insofar as worship is an expression of the
Christian vision, it is source for the articulation of doctrine; insofar
as theology is an expression of the Christian vision, it is the basis for
worship's practice and expression.

 Brunner expresses this mutual influence as follows: "To be
sure, the Agenda is more than a logical conclusion drawn from a
presupposed dogmatic premise. . . . But, on the other hand, dogma
must be effective in the composition of the Agenda as the formative
eidos (appearance, form), as the formative entelechy." [52] Because the
liturgical formulary is the concretization of a dogma, therefore it can
be translated into analytical form and the outcome is a study such
as Brunner's. Worship is a resource for a doctrine of worship, but
without a doctrine of worship "we will never arrive at the proper *usus,*
especially not in our present situation, which is so confused in many
respects. If error relative to what is done in worship is taught and
preached to the congregations and their servants, or if they, perhaps,
are told nothing at all, how can they arrive at a proper pneumatic
application?" [53] Wainwright expresses this mutual influence in a way that
takes liturgical expression seriously by giving a positive estimate to the
poetic mode in which liturgy operates. Usually theology looks upon
the language of worship as an awkward and inept expression of the
Christian vision. A "liturgical way of doing theology" involves grounding theology in liturgical speech and action.

 From the perspective of liturgical theology, there is a problem
with describing worship as an "expression" of the Christian dogma
or concentrated vision. It opens one to the idea that dogma or vision
can precede their expression, as "I" precede "my body." It leaves the
dichotomy untouched. It leaves the impression that there is a truth
to be embodied, which can be done either in a coherent articulation
(theology) or a concentrated existential vision (liturgy), and the current
can flow in both directions between the law of prayer and the law
of belief because they each express the abstract faith. But proper control
can be guaranteed only if the law of belief holds the reins over the
law of prayer. Worship may provide the existential matrix, but doctrine
exercises control over worship because the latter is not theological.

A Transition to Liturgical Theology

When *lex orandi* and *lex credendi* are understood in a mutual relationship, with the current flowing in both directions, it is an indication to me that liturgy is being spoken about only in its thin sense.[54] On this level it is true. But it is not the level to which I am trying to bring our understanding of liturgy.

The question liturgical theology wants to ask is why the raw material of worship must be translated into a second order form before it can be called theology, and why only second order theology can exercise a guardianship over orthodoxy. Liturgical theology should certainly be concerned with correct doctrine. Liturgical theology is theology, and not merely the investigation of rubrics, esthetics, and ceremonial ritual. But is the only form adequate for this theological work an academic one? Have liturgy and theology been so dichotomized that we believe the assembly to be bereft of theological guidance without theology books? There is a broader definition of liturgy and a deeper definition of *theologia*. In this definition, the community's transformation in liturgical encounter with God is understood to truly be a *theologia prima,* and Christian theology arises from the Church-at-liturgy like civilization arises *in* and *as* play. The liturgical assembly itself is "a theological corporation."[55] It is quite true that the academic theologian is formed by his or her existential participation in the Christian community, but liturgies do more than titillate second order theologians. Liturgies are not just expressions of theology; they are the basis for theologizing. But this is contingent on a different understanding of the purpose of liturgical language.

Jean Ladriere gives us some help in grasping this in his essay "The Performativity of Liturgical Language."[56] He puts the question this way:

> The basic problem is to discover how liturgical language works. Clearly this kind of language cannot be analysed in terms proper to information theory: it does not consist in the reporting of events, the description of objects, the formulation of theoretical hypotheses, the statement of experimental findings, or the handing on of data. It is characterized in that it is a certain form of action; it puts something into practice: in short, it possesses an "operativity." It is not merely a verbal commentary on an action external to itself; in and of itself, it is action.[57]

These are utterances which bring a new state of affairs into being. Employing J. L. Austin's categories, Ladriere notes that some types of linguistic utterances can be called "performative," meaning they perform an action by virtue of their sheer enunciation. Promises are like this. By saying the words, "I promise," a person creates an obligation—the person puts himself in a situation that did not exist before the promise was made. This is brought about in no other way than by virtue of making the promise. When the priest asks the bride and groom if they take the other to be their husband or wife, he is not asking a question out of curiosity; he is not asking for information; he is not asking for a description or report. And when the bride and groom reply "I do" they are not giving verbal commentary. The statement possesses an operativity. (Of course, the speech-act could be made by symbolic gesture as well as by symbolic speech.)

This theory of illocutionary speech acts, suggests Ladriere, "enables us to reformulate our problem more precisely, as follows: What is the characteristic illocutionary power of sentences in liturgical language?"[58] In other words, what does liturgical language do? Or to put on it the spin Wittgenstein would prefer, what do people do with liturgical language? The answer is complex, not simple. There are multiple deployments of illocutionary speech acts in a liturgy. Liturgical language features sentences which are tantamount to exhortation, confession, interrogation, adulation, statements of beliefs, wishes, and imperatives, among others. But all these statements together make up one language which "definitively constitutes the totality of liturgical language."[59] The unity of liturgical language depends upon all these language types operating together. In terms of my analogy from chapter one, this is the grammar a liturgist must learn. Ladriere thinks that liturgical language, conceived of as a whole, possesses a threefold performativity: It includes existential induction, institution, and presentification.

He defines existential induction as "an operation by means of which an expressive form awakens in the person using it a certain affective disposition which opens up existence to a specific field of reality."[60] The term *affectivity* is not used here in the sense of emotion or feeling, "but of that form of constitutive receptivity which makes us capable of adjusting to reality in its several manifestations: to the reality of salvation which comes to us from God by the mediation of Jesus Christ. . . ."[61] The same utterance—for example, "Lord have mercy"—may be made by different persons, or at different times, but each time it is uttered it places the speaker in relation to a specific field of reality and opens in the speaker a certain affective disposition. This is true whether spoken in the first person and affecting oneself alone, or spoken collectively as if there were only one speaker.

> Liturgical language uses certain characteristic performative verbs, such as "to ask," "to pray," "to give thanks." . . . Such verbs express illocutionary acts presupposing certain attitudes: trust, veneration, gratitude, submission, contrition, and so on. These attitudes come into effect at the very moment when, by virtue of the enunciation of the sentence, the corresponding act takes place. The performative verb is not a description of the attitude which its enunciation presupposes; its function is not to indicate the existence of this attitude, but is, so to speak, the attitude itself: it makes it exist. . . .[62]

These attitudes form a system (remember, liturgical language consists of a multiplicity of illocutionary acts but held together in a pragmatic unity). In its very functioning, says Ladriere, such liturgical language puts into effect certain specific acts which will, by their enacted utterance, have repercussion in the affectivity of the speakers.

When the performative utterance awakens this affective formation in the speaker, it accomplishes the two other tasks of liturgical language. The second task is institution. Liturgical language institutes a community. In this meeting the community is initiated as their speech acts create a common, objective space. Ladriere explains by saying, "Language is not the expression of a community constituted before it and apart from it and is not the description of what such a community would be, but the location in which and the instrument by means of which the community is constituted."[63] The third task of liturgical language is presentification. The language makes present for the participants a reality whose efficacy they take into their own life. It makes it present not as a spectacle to be spoken about or expressed, but as a mystery that comes to pass.

Liturgical theology thinks illocutionary speech (including symbol-acts) creates the community that comes into being when liturgical rite is transacted. To speak liturgical language faithfully demands a disciplined position toward God, self, and world: thus liturgical asceticism. Liturgical theology proper will have to do with an attitude that comes into being through ritual structure. According to Nathan

Mitchell, this is a recent front of study among students of ritual. Scholars such as Michel Foucault, Catherine Bell, and Talal Asad place ritual not on the shelf of symbol systems, but on the shelf called a "technology of the self." In Mitchell's words, "The final intentionality of rite is not 'to produce meanings' but to produce a ritually inscribed body (both personal and corporate) that knows how, liturgically, to 'do' a redeemed world." To make his point, he appeals to one of the founding ascetics, Benedict.

> In [the *Rule of Benedict*], "rite" was not yet recognized as a separate, specialized category of human behavior (the way modern liturgists and anthropologists like to think of it). Monastic liturgy and ritual were not yet seen, in the early sixth century, as formal activities that are inherently "symbolic, structured, canonical, invariable, non-technical, traditional, and repetitive" in nature. Indeed, RB thought of the monks' three principal daily occupations — chanting the Divine Office *(opus Dei),* manual labor, and "holy reading" *(lectio divina)* — as the *same kinds of activity* requiring roughly the *same amount* of time.[64]

To understand liturgical theology, the grammar of liturgy must be deepened to include *theologia prima,* and our concept of that theology itself must be deepened until it is contingent upon liturgical asceticism.

I do not propose that liturgical practice should be immune to theological critique. Far from it. In fact, such a position would imply that liturgy has only to do with personal expression (in which case, the only basis one would have by which to judge liturgy is whether it "turns you on"), and that is exactly the position liturgical theology is trying to overcome. There must indeed be a theological critique of liturgy or else the dichotomy remains in place whereby liturgy has to do with esthetics (not theology) and theology has to do with doctrine (not liturgy). Liturgical theology's quarrel is not with a theological critique of a liturgical practice, but it is a quarrel about who is qualified to make it. Liturgical theology affirms that the *lex orandi* capacitates a liturgist for *theologia prima.* The *lex orandi,* as it comes into being in the liturgical rite, is theological.

If, however, worship and doctrine are each, in their own way, expressions of the Christian vision, and if they stand in a bi-directional relationship as theologies of/from worship have it, then the question of norm is ultimately reduced to a matter of historical precedence. Thus, historians look for times when a shift in liturgical expression influenced doctrine, and for other times when a shift in doctrinal expression influenced liturgy. But this is still talking about liturgy in its thin sense. In its thick sense, the performance of the liturgical rite brings reality to be, it does not merely bring it to expression. This is the reason why liturgical theology argues that *lex orandi* establishes *lex credendi*. It is not because historical instances can be found where a practice precedes a teaching; it is not because worship is the place where the vision comes into sharp focus and is found appealing; it is not because subconscious experience precedes conscious thought, or because liturgical language is more paradoxical than analytical thought. The law of prayer establishes the law of belief because liturgy is *theologia prima*.

Kavanagh concedes that for many "this puts us on strange ground indeed, for since the high Middle Ages with the advent of the university and of scientific method, we have become accustomed to the notion that theology is something done in academies out of books by elites with degrees producing theologies of this and that. Theological curricula are filled with such efforts." Becoming accustomed to this strange ground will require the acknowledgment that "liturgical theology comes closer to doing *theologia prima* than *theologia secunda* or a 'theology of the liturgy,' and that doing primary theology places a whole set of requirements on the theologian which are not quite the same as those placed on a theologian who does only secondary theology."[65] Therefore, to make this clearer I have acknowledged tradition's treatment of asceticism as an ingredient to theology. The prerequisite for academic theology is education; the prerequisite for liturgical theology is holiness. This brings us to the threshold of liturgical asceticism again. If the subject matter of theology is God, humanity, and cosmos, then the theological struggle goes on in the nave as well as in the study. It is neither as if believers have an inchoate understanding that cannot be called theology until it is cast in formulae by academics; nor as if primary theology is amateurish thinking that is better expressed by professionals; nor as if secondary theologians are privy to data that they must transmit to the less informed.

It is a truism to say encounter with God precedes reflection upon that encounter; but this is still not yet enough to explain liturgical theology. Liturgy is encounter with God, yes, but furthermore it is a living adjustment—meaning a theological response—to the Holy One. The dichotomy that places raw experience in the sanctuary but reserves theology for the lecture hall is here rejected. The assembly makes response, too, and although their response is different in form from the organized, analytic, systematic, researched response that makes up secondary theology, it is a theological response nevertheless. As Kavanagh states, "To detect that change in the subsequent liturgical act will be to discover where theology has passed, rather as physics detects atomic particles in tracks of their passage through a liquid medium."[66]

The assembly's response can be characterized as truly theological only if our definition of theology is not excessively narrow, and our definition of liturgy sees ritual as a ruled, grammatical activity. The liturgical assembly is a theological corporation. The adjustment made by those who encounter God's holy presence in word and sacrament is an instance of *theologia prima*. There are many reasons to reflect further, in a more systematized fashion, but this does not disqualify primary theology as theology. Secondary theology is but one species in the genus. Say it this way. Not all worship is liturgical, but there is such a thing as liturgical worship. Not all prayer is liturgical, but there is liturgical prayer. Not all space, time, sacrifice, or assembly is liturgical; but there is liturgical space, liturgical time, liturgical sacrifice, and liturgical assembly. And in this case, not all theology is liturgical, but there is liturgical theology. It is an instance of corporate theologizing which is done in liturgical community and not in private isolation. Thus, as we have said, the corporate theological experience is normative for private theology, and this theological experience is found in concrete liturgical acts and not in abstracted ideas about liturgy.

Kavanagh writes, "If theology as a whole is critical reflection upon the communion between God and our race . . . then scrutiny of the precise point at which this communion is most overtly deliberated upon and celebrated by us under God's judgment and in God's presence would seem to be crucial to the whole enterprise."[67] The distinctive character of liturgical theology stems from the fact that it is in the liturgy, under God's judgment and in God's presence, that *theologia prima* is done. Whether the theologian be a monk in the cell, a believer in the pew, or an academic in the study, the subject matter being considered is the Church's corporate theological adjustment to encounter with the Father through Christ in the Holy Spirit. Theology of worship, and theology from worship, can both provide important help about important questions, but they begin from a different place on the theological map. And, for the most part, liturgical theology has not been given any place at all in the theological taxonomy because it begins with the eighth-day rite, instead of with conceptualizations. Liturgical theology is distinct both in its methodology (it begins with concrete liturgies) and in its form (it is primary theology).

---

1. Aidan Kavanagh, *On Liturgical Theology*, 89.

2. _____, 84.

3. Robert Taft, "The Structural Analysis of Liturgical Units: An Essay in Methodology," *Worship* 52 (July 1978) 315.

4. _____, 317.

5. Aidan Kavanagh, *On Liturgical Theology*, 73–74.

6. Alexander Schmemann, "Theology and Liturgical Tradition," *Worship in Scripture and Tradition*, ed. Massey H. Shepherd (New York: Oxford University Press, 1963) 175.

7. In the first edition I included a fourth distinction, which I have dropped here for clarity. A very simple distinction was intended. If, as I claim, liturgical theology is worked out and contained in the structure of a liturgical rite, then it actually exists in liturgies. What, then, shall I call books *about liturgical theology?* What shall I call a book that describes what liturgical theology is and makes apology for it? What is Kavanagh's *On Liturgical Theology*, or Schmemann's *Introduction to Liturgical Theology*, or this very attempt of mine? Someone might call them "liturgical theology," but I think not. A live human body differs from a book *on* human anatomy. Kavanagh cleverly identifies his book as on liturgical theology. An apology for the concept is not the same as the thing itself.

8. J. Huizinga, *Homo Ludens: A Study of the Play-Element in Culture* (Boston: The Beacon Press, 1950) 173.

9. Aidan Kavanagh, *On Liturgical Theology*, 97.

10. Gabriel Marcel, *Mystery of Being*, vol. I (Chicago: Gateway Edition, Henry Regnery Company, 1950) cf. 120ff.

11. Regin Prenter, *Creation and Redemption* (Philadelphia: Fortress Press, 1968) 4.

12. _____, 39.

13. _____, 42.

14. _____, 491.

15. Vilmos Vajta, *Luther on Worship* (Philadelphia: Muhlenberg Press, 1958) preface, xi.

16. _____, xi–xii.

17. _____, xi.

18. _____, 12–13.

19. _____, 27, FN 1. See, for example, Luther's discussion of testament in *The Babylonian Captivity of the Church* in Luther's Works, vol. 36 (Philadelphia: Fortress Press, 1959) 38ff.

20. _____, 28.

21. _____, 77.

22. _____, 150–51.

23. _____, 173. The Enthusiasts seemed to think that keeping liturgical form would crush Christian liberty. Luther humorously says, "Thank goodness we have strong enough skulls to wear a tonsure, our stomachs and bellies are healthy enough to fast and eat and digest fish on Friday and Saturday, especially since they allow us to drink good wine with it (doubtless for added chastisement), and we have shoulders and bones strong enough to wear chasubles, surplices, and long robes." Footnote, 174.

24. Aidan Kavanagh, *On Liturgical Theology*, 117–18. Kavanagh does not offer historical detail regarding what these factors were, but by the time of the sixteenth century liturgy had waned "into a form of doxological education conducted by secondary theologians who possessed academic degrees. . . ." (118).

25. A stronger critique, bordering on overkill, may be offered of sacramentology when it is treated in isolation from liturgical ritual. Does the reader share the uneasy sensation I have when sitting down at a table that has not yet been cleaned up from a meal? Crumbs on the booth chair, dabs of grease on the milk glass rim, knives and forks jumbled. Why is it distasteful? Because one was not in on the activity of which this is an after-the-fact sign. Cleaning up is different if it is the closing act of the activity of dining, but if one has not been a participant in the action, then the crumbs are a step removed from the activity they signify, now past. This is how some sacramentology feels when it analyzes (abstractly instead of liturgically) the dried wine and the crumbs of bread left behind after the activity. A liturgical theology of sacrament would take into account the life-giving activity between human and divine, and not simply bus the theological dishes.

26. Robert Taft, "How Liturgies Grow: the Evolution of the Byzantine 'Divine Liturgy,'" *Orientalia Christiana Periodica*, 43 (1977) 360.

27. Regin Prenter, "Liturgy and Theology," in *Theologie und Gottesdienst: Gesammelte Aufsatze* (Gottingen: Forlaget Aros Arhus, 1977) 147.

28. Aidan Kavanagh, *On Liturgical Theology,* 126.

29. Vilmos Vajta, "Creation and Worship" in *Studia Liturgica,* 2 (1963) 29.

30. _____, 30.

31. _____, 30.

32. _____, 32.

33. _____, 32–33.

34. _____, 33.

35. _____, 33.

36. Peter Brunner, *Worship in the Name of Jesus* (St. Louis: Concordia Publishing House, 1968).

37. _____, 25.

38. _____, 36.

39. _____, 217.

40. _____, 225.

41. _____, 234.

42. Geoffrey Wainwright, *Doxology* (New York: Oxford University Press, 1980). I hope that my punctuation has correctly communicated his intent; there is none on the title page.

43. Geoffrey Wainwright, *Eucharist and Eschatology* (London: Epworth Press, 1971). This was republished in 2002 by OSL Publications (the publishing ministry of The Order of Saint Luke).

44. Geoffrey Wainwright, *Doxology,* preface.

45. _____, 1.

46. _____, 3.

47. _____, 8. Wainwright mentions that his use of the word *ritual* is not pejorative, as in "merely ritual." "On my sense of the word, even those communities that pride themselves on their freedom from 'ritual' will generally be found to use ritual; only they will not be aware of it, and so will be unable either to enjoy its pleasure to the full or to be properly vigilant about its dangers."

48. _____, 3.

49. _____, 161.

50. _____, 218.

51. _____, 250.

52. Peter Brunner, *Worship in the Name of Jesus,* 290.

53. _____, 25.

54. Wainwright quotes Pope Pius XII approvingly when the latter wrote in *Mediator Dei* that "this is the origin of the well-known and time-honoured principle: 'Let the law of prayer establish the law of belief,' *legem credendi lex statuat supplicanti. . . .* [But] If we wanted to state quite clearly and absolutely the relation existing between the faith and the sacred liturgy we could rightly say that "the law of our faith must establish the law of our prayer,' *lex credendi legem statuat supplicandi.*" I think this document is also referring to liturgy at a different level than the one I will try to make clear in chapter 4.

55. In a response by Kavanagh. Wainwright wrote, "A Language in Which We Speak to God," and Kavanagh wrote, "Response: Primary Theology and Liturgical Act," both in *Worship* 57 (July 1983) 309–24.

56. Jean Ladriere, "The Performativity of Liturgical Language," in *Concilium: Liturgical Experience of Faith* (New York: Herder & Herder, 1973) 50–61. See also Gerald V. Lardner, "Communication Theory and Liturgical Research," *Worship* 5 (1977) 299–306.

57. _____, 51. Doesn't his description of what liturgical language is not, correspond exactly to what worship would do as expression of doctrine? It reports, states, describes, formulates, and hands on data.

58. _____, 54.

59. _____ .

60. _____, 56.

61. _____, 58.

62. _____, 57.

63. _____, 59.

64. Nathan Mitchell, "Ritual as Reading," in *Source and Summit: Commemorating Josef A. Jungmann,* ed. Joanne Pierce & Michael Downey (Collegeville: The Liturgical Press, 1999) 170. Asad calls liturgy a "practice among others essential to the acquisition of Christian virtues."

65. Aidan Kavanagh, *On Liturgical Theology,* 74–75.

66. _____, 74.

67. _____, 78.

Chapter 3

The Pioneering Work
of Alexander Schmemann

Alexander Schmemann was a pioneer in articulating the definition
of liturgical theology that I am seeking. In his capacity as teacher for
three decades at St. Vladimir's Orthodox Theological Seminary, and
dean for two of them, he tried to unite liturgy and theological studies
for his students, and it is this integrating vision that interests me
here.[1] He wrote about liturgical theology in numerous articles over
his career,[2] in his book *Introduction to Liturgical Theology*,[3] and some
methodological comments can be found scattered throughout his final
book, published posthumously, *The Eucharist*.[4] For a complete picture
of his thought, we should look at all these sources, but I have divided
that complete picture into two parts. In this chapter I will gather
together his methodological remarks about what liturgical theology is,
and why it is important. I will confine myself to his corpus, summarizing
it without evaluative comment[5] and without analyzing connections
with other scholarship. Then in chapter seven I will concentrate upon
his last book, which is an example of liturgical theology.

An Organic Definition

In Schmemann's own account there is a distinct difference between
what he calls liturgical theology, on the one hand, and theology of liturgy, on the other. (I have simply nuanced his latter category by distinguishing two ways of going about it.) There is a risk that this distinction
will be misunderstood as an effort to confine the study of liturgy in
the former, and the study of theology in the latter. So let me begin
with a startling quote by Schmemann. He says, "In the approach which

I advocate by every line I ever wrote, the question addressed by liturgical theology to liturgy and to the entire liturgical tradition is not about liturgy but about 'theology,' i.e. about the faith of the Church as expressed, communicated and preserved by the liturgy."[6]

This is an enigmatic remark coming from a man whose work is famed in the field of liturgics, and it forces us to ask what he means by "theology." How can Schmemann maintain that the agenda of liturgical theology is not liturgical but theological? Does he not know that he is perceived as someone whose major purview is such topics as the evolution of rite, rubric, piety, cult, and symbols in liturgy? He has been characterized this way, but he explicitly denies it: "The fact, however, is that such is not my concept of liturgical theology. . . ."[7] Schmemann must therefore have a particular understanding of theology in mind if he is going to assert that the question addressed by liturgical theology is not about liturgy but about theology. Indeed he has. He understands liturgical theology to be the faith of the Church itself coming to be.

It is tempting to suppose one could understand the complex term *liturgical theology* by summing the definition of each simple constituent part—a sort of conjunctive definition made up of two segments. Under such a definition it would appear that there are two independent enterprises which some imaginations might relate, and others might not. There would be the field of liturgiology, which busies itself with uncovering historical liturgical data, and the additional task of theology, which may (or may not) make use of this supplied data when doing theology, or even when considering a theology of worship. Under this conjunctive definition, then, theology would involve itself with matters liturgical either when it turns its attention to liturgy as an object of study (my theology of worship), or when it utilizes liturgy's texts and practices as a source of data (my theology from worship). The two fields would thus be connected at the periphery, as when two circles touch at one point of their arcs.

Schmemann considers this way of defining liturgical theology inadequate, albeit common. It is inadequate because it fails to integrate liturgy and theology into an organic whole. For him, the complex definition of liturgical theology determines the definition of each constituent part.

> Liturgical theology—and I cannot over-emphasize this—is *not* that
> part of theology, that "discipline," which deals with liturgy "in itself," has
> liturgy as its specific "object," but, first of all and above everything else,
> the attempt to grasp the "theology" as revealed in and through liturgy.
> There is, I maintain, a radical and indeed irreducible difference between
> these two approaches to liturgical theology whose task then obviously
> depends on whether one opts for one or the other.[8]

Schmemann's definition of liturgical theology is organic such that the
former word identifies the ontological condition for the latter.

    This organic understanding cannot be had cheaply, though.
When Schmemann sets the terms for his definition, it is with the goal
that both theology and liturgy be understood in harmony with the
organic term *liturgical theology*.

> There is much confusion and ambiguity in the use of certain terms. One
> speaks, for example, of liturgical theology, of a liturgical "ressourcement"
> of theology. For some, this implies an almost radical rethinking of
> the very concept of theology, a complete change in its structure. The
> *leitourgia*—being the unique expression of the Church, of its faith and of
> its life—must become the basic *source* of theological thinking, a kind of
> *locus theologicus* par excellence. There are those, on the other hand, who,
> while admitting the importance of the liturgical experience for theology,
> would rather consider it as a necessary object of theology—an *object*
> requiring, first of all, a theological clarification of its nature and function.[9]

    I would like to call attention to Schmemann's use of *leitourgia*
at its first occurrence in this chapter. So many diminished meanings
are associated with liturgy that sometimes, to underscore that he is using
the term in a deeper way, Schmemann uses the Greek term instead.
This is not a consistent practice, but when he uses *leitourgia* it is generally
to give us pause. It is as if he wants the opportunity to start with a
blank slate and fill it up with the proper meaning. Said another way,
he is transplanting a word from another language in order to be
able to deliberately determine its grammar in the language game he is
explaining. I have already echoed such a distinction in chapter one when
I distinguished a thin sense of liturgy from a thick sense, and I will
follow Schmemann's practice in chapter four when I will begin deliberately using leitourgia to identify that thick definition.

    Schmemann thinks some people see liturgy as a source for
theological reflection, and others see it as an object of theological

study—but note that both distinguish theology, on the one hand, from liturgy, on the other. There is liturgy and there is theology, and somehow these two must be related to one another, either as source or object, because they are discrete activities. Theology might borrow data from liturgy, or it might make liturgy an object of scrutiny, but this is quite different from saying that liturgy is theological. Both of these views appeal to historical antecedents. They are each "based to some extent on a conscientious desire to recover positions that are supposed to have been held previously. And, indeed, one can discern in the history of the Church two main types or patterns of relationship between theology and the *leitourgia*."[10]

The first pattern of relationship, that which treats liturgy as resource for theology, has of late been identified with the patristic tradition. Schmemann will make it clear later that our modern perception fails to do justice to what the Fathers actually meant, but here he is describing a popular notion about the connection between liturgical experience and theological thought in the Fathers. To say liturgy is the living source of all Christian thought is taken by this viewpoint to mean that theological dogma is authenticated or authorized when it finds antecedence in liturgical expression. It takes the axiom *lex orandi est lex credendi* to mean "that the liturgical tradition, the liturgical life, is a natural milieu for theology, its self-evident term of reference."[11] The second pattern of relationship is called scholastic by Schmemann. By this he does not simply mean a historical school or period, but any structure in which theology has an independent status, such that the "position of worship in relation to theology is reversed: from a *source* it becomes an *object*, which has to be defined and evaluated within the accepted categories. . . . Liturgy supplies theology with 'data,' but the method of dealing with these data is independent of any liturgical context."[12]

It would be a temptingly easy solution to identify the patristic tradition as liturgical theology and the scholastic tradition as theology of liturgy. It would make it easy to see proponents of the liturgical movement as advocates for a superior patristic pattern over a deviant scholastic pattern. But to Schmemann's mind it is not this easy.

> It is at this point that the question must be asked: Can either of these two attitudes, in their pure expression, be acceptable to us today, and be the starting point of a reconsideration of the relationship between worship and theology? It seems to me that in the modern discussion of the liturgical

problem, one essential fact is very often overlooked, or at least not given sufficient attention. Yet it is this fact that makes the liturgical problem of our time much more complex than it may seem. I define it as the *metamorphosis of the liturgical consciousness*.[13]

The problem of arriving at a proper definition of liturgical theology cannot be solved as simply as repeating the slogans of the Fathers because our understanding of both theology and liturgy has changed. Not only has theology come to be perceived scholastically, but there also exists a liturgical crisis in which the understanding of *leitourgia* has shifted. In a moment we shall more fully examine how Schmemann understands this metamorphosis, but in brief it can be described as the loss of the eschatological dimension of worship (which, in turn, he attributes to a form of modern reductionism that confuses symbol with representation). In other words, we no longer see *leitourgia* as symbolic icon of the heavenly liturgy.

To recapitulate, we are faced with two alternatives: the one sounding like liturgical theology, but in fact missing the mark because even though it makes much noise about utilizing liturgical sources like texts and practices, it continues to understand theology as an activity independent of and in addition to liturgy; the other being a theology of liturgy that considers liturgy to be one of many possible objects of theological discourse. Liturgical theology, as Schmemann understands it, is far more radical than either of these alternatives, because it restores theological status to liturgical tradition itself, a status that has long been monopolized by second-order, academic theology.

> The liturgical movement is the first attempt to break this monopoly, to restore to liturgical tradition its own theological status. In this it radically differs from all ritualistic or pietistic revivals of the past, with their emphasis on the psychology or the edifyingly mystical atmosphere of worship. . . . Its fundamental presupposition is that the liturgy not only has a theological meaning and is declarative of faith, but that it is the living norm of theology; it is in the liturgy that the sources of faith—the Bible and tradition—become a living reality.[14]

According to Schmemann, the liturgy is not an object to observe, or a resource to quarry from, or a milieu to work out of; liturgy is the condition for theology. This radicalizes our modern perception of the patristic pattern.

The formula *lex orandi est lex credendi* means nothing else than that theology is *possible* only within the Church. . . . The problem of the relationship between liturgy and theology is not for the Fathers a problem of priority or authority. Liturgical tradition is not an "authority" or a *locus theologicus;* it is the ontological condition of theology, of the proper understanding of *kerygma,* of the Word of God. . . . [15]

A conjunctive definition of liturgical theology is not truly overcome by an organic definition until we understand that liturgy is theological. Both liturgy and theology suffer a distortion when they are severed from one another. The goal of the liturgical theologian is not to insinu-ate liturgy into theology, or to persuade the theological community to include more sacramentaries in its bibliography pages, or urge that a more doxological spin be placed on our language. The goal of liturgical theology is to gainsay the presupposed dichotomy insofar as it exists at all.

How is liturgy the ontological condition for theology, and what are the consequences to theology when it is detached from its ontological condition? In numerous places Schmemann describes the crisis it causes in theology. He thinks theology suffers an unhealthy pluralism,[16] disabling the communication it should share with the Church. Such isolated theology

seems deeply alienated from the Church, from her real life and needs. . . . Theology is no longer the conscience and the consciousness of the Church, her reflection on herself and on her problems. It has ceased to be *pastoral* in the sense of providing the Church with essential and saving norms; and it has also ceased to be *mystical* in the sense of communicating to the people of God the knowledge of God which is the very content of life eternal. A theology alienated from the Church, and a Church alienated from theology.[17]

Theology is in crisis when it is divorced from the life of Christians living the Church's faith. Yet that is what has happened to theology because it has been made into an exclusively intellectual activity, a subdiscipline of the academy.

Theologians avoid discussing the trivial reality of the Church's life, and do not even dream about influencing it in any way. In turn, the Church, i.e. the bishops, priests and laity, are supremely indifferent to the writings of the *theologians,* even when they do not regard them with open suspicion. . . . No wonder, therefore. . . . theology is guided in its inner life not by the experience, needs or problems of the church but by individual interests of individual theologians.[18]

Etymologically, the word *theology* means "talk about God," but this generic definition does not get us very far. Who is engaging in this talk, and for what purpose? The theology that Schmemann wishes to identify is one done by and for the Christian community. "Ideally theology is the conscience of the Church, her purifying self-criticism, her permanent reference to the ultimate goals of her existence."[19] Ideally, theology refers humanity and the cosmos constantly to God. When theology is liturgical, then it remembers its reason for speaking.

Theology suffers a crisis when its logic no longer comes from the liturgy, which is God's action in the community of faith, for then *lex credendi* no longer flows out of *lex orandi*. This is the crisis that Schmemann characterizes as scholastic theology, school theology. "The basic defect of school theology consists in that, in its treatment of the sacraments, it proceeds not from the living experience of the Church, not from the concrete liturgical tradition that has been preserved by the Church, but from its own *a priori* and abstract categories and definitions, which hardly conform to the reality of church life."[20] In what Schmemann calls scholastic theology, *lex credendi* is ruptured from *lex orandi* and the theologian takes it upon himself to decide what is important. If theology is "above all the search for words appropriate to the nature of God,"[21] and if worship and theology should be organically connected, then their severance results in distortion. "If today both theology and liturgy have ceased, at least to a substantial degree, to perform within the Church the function which is theirs thus provoking a deep crisis, it is because at first they have been divorced from one another; because the *lex credendi* has been alienated from the *lex orandi*."[22]

A theology that is liturgical is not one which has liturgy as its object, as if the spotlight of theological discourse momentarily shines upon worship. The question addressed by liturgical theology is not about liturgy; it is about theology. That is why research into the Church's liturgical ordo (that collection of rules and prescriptions which regulate the Church's worship) is research into the Church's theology. To study the Church's faith in its liturgical form is to encounter the Church's theological faith as well. Schmemann notes, "What I tried to say in my book *[Introduction to Liturgical Theology]*, and also in some other writings, is that the 'essence' of the liturgy or *'lex orandi'* is ultimately nothing else but the Church's faith itself or, better to say, the manifestation, communication and fulfillment of that faith."[23] A theology of liturgy sees liturgy as an expression of the faith, while Schmemann's method of liturgical theology sees liturgy as an epiphany of the faith. They begin from different frameworks.

Thus Schmemann's essential definition: "As its name indicates, liturgical theology is the elucidation of the meaning of worship."[24] But what is elucidated? Where lies the meaning of worship? Not in superficial and arbitrary symbolism, not in rules and rubrics, not in "how to" manuals, not in the closing chapter on "ceremonial" in the systematic sacramentology. Although this is what the liturgical study has sometimes disappointingly contented itself with, Schmemann insists that it is not the point of liturgical theology. Having noted the effect that the rupture of liturgical theology has had upon theology, he also notes the affect the rupture has had upon the deterioration of liturgics.

> What is called liturgics in the religious schools was usually a more or less detailed practical study of ecclesiastical rites, combined with certain symbolical explanations of ceremonies and ornaments. Liturgical study of this kind, known in the West as the study of "rubrics," answers the question how: how worship is to be carried out according to the rules, i.e. in accordance with the prescriptions of the rubrics and canons.[25]

Liturgical theology's ultimate concern is not with texts as resources, but with the Church's living faith itself. Questions about the liturgical ordo are penultimate to the theological issue that ultimately concerns the liturgical theologian. Since the meaning of liturgy is God's act upon God's people, its interpretation is nothing less than the elucidation of the mystery of divinely bestowed new life, i.e. theology. As the explanation of worship, liturgical theology

> ought to be the elucidation of its theological meaning. Theology is above all explanation, "the search for words appropriate to the nature of God," i.e. for a system of concepts corresponding as much as possible to the faith and experience of the Church. Therefore the task of liturgical theology consists in giving a theological basis to the explanation of worship and the whole liturgical tradition of the Church. . . .
>
> If liturgical theology stems from an understanding of worship as the public act of the Church, then its final goal will be to clarify and explain the connection between this act and the Church, i.e. to explain how the Church expresses and fulfils herself in this act.[26]

The Underlying Ecclesiology

Suppose it is agreed that theology is a "logos" (talk about; a stab at meaning). The approaches still differ on the matter of what to talk about. A theology of liturgy will talk about worship; liturgiology will talk about ritual development; but surely neither of these are theology, whose proper subject matter is God! Liturgical theology does not talk about ritual, Schmemann insists; it talks about God. But this is because when it talks about liturgy, it is talking about God liturgically present. Liturgy is the presence of that about which the theologian speaks, viz. the reign of God, the kingdom at hand, the life of adoption, Christ among us, redeemed life, eschatological existence. Theology is talk about God in self-revealing action, and liturgical theology can be considered genuine theology because God acts in the liturgy. The reason why liturgical theology unpacks the faith of the Church is because in the liturgy the Church experiences itself as the handiwork of God. Here God's creative proclamation is manifested and faith is actualized. Liturgy, then, is not just a resource for theology, but its root. And liturgical theology may be said to be eucharistic, not mainly in the sense that the Eucharist is an object of theological contemplation and analysis, but in the sense

> that in the moment of the Church the Eucharist is the *moment of truth* which makes it possible to see the real "objects" of theology: God, man and the world, in the *true light,* which, in other words, reveals both the *objects* of theology as they really are and gives the necessary *light* for their understanding. . . . Theology, like any other Christian service or *"leitourgia"* is a *charisma,* a gift of the Holy Spirit. This gift is given *in the Church.* . . .[27]

To understand liturgical theology in this manner, one must see liturgy as an eschatological event. According to Schmemann, eschatology is not so much a doctrine as it is a dimension of faith and theology. "It permeates and inspires from inside the whole thought and life of the Church. . . . If [the kingdom] is to have a consistent orientation and this means precisely a theology, this theology must be rooted, first of all, in the recovered Christian eschatology."[28] Christian eschatology requires recovery because it is absent; the consequence has been this metamorphosis of the liturgical consciousness. "It is not Christian worship that changed, but it is comprehension by the believers, by the Christian community. In a simplified form one can say that, in the consciousness of the community, the *leitourgia* became once again a cult. . . ." [29] What the patristic period knew naturally and existentially has been forgotten by today's liturgical consciousness. Pointing out the eschatological presuppositions and consequences of liturgy to the patristic age would be like pointing out water to a fish, but that sensibility is removed from us now, and so pointing out eschatology is like pointing to the distant future. The Fathers knew that the Church belongs to the age to come even while it dwells in this world and fulfills its mission to witness to the *eschaton*—the lordship of Christ. The eschatological dimension of the Church, Schmemann says, means the body of Christ is not and can never be of this world; it means the new life of the age which, in terms of this world, is still to come. And yet the Christian liturgist is already inaugurated into that life. If this is forgotten, then liturgy becomes synonymous with the ritual form itself, instead of being experienced as the ritual enactment of the eschatological Lordship of Christ. Schmemann agrees that such forgetfulness is common, and that we have neglected the eschatological reality in favor of the ritual actions. He makes a startling proposition in order to awaken us from our stupor: Liturgy is the end of cult, expressed in cultic form.

Schmemann does not deny that Christian liturgy occurs under ritual form, nor that its antecedents are in Jewish cultic traditions, but he insists that in the Christian context these cultic categories are understood in a wholly transformed way. This transformation "consists in *the abolishment of cult as such,* or at least in the complete destruction of the old philosophy of cult." [30] This concept of cult stands upon an alleged opposition between the sacred and the profane. Cultic action becomes necessary where something or someone or some action stands in need of being made sacred. Untransformed cult is "a sacred action, or rite, performed in order to establish 'contact' between the community and God. . . . A 'cult' by its very essence presupposes a radical distinction between the 'sacred' and the 'profane,' and, being a means of reaching or expressing the 'sacred,' it posits all the nonsacred as 'profane.' " [31] Christian liturgy is not a cult in this sense because within the Church the conflict between the sacred and the profane has been reconciled. Yet this seems to be precisely what has been forgotten in our modern, metamorphosized consciousness. As a result, religion is confined to the temple. "In the popular approach—and 'popular' by no means excludes the great majority of the clergy—the Church is, above all, a 'cultic' or liturgical institution, and all her activities are, implicitly or explicitly, directed at her liturgical needs. . . . The Church is essentially an institution existing for the fulfillment of the 'religious needs' of her members. . . ."[32] When the early Christians chose the term *leitourgia* it signaled that they did not think themselves to be doing cult, but they were doing the eschatological work of making Christ's kingdom present. "The fact that the Church adopted [the term *leitourgia*] finally for her cult, and especially for the Eucharist, indicates her special understanding of worship which is indeed a revolutionary one."[33] *Leitourgia* means to put on Christ; the Church is herself the presence of the eschaton, the actuality of restored life which is ours in Christ. The unique function of the divine liturgy is to " 'make the Church what she is'—witness and participant of the saving *event* of Christ, of the new life in the Holy Spirit, of the presence in 'this world' of the Kingdom to come."[34] Theology's subject matter is this saving event, and thus theology is liturgical in the sense that theology's ultimate term of reference is the faith of the Church, a faith created not by propositions but by the real experience of this saving event.

The term *leitourgia* originally meant "an action by which a group of people become something corporately which they had not been as a mere collection of individuals—a whole greater than the sum of its parts. It meant also a function of 'ministry' of a man or of a group on behalf of and in the interest of the whole community."[35] This is so intimate to the Church's identity that Schmemann can put the point more strongly. The Church does not have a ministry; rather, "The Church itself is a *leitourgia*, a ministry, a calling to act in this world after the fashion of Christ, to bear testimony to Him and His kingdom."[36] That is why the Eucharist is the very epiphany of the Church's identity: Here the Church enacts the eschatological ministry that was given it by Christ. But today confusion reigns about this. "The experience of worship has long ago ceased to be that of a corporate liturgical act. It is an aggregation of individuals coming to church, attending worship in order to satisfy individually their individual religious needs, not in order to *constitute* and to *fulfill* the Church."[37]

Leitourgia is the sacramental presence of God in the eschatological community, whose kingdom identity is manifested and comes to being in the celebration of the Divine Liturgy in order to be a light to the world so that those in darkness might witness the joy which the cosmic redemption has restored to humanity. Schmemann calls the loss of this eschatological corporate identity a liturgical crisis. The crisis has not been caused by a change in worship's structure, but by an error in our minds about the basic purpose of worship. Something has been reversed.

> The fact is that worship has ceased to be understood as a function of the Church. On the contrary, the Church herself has come to be understood as a function of worship. . . . The Church cannot be equated or merged with "cult"; it is not the Church which exists for the "cult," but the cult for the Church, for her welfare, for her growth into the full measure of the "stature of Christ" (Ephesians 4:13). Christ did not establish a society for the observance of worship, a "cultic society," but rather the Church as the way of salvation, as the new life of re-created mankind.[38]

A function is the purpose for which something exists; it is the activity of the thing; it is what something is designed for. A function is the action for which something is particularly fitted or employed. By saying worship is the function of the Church, Schmemann is saying that worship is the action for which the Church is designed, the activity for which members of the body of Christ were fitted at baptism. But now, in a confusing reversal, the Church has instead come to be seen as a function of worship, and this has caused "a very significant shift in the understanding of the sacraments. They have become private services for individual Christians, aimed at their personal sanctification, not at the edification of the Church."[39] Thus we treat worship as a means for our individual salvation. We attend liturgy, receive sacraments, and offer worship in order to be saved. Schmemann calls this a secularization of worship, and observes that "no word is used more often by secularism in its dealing with religion than the word *help*. 'It helps' to belong to a religious group, to be identified with a religious tradition, to be active in the Church, to pray; 'it helps,' in short, to 'have religion.' "[40]

The Church Fathers understood the matter differently. Rather than thinking that the Eucharist's main function was to help us, they looked upon the Divine Liturgy as the occasion of the Church's participation in God's kingdom. It was stepping out of this world's calendar into an "eighth day." The concept of the eighth day had widespread influence in the early Church and Schmemann makes frequent use of it. God created in six days and rested on the seventh, but when *anthropos* had fallen into sin God had to act again, and there was an eighth day. It is the day of Christ's resurrection, and to live in the eighth day is to live out of Christ's resurrecting power. And every eighth day the Church gathers for *leitourgia*.

> For the early Church the Lord's Day was not a substitute for the sabbath; . . . The appearance of [the day introduced by the Church] is rooted in the expectation of salvation. . . . It was precisely in connection with or as a result of this eschatology that there arose the idea of the Lord's Day, the day of Messianic fulfillment, as the Eighth Day, "overcoming" the week and leading outside of its boundaries.[41]

What is the kingdom of God? Where is it experienced? How does it become the root of the Church's theological word? The early Church, at least, had an answer to such questions: "To her the Kingdom of God was revealed and made 'known' every time she gathered on the eighth day—the day of the *Kyrios* [Lord]—'to eat and drink at Christ's table in His Kingdom' (Luke 22:29–30), to proclaim His death and confess His Resurrection, to immerse herself in the 'new eon' of the Spirit."[42] Worship is the function of the Church by which witness is made to God's redemptive act in Christ which restores relationship between God and the world. The Church fulfills its nature and manifests itself most fully at the eucharistic table when estrangement between God and the world is overcome, and the giver is acknowledged with thankfulness. The Church is the sacramental anticipation of the world still to come, and as such she is the first fruits of the messianic banquet, and the liturgy is precisely the passage from this world into the new age.

When the Church is said to be a new creation, therefore, it is not in the sense of being a novel cultic relationship, but in the sense of being the manifestation of our restored relationship with God, a relationship for which humanity was created. According to the Christian story, human beings are distinguished from other creatures by their capacity to be *homo adorans*. "All rational, spiritual and other qualities of man, distinguishing him from other creatures, have their focus and ultimate fulfillment in this capacity to bless God . . . '*Homo sapiens*,' '*homo faber*' . . . yes, but, first of all, '*homo adorans*.' The first, the basic definition of man is that he is *the priest*."[43] The original sin of humankind is not that religious duties were neglected, but that religion was turned into a duty at all. Sin made men and women think of God in terms of law, and sin in terms of breaking laws.

In our perspective, however, the "original" sin is not primarily that man has "disobeyed" God; the sin is that he ceased to be hungry for Him and for Him alone, ceased to see his whole life depending on the whole world as a sacrament of communion with God. The sin was not that man neglected his religious duties. The sin was that he thought of God in terms of religion, i.e., opposing Him to life. The only real fall of man is his noneucharistic life in a noneucharistic world.[44]

The cultic means of overcoming a separation ends when the separation has ended. This is the context in which it can be affirmed that *leitourgia* is the end of cult. Religion attempts the reunification of God and humankind; Christ achieves it. So *leitourgia* is not cult, even if it uses cultic forms. In Christ the whole world was redeemed, not just sacred pockets of it, and the Church's liturgy specifically witnesses to this cosmic redemption. In Christ "eucharistic life was restored to man. For He Himself was the perfect Eucharist; He offered Himself in total obedience, love and thanksgiving to God. God was His very life. And he gave this perfect and eucharistic life to us. In Him God became our life. . . . [This Eucharist] is the movement that Adam failed to perform, and that in Christ has become the very life of man. . . ."[45] In Christ, life was returned as sacrament and communion to a material creation that Adam's sin had rendered lifeless. The Church's entire life is a ministry, a *leitourgia*, because it bears witness simply by being what it is: redeemed, transfigured, and joyful. "The Eucharist is the entrance of the Church into the joy of its Lord. And to enter into that joy, so as to be a witness to it in the world, is indeed the very calling of the Church, its essential *leitourgia*, the sacrament by which it 'becomes what it is.' "[46]

The Church is a new creation, the scriptures say, but what is that? The Church is not a different creation; it is creation made new. The Church is not a second, subsequent, alternative creation; it is the Genesis creation fulfilled at Christmas and Pentecost. The Church exists as the eschatological sign of, and instrumental passage into, what this creation will become.

> She is the *passage* of the "old" into the "new"—yet what is being redeemed, renewed and transfigured through her is not the "Church," but the old life itself, the old Adam and the whole of creation. And she is this "passage" precisely because as institution she is "bone of the bones and flesh of the flesh" of this world. . . . She is indeed *instituted* for the world and not as a separate "religious" institution existing for the specifically religious needs

of men. . . . The Church is thus the restoration by God and the acceptance by man of the original and eternal destiny of creation itself. . . . As institution the Church is in *this world* the sacrament of the Body of Christ, of the Kingdom of God and the world to come.[47]

The Church is the renewal of the world, not a replacement of it. The Church is that part of the cosmos (spiritual and material) which has undergone transfiguration in anticipation of the final transfiguration.

Liturgy is God's act of cosmic sanctification, and the Christian cult is where this divine activity breaks surface: Therein lies liturgy's eschatological significance, and the reason why it is a "Divine Liturgy" and not a human ritual. As first fruits of this cosmic drama, the Church is more than the sum of its members; it is the passage of the old world into new life. The Church is the presence in this world of the world to come. The Church is a new creation insofar as it is enactment, or epiphany, or manifestation, of a transformed relationship with God, a relationship which is not our own doing but is God's gift in Christ. As Kavanagh put it, liturgy is "doing" the world the way the world was meant to be done.

This is the sense in which liturgy is the ontological condition for theology: Theology is rooted in the Church's liturgical celebration. Liturgy is the accomplishment of the salvation of which theology speaks. Start with too shallow a grammar of liturgy, and calling it the *locus theologicus* will appear ludicrous. But as Schmemann means it, the Church's public liturgy is not merely an expression of the community's vision; it is the very epiphany of God's transforming work upon the world. Theology's task is to "bear witness to this truth, and there is no end to this task. Each theologian will see it only partially and partially reflect it, and each one will remain free, indeed, to reflect it according to his own particular charisma and vocation, but just as all charismata have one and the same source, all vocations ultimately contribute to the edification of one catholic theology of the Church."[48] One can also say that theology is the articulation of faith, if one remembers that faith is not an assent to doctrine but a "living relationship to certain events: the Life, Death, Resurrection and Glorification of Jesus Christ, His Ascension to heaven, the descent of the Holy Spirit, . . . a relationship which makes [the Church] a constant 'witness' and 'participant' of these events. . . ."[49] That is why the faith is not detachable from its ritual enactment. In liturgy, the Church is witness to and participant in these events as present experience. This is why theology, as reasonable discourse about this experience, "is 'description' more than 'definition' for it is, above all, a search for words and concepts adequate to and expressive of the living experience of the Church; for a reality and not 'propositions.' . . . [The Church is] the very epiphany of these events themselves. And she can teach about them because, first of all, she knows them; because she is the experience of their reality. . . . Her *lex credendi* is revealed in her life."[50]

A CRISIS OF SYMBOL

Regrettably, the eschatological element has bled out of *leitourgia,* and we are left with a ritual reduced to cultic categories alone, accompanied by the return of the sacred and profane division. "The *leitourgia* became once again a cult, i.e. a system of sacred actions and rites, performed in the Church, for the Church and by the Church, yet in order not to make the Church 'what it is,' but to 'sanctify' individual members of the Church, to bring them in contact with God."[51] Why? What were the causes for this pseudomorphosis of the liturgical consciousness? Why did a corporate and cosmic act become individualized therapeutic help? How did the Church come to be seen as a sacred enclave in a profane environment where troubled individuals could go for help with their religious needs? A reduction has occurred here, one in which the ecclesiological meaning of the Eucharist and the eucharistic dimension of ecclesiology have been forgotten. It is, Schmemann charges, a reduction typical of an approach that he calls by the name "scholastic theology" that has infected both the east and west. Liturgy is now isolated from Eucharist as the sacrament of the kingdom, the Eucharist is now separated from the Church's eschatological existence, and *lex credendi* is now divorced from *lex orandi* and wedded to school theology. What is the source of this liturgical crisis which so dramatically affected liturgical theology?

Schmemann answers by pointing to the skewed perception of liturgy and Church that results when symbol is reduced to representation or illustration. Instead of the Church's Divine Liturgy being the sacramental presence of God *in actu,* liturgy is taken to represent a certain event of the past for our meditation. The liturgy is treated as illustrative symbol of a reality, on the assumption that the symbol is not the reality but only directs our attention to it. "The reasons for this lie in the fact that 'symbol' here designates something not only *distinct* from reality but in essence even *contrary* to it."[52] When this happens—when symbol ceases to designate something real—then two consequences follow: "where one is concerned with 'reality' there is no need for a symbol, and, conversely, where there is a symbol there is no reality. This led to the understanding of the liturgical symbol as an 'illustration,' necessary only to the extent that what is represented is not 'real.'"[53] The reductionism that plagues us treats symbol as antithetical to reality, instead of a disclosure and conveyance of reality. And then what is left to symbolism? So reduced, it can only recall to us the significance of an event by serving as a particularly vivid audio-visual aid (a literal *souvenir*). Rites are equivalent to didactic dramatizations. When this reductionism invades ecclesiology, it assumes liturgy is illustrative (of theological doctrine) rather than epiphanous (of eighth day life).

One example of this misplaced opposition between symbol and reality can be observed by comparing the scholastic approach to sacrament with the eschatological, symbolic approach. (I would like to note once more that when Schmemann uses the term *scholastic* he means an approach, not a historical era or specific individuals. To determine whether the eras and persons traditionally labeled "scholastic" do in fact exhibit this diminished approach to symbol would have to be decided on a case-by-case basis.) Schmemann thinks this is particularly evident in the way the consecratory formula was treated. He contrasts the scholastic approach with that of the early Church.

> In the study of the Eucharist, theological attention was focused exclusively upon the question: what happens to the elements, and how and when exactly does it happen? For the early Church the real question was: what happens to the *Church* in the Eucharist? The difference is radical; it shows perfectly clearly the nature of the change, from the eschatological to the ecclesiological "dimension" of the sacraments. Theology shifted to a purely "cultic" inquiry, which is centered always on the question of the validity and modality of a rite.[54]

Questions about the efficacy of the consecration were motivated by the need to be certain of Christ's real presence in the Lord's supper. But to Schmemann's mind, even feeling the necessity to have insuring certainty is evidence of a fear that Christ's presence has been degraded to the category of illustrative sign. And this could only happen because symbol was seen as the antithesis of reality instead of the revelation of reality. When symbol is understood as the opposite of what is real, sacrament is understood as an exception to nature. Then the sacrament must be a unique symbol to represent a unique reality, something *sui generis.*[55] From this perspective, sacrament is not revelation about the world, it is an exception within the world, distinct unto itself. Sacraments then constitute a special reality: "special in their being established directly by Christ himself, special in their essence as 'visible signs of invisible grace,' special in their 'efficacy' and, finally, special as the 'causes of grace' *(causae gratiae)*."[56] In this scholastic antithesis between symbol and reality, the consecratory formula serves to make the symbolic presence into a real presence.

> Any "confusion" of this reality with "symbolism" came to be seen as a threat to eucharistic "realism" and hence also to the *real presence* of the body and blood of Christ on the altar. This led to the reduction of the sacrament to the "consecratory formula"—which by its very narrowness "guarantees" in time and space the reality of the change—and this "fear" also led to the more and more detailed definition of the "modus" and "moment" of the change, as well as its "efficacy."[57]

Since the symbol cannot be real, the symbolic elements must be transubstantiated by the consecration into the reality itself.

This is not, Schmemann insists, the Orthodox understanding of the Real Presence. Since it is the Holy Spirit who is the sign of the new age, coming after the completion of Christ's work and bringing the new time, Orthodoxy stresses that it is the Holy Spirit who transforms bread and wine into spiritual food. This transformation is part of the transforming work of the Spirit. It does not happen because

> of some strange and miraculous power left by Christ with some people (priests) who therefore can perform this miracle by virtue of their power, but because we—the Church—are *in Christ,* i.e. in His Sacrifice, Love, Ascension, in the whole of His *movement* of deification, or transforming His Humanity by His Divinity; because, in other words, we are in *His* Eucharist and offer Him as our Eucharist to God. . . . The mystery of the Eucharistic transformation is thus the mystery of the Church herself, of her belonging to the new age and to the new life—in the Holy Spirit. For "this world" for which the Kingdom of God is yet to come . . . the Bread remains bread and the Wine remains wine. But in the wonderful and transfigured *reality* of the Kingdom, revealed and manifested in the Church, they are *verily* and *totally* the very Body and the very Blood of Christ.[58]

The mystery of the eucharistic transformation is the mystery of the Church liturgically being what she is for the sake of the world. The entire Church and the entire liturgy is the sacramental presence of Christ, not just the transubstantiated elements.

Because symbol is treated as antithetical to reality, and because ceremonial is treated as an ultimately nonessential framework for the validly performed sacrament, therefore school theology tends to deal with the sacraments independent of the liturgy. Schmemann, on the contrary, would have us see the whole liturgy as one sacramental, transforming act. That is why every chapter in his book *The Eucharist* begins "The Sacrament of . . ." Sacramentology must be rooted in liturgy in the same way that *lex credendi* is rooted in *lex orandi*. This is only another instance of the difference between the approaches of liturgical theology and theology of liturgy. In the latter, "something is lacking because the theologian thinks of the sacrament and forgets the liturgy. As a good scientist he first isolates the object of his study, reduces it to one moment, to one 'phenomenon'—and then, proceeding from the general to the particular, from the known to the unknown, he gives a definition, which in fact raises more questions than it answers."[59]

A sacrament is both cosmic and eschatological. It is cosmic because earth, heaven, and humanity is embraced and returned to God as His own; it is eschatological because these very creations are transfigured into the new earth, the new heaven, the new humanity, albeit still in hidden form. The Church, as sacrament, is therefore cosmic and eschatological.

> She is a sacrament in the cosmic sense because she manifests in "this world" the genuine world of God, as he first created it. . . . She is a sacrament in the eschatological dimension because the original world of God's creation, revealed by the Church, has already been saved by Christ. . . . Being a sacrament in the most profound and comprehensive sense of the term, the Church creates, manifests and fulfils herself in and through the sacraments.[60]

This is the ecclesiological meaning of the Eucharist, and the eucharistic dimension of ecclesiology. The liturgical crisis arises from the fact that both the cosmic and eschatological facets of ecclesial identity have been lost. Then symbol hides reality instead of disclosing it, and the Church's liturgy is thought to be the mere symbol of a reality that exists not in the actuality of the Church, but somewhere else, as something else. Symbol is misunderstood as the sign of an absent reality.

If liturgical symbol is to function the way it should, as epiphany and not as a representation one step removed, then faith is required. Such faith is not empirical knowledge, yet it is knowledge that can be communicated through the empirical symbol that renders the reality present. "Faith certainly is contact and a thirst for contact, embodiment and a thirst for embodiment: It is the manifestation, the presence, the operation of one reality within the other. All of this *is* the symbol (from *sumballo*, 'unite,' 'hold together')."[61] The relationship is not logical (this stands for that), nor analogical (this illustrates that), nor causal (this generates that). The relationship is epiphanous: this communicates the other. Faith sees Christ on the altar, in the elements, with the Church, in the ordained priesthood, within his Body the Church. The Church's ritual liturgy is the epiphany of eighth-day existence, which is eschatological life in the kingdom. This is what Schmemann means when he says the liturgy is the passage from earth to heaven.

The Church is sacramental not because it dispenses hypostasized grace, or because it is the warden of divine revelations, or because by the cultic power of its priests it can transubstantiate the symbol into the reality. On all these levels, the cultic acts do not yet reach their fulfillment as *leitourgia*. The liturgy does exist as cult, yes, but it is "a cult which eternally transcends itself, because it is the cult of a community which eternally realizes itself, as the Body of Christ, as the Church of the Holy Spirit, as ultimately, the new aeon of the kingdom. It is a tradition of forms and structures, but these forms and structures are no longer those of a 'cult,' but those of the Church itself, of its life 'in Christ.'"[62] The Church is sacramental because in the act of liturgical cult performed in fidelity to her Lord, she fulfills the cosmic reality which she eschatologically contains. That kingdom of God known by faith is still to come, but is already present, and that makes the liturgy of the Church fundamentally antinomical in nature.

This antinomy will persist until Christ's second coming. Until then the kingdom must be celebrated in symbolic cult (which is not at all to say that the kingdom is confined to cult). "In this world, the *eschaton*—the holy, the sacred, the 'otherness'—can be expressed and manifested only as 'cult.'"[63] In the liturgical rite, wherein the gathered Church becomes something corporately which it had not been as a mere collection of individuals, the kingdom is expressed: in the sense of "pressed out," conveyed, manifested, epiphanized, made known to those with eyes of faith to see it. For those who believe it and accept it, the kingdom is already here and now, but not yet in glory. "The Lord's glorification does not have the compelling, objective evidence of His humiliation and cross. His glorification is known only through the mysterious death in the baptismal font, through the anointing of the Holy Spirit. It is known only in the fullness of the Church, as she gathers to meet the Lord and to share in His risen life."[64] Because the Church is in this world but not of it, because the cosmos has been redeemed by Christ but this redemption is not yet fulfilled (the world is not yet filled full of God's Spirit), therefore the eschaton is expressed and manifested as cult. "Not only in relation to the world, but in relation to itself as dwelling in the world, the Church must use the forms and language of the cult, in order eternally to transcend the cult, to 'become what it is.' "[65]

This antinomy also explains why the journey to the kingdom begins with leaving. Entrance into Christ in the cultic acts of the liturgy is "an entrance into a fourth dimension which allows us to see the ultimate reality of life. It is not an escape from the world, rather it is the arrival at a vantage point from which we can see more deeply into the reality of the world."[66] The first liturgical act of the eighth day is for Christians to leave their beds and homes and gather at the assembly (the term by which the Church's worship was called in the New Testament: *synaxis*). This is already a sacramental act taking place, for Christians " 'come together in one place,' to bring their lives, their very 'world' with them and to be more than what they were: a new community with a new life," not in order to add a religious dimension to the natural world but "to *fulfill the Church,* and that means to make present the One in whom all things are at their *end,* for all things are at their *beginning.*"[67]

WHERE TO FIND LITURGICAL THEOLOGY: A METHOD

Now we are at last in a position to see the true task and method of liturgical theology. Apart from this ecclesiology, liturgical theology will always be underestimated. The Church does not assemble so that individuals can discretely participate in their private means of grace. Instead Schmemann understands *leitourgia* to be an action by which a group of people become something corporately, which they had not been as a mere collection of individuals, in order to perform a ministry on behalf of and in the interest of the whole community. The whole community in this case are all the sons of Adam and daughters of Eve, that is, everyone in the clan to which Christ belongs. "Thus the Church itself is a *leitourgia*, a ministry, a calling to act in this world after the fashion of Christ, to bear testimony to Him and His kingdom."[68] The liturgy exists in order to constitute Church, which is the epiphany of the kingdom.

It is crucial for understanding Schmemann's agenda of liturgical theology to see how *leitourgia* and ecclesiology are intertwined, because that explains why liturgical theology is found nowhere else but in the liturgical tradition of the Church. "If liturgical theology stems from an understanding of worship as the public act of the Church, then its final goal will be to clarify and explain the connection between this act and the Church, i.e. to explain how the Church expresses and fulfills herself in this act."[69] The *lex credendi* is found in the Church's worship itself, which is to say in its ordo or structure or concrete historical shape. Thus "the first principle of liturgical theology is that, in explaining the liturgical tradition of the Church, one must proceed not from abstract, purely intellectual schemata cast randomly over the services, but from the services themselves — and this means, first of all, from their ordo."[70]

To have access to the subject matter of liturgical theology, one must look at real liturgies in detail (I am here opposing real liturgies to ideas of worship). In this ecclesiology, the assembly somehow enacts the mystery; it does not merely reflect it, and therefore those who strive to bespeak this mystery will find their subject matter in these concrete enactments, not in ideation about the phenomenon of worship in general. It is a mistake (even if a long-practiced one) to first invent a theory of worship and then look for liturgical texts or practices to support the *a priori* theory. Because liturgy does not exist in general, the task preparatory to liturgical theology is historical analysis of liturgical structure and evolution. There are no short-cuts here. The structure of liturgy is not our invention, and it will not be charted by the creative work of theological theorists but by the careful work of liturgiologists.

Furthermore, since liturgy is the faith of the Church in motion, the *lex orandi* which establishes *lex credendi* is not located on the pages of prayer books but in the dynamic action of the liturgy. After all, rite is more than text.

Worship simply cannot be equated either with texts or with forms of worship. It is a whole, within which everything, the words of prayer, lections, chanting, ceremonies, the relationship of all these things in a "sequence" or "order" and, finally, what can be defined as the "liturgical coefficient" of each of these elements (i.e. that significance which, apart from its own immediate content, each acquires as a result of its place in the general sequence or order of worship), only all this together defines the meaning of the whole and is therefore the proper subject of study and theological evaluation.[71]

What is needed, then, is historical analysis of the structure of concrete liturgies, which is why this study must have its own distinctive method. Liturgical theology will occupy a special place in the general system of theological disciplines, and should have a place in the theological taxonomy. "Liturgical theology is therefore an independent theological discipline, with its own special subject—the liturgical tradition of the Church, and requiring its own corresponding and special method, distinct from the methods of other theological disciplines. Without liturgical theology our understanding of the Church's faith and doctrine is bound to be incomplete."[72] The attempt to reach meaning apart from structural analysis is a mistake. What needs to be read is rite. This is a profound and arduous task, but its forfeit risks arbitrariness in the use of liturgical material.

By his organic definition of liturgical theology, Schmemann wants to overcome the divorce of liturgy from theology and theology from liturgy. Can the alienation be overcome?

Enough has been said . . . to enable us to give this question a positive answer: Yes, it can. But only if the theological mind recovers its "wholeness" broken by centuries of western captivity; if it returns to the old yet always valid expression of that wholeness: *lex orandi est lex credendi*. And this implies, as its first condition, a double task: a liturgical critique of theology, and a theological critique of the liturgy.[73]

Some may be surprised to hear Schmemann admit the need for a theological critique of the liturgy after all his talk about liturgy being the ontological condition for theology, but if so, they have not been paying attention. There is a valid theological critique of liturgy. Schmemann only contends that it will not be done by the approach a theology of liturgy would offer: searching for a doctrinal key to the liturgical rite, constructing a theological plumb line for the reform of liturgy, formulating a theology of worship with which liturgy must comply. In order to understand the kind of theological critique Schmemann has in mind, we must begin by seeing how liturgy gives birth to theology.

If liturgical theology is not to be pulled out of the air like a magician's rabbit, then its students must begin with the ordo. "Historical liturgics establishes the structures and their development, liturgical theology discovers their meaning: such is the general methodological principle of the task."[74] The starting point is a liturgiology that examines the prayers and rites and actions with which Christians through the ages have interacted with the living presence they encounter in liturgical assembly. And this means more than a mere surface reading of the texts. To discover the meaning in the deep structure of the liturgy one must investigate specific rites, canonical injunctions, symbols, concepts, stories, and cultic actions. These basic structures "fix the 'liturgical coefficient' of each element and point to its significance in the whole, giving to worship a consistent theological interpretation and freeing it from arbitrary symbolic interpretations."[75] Perhaps liturgiology stands to liturgical theology somewhat as exegesis stands to biblical theology.

Schmemann believes the theological task is to find the meaning of the ordo exactly in its structures, since liturgy is not merely an illustrative representation of a theological principle. Liturgical theology is "the *locus theologicus par excellence* because it is its very function, its *leitourgia* in the original meaning of that word, to manifest and to fulfill the Church's faith and to manifest it not partially, not 'discursively,' but as living totality and catholic experience."[76] In its totality, the *lex orandi* will establish *lex credendi*, but those laws of belief will be found first in the liturgical structures, and afterward on the academician's bookshelf. This implies

> an organic and essential interdependence in which one element, the faith, although source and cause of the other, the liturgy, essentially needs the other as its own self-understanding and self-fulfillment. It is, to be sure, faith that gives birth to, and "shapes," liturgy, but it is liturgy, that by fulfilling and expressing faith, "bears testimony" to faith and becomes thus its true and adequate expression and norm: *lex orandi est lex credendi.*[77]

It is therefore a misinterpretation of Schmemann's principles to conclude he believes every theological doctrine must be supported by a liturgical rubric (and the older, the better). It is not his purpose to say that every teaching of the Church must find direct correspond to a liturgical text. This does injustice both to liturgy, which is not meant to be a historical source book, and to theology, which has its own integrity and is not merely exegesis of liturgical history. What Schmemann's understanding of liturgical theology does say, insistently, is that since the liturgy is the corporate epiphany of faith (the ritual locus of *lex orandi*), it is normative for *lex credendi*.

Since liturgical theology apprehends the faith of the Church as it is epiphanized in liturgical structure, therefore the first methodological step is to look at the deep structures of the rite. Unfortunately, there has been a three-way rupture between cult, theology, and piety. Liturgical cult is no longer the expression and norm of either reasonable faith (theology) or affective faith (piety). If theology and piety run autonomous courses, then "theology exhausts itself in purely formal and truly irrelevant definitions of sacrifice and transubstantiation, while piety little by little subordinates the Eucharist to its individualistic and pietistic demands."[78] The theological critique Schmemann intends does not come from beyond, but arises from within the liturgical matrix of cult, theology, and piety. He elaborates on what this means through a paradigmatic example.

In the early Church there was a self-evident connection and interdependence between the Lord's Day, the Eucharist and the Ecclesia (the coming together of the faithful as "church"). The Lord's Day was an eighth day in the cosmos in which the Christian's eschatological status was symbolized at the eucharistic altar by the gathering together of a new people, the Church. Although this connection still exists liturgically (since Christians do assemble on the Lord's day for Eucharist) it is clear that this connection is neither understood nor experienced in the way it was by the early Church.

> Why? . . . The connection itself remained a part of the *lex orandi* but it ceased to be related in any way to the *lex credendi*, was no longer regarded as a theological *datum* and no theologian has even bothered to mention it as having any theological significance, as revealing anything about the Church's "experience" of herself, the World and the Kingdom of God. Thus the Lord's Day became simply the Christian form of the Sabbath, the Eucharist one "means of grace" among many, and the Church—an institution with sacraments but no longer sacramental in her very nature and "constitution."[79]

The Lord's Day, the Lord's Body (Eucharist), and the Lord's Body (Church) should be mutually illuminating. The cosmic, eschatological and ecclesiological dimensions should cast light upon each other. Like they interpenetrate in the historic structure of liturgical practice, they should interpenetrate in our theological consciousness. If *lex orandi* establishes *lex credendi* properly, then a) the assembly will be understood in its context of the eighth day and at Eucharist, b) the Eucharist will be understood to be for the assembly and on the eighth day, and c) the eighth day will be understood as already presenting a foretaste of the messianic banquet in order to create a new humanity, the Church, which has fellowship with God on the basis of Christ's symbolical and sacrificial presence, making it his body.

These dimensions do not accidentally coincide in liturgical structure, but they epiphanize redemptive theology. Apart from this liturgical substance, how could one discourse about redemption, God's kingdom, Christology, sacraments, God's self-revelation, forgiveness, atonement, eschatology, ecclesiology, etc.? In another place Schmemann itemizes the components of the liturgical matrix as assembly, the Eucharist, and Church, and simply says "the fundamental task of liturgical theology consists therefore in uncovering the meaning and essence of this unity."[80] To do so would be to find the Church's *lex credendi* in the Church's *lex orandi.*

Schmemann is not trying to meld theology and liturgy; to suggest such a thing is already a sign of the mutual alienation of theology from liturgy. The liturgical critique of theology does not mean theology should have liturgy as its sole object of study, or that theological statements should be sprinkled with phrases from the sacramentary, or that doctrine is authenticated by footnoting rubrics. It does, however, mean that theology has its "ultimate term of reference in the faith of the Church, as manifested and communicated in the liturgy."[81] This would require a conversion not of the theologian's methods, but of the theologian. Even if the theologian "has mastered to perfection the necessary asceticism of intellectual discipline and integrity," there is a further demand; "he now has to learn how to immerse himself into the joy of the Church. . . . He has to rediscover the oldest of all languages of the Church: that of her rites, the rhythm and the *ordo* of her *leitourgia.* . . . He has to become again not only the student of the Church's faith but, above all, its *witness.*"[82]

It comes clear at last what Schmemann means by a theological critique of the liturgy. It is performed by the Church's tradition itself (that oldest of languages which any individual critic must learn). The role of tradition is to protect the *lex orandi* by means of the Church's *lex credendi*, this law of belief which itself was born in the Church's womb of prayer. There were long centuries when liturgy was divorced from theology, and then tradition's theological critique was "obscured by several strata of pseudo theological and pseudo pious explanations and interpretations, by a superficial pseudo symbolism, by individualism and legalism. And it is not easy today . . . to rediscover and to communicate the real 'key' of the Orthodox liturgical tradition, to connect it again to the *lex credendi*."[83] Connecting again the key of liturgical tradition to the Church's *lex credendi* is a theological obligation. It is not a duty that falls to ritual studies or historical review or canon law; it falls to liturgical theology. While liturgical theology must take the historical aspect into account, it must not become transfixed by the rules of the ordo to such a degree that it fails to consider the theological structure of the ordo. If it does, then it fails to be theology, and cannot offer its critique. Tradition critiques liturgy, but theology discovers (and assuredly does not invent) the tradition in the ordo.

If the ordo was just a list of rules, then history (liturgiology) could suffice. But the ordo is not the list of rules; it is the principle that animates those rules. That's why, although the historical aspect is absolutely indispensable, it "not only can never be an end in itself, but, in the last analysis, it is only from a theological perspective that it can receive its most important and proper questions. Very good and knowledgeable historians, because of their theological ignorance, have nevertheless produced monuments of nonsense comparable to those produced by the theologians of liturgy ignorant of its history."[84] The ordo is not the regulations alone, but the grammar which the rubrics embody. Uncovering this is what Schmemann calls the "problem of the ordo."

> To find the ordo behind the "rubrics," regulations and rules—to find the unchanging principle, the living norm or "logos" of worship as a whole, within what is accidental and temporary: this is the primary task which faces those who would regard liturgical theology not as the collecting of accidental and arbitrary explanations of services but as the systematic study of the *lex orandi* of the Church. This is nothing but the search for or

identification of that element of the Typicon which is presupposed by its whole content, rather than contained by it, in short, its general "philosophy." It is the elucidation of those principles and premises upon which all the regulations contained within it are founded.[85]

Conclusion

Schmemann's statement at the beginning of this chapter no longer looks so amazing. The question addressed by liturgical theology to liturgy and to the entire liturgical tradition is not about liturgy, but in fact is about theology. The question is about tradition. The essence of the liturgy is ultimately nothing else but the Church's faith itself. The interpretive task is to grasp the theology as revealed in and through the liturgy. The "general philosophy" is not written within the typicon itself because "the written Ordo arose after worship, and arose not as the elucidation of its theory, or as the outline of a liturgical rite for given conditions, or even as an aid for deciding disputed questions of liturgical practice."[86] Written rubrics are to worship as what canons are to the structure of the Church: The canons do not create the Church; they arise for the defense, clarification, and definition of a structure that already exists. Likewise, the written ordo does not determine the law of worship, but it presupposes the *lex orandi*. This law of worship is operative in the evolution of ritual structure and can be read there by those trained to read the rites of the Church. "The written Ordo does not so much determine the law of worship as it adapts this law to this or that need. And this means that it presupposes the existence of this law or 'general element.' The search for, elucidation and explanation of, this basic principle constitutes the problem of the Ordo."[87] We should expect nothing else from liturgy, which is led by the living Spirit and not by dead rules. Schmemann stresses,

> The liturgy has to be explained once again as the *leitourgia of the Church*— and this is the task of the theologian. But for this task, the real liturgical tradition must be rediscovered—and this is the task of the liturgiologist. If it is for theology to purify the liturgy, it is for the liturgy to give back to theology that eschatological fullness, which the liturgy alone can "actualize"—the participation in the life of the Kingdom which is still to come.[88]

Liturgical theology gives voice to the *lex orandi* of the liturgy, and when it does, the Church's *lex credendi* can simultaneously be heard, for it rises from this source.

1. Alexander Schmemann was born in Estonia in 1921 to Russian émigrés, and grew up in France where he was educated. He was ordained a Russian Orthodox priest in 1946. He completed theological studies at the Orthodox Theological Institute of St. Sergius in Paris, the center of Russian Orthodox studies after the Revolution. After teaching there briefly, he came to St. Vladimir's Orthodox Theological Seminary in 1951, and served as dean of the seminary from 1962 until his death from cancer in 1983.

2. The quotations in this chapter are from the sources where they originally appeared. After the first edition of this book appeared, Thomas Fisch collected most of these articles into a convenient book entitled *Liturgy and Tradition: Theological Reflections of Alexander Schmemann* (Crestwood, NY: St. Vladimir's Seminary Press, 1990).

3. Alexander Schmemann, *Introduction to Liturgical Theology* (Crestwood, NY: St. Vladimir's Seminary Press, 1966).

4. _____, *The Eucharist* (New York: St. Vladimir's Seminary Press, 1987).

5. Except to honor my own indebtedness. I went to graduate school with every expectation of doing a theology of worship. In an independent study during my first year, Aidan Kavanagh proposed that we read together everything Schmemann had written, since Kavanagh was thinking about his 1981 Hale Memorial Lectures, subsequently published as *On Liturgical Theology*. Schmemann and Kavanagh derailed me completely: This liturgical theology was not the same as the systematics I was expecting to perform. The rest of my graduate study was spent trying to satisfy myself with an adequate definition.

6. Alexander Schmemann, "Liturgical Theology, Theology of Liturgy, and Liturgical Reform," *St. Vladimir's Quarterly* 13 (No. 4, 1969) 128.

7. This is W. J. Grisbrooke's characterization, and Schmemann denies it in "Liturgical Theology, Theology of Liturgy, and Liturgical Reform," 217.

8. Ibid., 218.

9. _____, "Theology and Liturgical Tradition," *Worship in Scripture and Tradition*, ed. Massey Shepherd (Oxford: Oxford University Press, 1963) 166.

10. _____, 167.

11. _____.

12. _____, 168.

13. _____, 170.

14. _____, 169–70.

15. _____, 175. Schmemann does sometimes call liturgy a *locus theologicus* but can use the term two different ways, distinguishing between *locus* as a data source or as the ontological condition. We shall try to keep this distinction vivid.

16. There is such a thing as a healthy pluralism; e.g. "there certainly were substantial differences among the Fathers, but they did not break the basic unity of a common experience and vision." But today's theology suffers an unhealthy form. "Orthodox theologians do not seem to understand one another, so different are the respective 'keys' in which they approach the same problems, so opposed to one another their basic presuppositions and thought forms. This leads either to meaningless polemics . . . or to a kind of 'peaceful coexistence' of theological orientations mutually ignoring one another." "Liturgy and Theology," *The Greek Orthodox Theological Review,* 17 (Spring 1972) 86.

17. Ibid., 87.

18. Alexander Schmemann, "Theology and Eucharist," *St. Vladimir's Seminary Quarterly,* 5:4 (1961) 11.

19. _____.

20. _____, *The Eucharist* (Crestwood, NY: St. Vladimir's Seminary Press, 1987) 13.

21. _____, *Introduction to Liturgical Theology* (Crestwood, NY: St. Vladimir's Seminary Press, 1966) 14.

22. _____, "Liturgy and Theology," 89.

23. _____, "Liturgical Theology, Theology of Liturgy, and Liturgical Reform," 217.

24. _____, *Introduction,* 14.

25. _____, 9.

26. _____, 14.

27. _____, "Theology and Eucharist," 22.

28. _____, "Prayer, Liturgy and Renewal," *The Greek Orthodox Theological Review,* 16:1 (1969) 12.

29. _____, "Theology and Liturgical Tradition," 176.

30. _____, 172. Schmemann's double, antinomical use of the word may be confusing. Kavanagh seems to make the same point, using the term *rite* instead of *cult,* and his remark may help to clarify. "Rite involves creeds and prayers and worship, but it is not any one of these things, nor all of these things together, and it orchestrates more than these things. Rite can be called a whole style of Christian living. . . . Rite in this Christian sense is generated and sustained in this regular meeting of faithful people in whose presence

and through whose deeds the vertiginous Source of the cosmos itself is pleased to settle down freely and abide as among friends. A liturgy of Christians is thus nothing less than the way a redeemed world is, so to speak, done." Aidan Kavanagh, *On Liturgical Theology*, 100.

31. _____, "Theology and Liturgical Tradition," 172.

32. _____, "Theology and Eucharist," 13.

33. _____, 17.

34. _____, 17.

35. _____, *For the Life of the World* (Crestwood, NY: St. Vladimir's Seminary Press, 1973) 25.

36. _____.

37. _____, "Theology and Eucharist," 13.

38. _____, *Introduction*, 23.

39. _____, "Theology and Eucharist," 18.

40. "Problems of Orthodoxy in America: III. The Spiritual Problem," *St. Vladimir's Seminary Quarterly*, 9:4 (1965).

41. Alexander Schmemann, *Introduction*, 61.

42. _____, "Prayer, Liturgy and Renewal," 11.

43. _____, *For the Life of the World*, 15.

44. _____, 18.

45. _____, 34–35.

46. _____, 26.

47. _____, "Theology and Eucharist," 15.

48. _____, 23.

49. _____, "Liturgy and Theology," 90.

50. _____.

51. _____, "Theology and Liturgical Tradition," 176.

52. _____, *The Eucharist*, 30.

53. _____.

54. _____, "Theology and Liturgical Tradition," 177.

55. Alexander Schmemann takes Dom Anscar Vonier as his foil, and the latter so labels the sacrament when he writes, "The world of the sacraments is a new world, created by God entirely apart from the natural and even from

the spiritual world. . . . [The sacraments] have their own form of existence, their own psychology, their own grace. . . . We must understand that the idea of the sacraments is something entirely *sui generis*." The passage is from *A Key to the Doctrine of the Eucharist* (Maryland: The Newman Press, 1948) 41ff., and quoted by Schmemann in *The Eucharist*, 32.

56. Alexander Schmemann, *The Eucharist*, 32.

57. _____, 37–38.

58. _____, *Liturgy and Life: Christian Development through Liturgical Experience* (New York: Department of Religious Education, Orthodox Church in America, 1974) 60. The Latin Church concurs that the Holy Spirit has a role in the eucharist, and understands the epiclesis to have been implicit in the canon. To make that clear, the epiclesis has been made explicit in all recent Roman canons. The danger of a narrowed perception of Christ's presence was due to various historical factors, but the *Catechism of the Catholic Church* affirms a full ecclesial presence of Christ in the Word, the prayer of the community, in the poor and sick and imprisoned, in each of the sacraments, in the sacrifice of the Mass, in the person of the minister, and uniquely and especially in the eucharistic species (CCC, 1373). The various ways in which Christ is present was affirmed in *Mysterium Fidei* by Paul VI (par. 35–39).

59. _____, *For the Life of the World*, 42.

60. _____, *The Eucharist*, 35–36.

61. _____, 39.

62. _____, "Theology and Liturgical Tradition," 175.

63. _____, 174.

64. _____, 174.

65. _____, 174.

66. _____, *For the Life of the World*, 27. This occurs weekly, but it is also the image under which the entire season of Lent must be discussed: "When a man leaves on a journey, he must know where he is going. Thus with Lent. Above all, Lent is a spiritual journey and its destination is Easter. . . . The liturgical traditions of the church, all its cycles and services, exist, first of all, in order to help us recover the vision and the taste of that *new life*. . . . [The worship of the Church] was from the very beginning and still is our entrance into, our communion with, the *new life of the Kingdom*. . . ." *Great Lent: Journey to Pascha* (Crestwood, NY: St. Vladimir's Seminary Press, 1974) 11, 13.

67. _____.

68. _____, *The Eucharist*, 25.

69. _____, *Introduction*, 14.

70. _____, *The Eucharist*, 14.

71. _____, *Introduction*, 15–16.

72. _____.

73. _____, "Liturgy and Theology," 95. This is an appropriate place to remind the reader that when Schmemann refers to "scholasticism" and a "western captivity," he does not mean the Western tradition *per se,* or Thomas Aquinas, or any particular strand of scholastic teaching. He means an approach to theology conducted in rational isolation from the full theological life of the Church which is liturgical, spiritual, mystical, sacramental. Rooting theology in the Church's life instead of merely in the academy would restore a wholeness to theology. This does not mean adopting an uncritical stance. It is exactly Schmemann's purpose in this quote to point out that a theological critique of the liturgy is necessary; he is only asking what kind.

74. _____, *Introduction*, 18.

75. _____, 18.

76. _____, "Liturgical Theology, Theology of Liturgy, and Liturgical Reform," 219. Here the term *locus theologicus* obviously means something different from a source of theological data.

77. _____, 218.

78. _____, "Liturgy and Theology," *Liturgy and Tradition*, 60.

79. _____, 220.

80. _____, *The Eucharist*, 11–12.

81. _____, "Liturgy and Theology," 95.

82. _____, 98.

83. _____.

84. _____, 99–100.

85. _____, *Introduction*, 32–33.

86. _____.

87. _____.

88. _____, "Theology and Liturgical Tradition," 178.

Part II

Liturgy and *Leitourgia*

Chapter 4

What Does Liturgical Theology Look Like?

Chesterton noticed the fluctuation of ideas and moods and philosophical positions that rise and fall over time. He thought we have had "nothing but movements; or in other words, monomanias. But the Church is not a movement but a meeting-place; the trysting-place of all the truths in the world."[1] I should like to borrow this poetic image and suggest that liturgy is the trysting place of God. (To tryst: an agreement, as between lovers, to meet at a certain time and place.) God, our Divine Lover, has agreed to meet *anthropos* on holy ground. The liturgy is thus in line with the great biblical trysts God held in the Garden of Eden with Adam and Eve at the cool of the evening; atop Sinai at the burning bush with Moses after his ascetical ascent;[2] at the tabernacle when the *shekinah* of cloud and fire signaled God was at home, like a porch light turned on. The liturgical altar is the trysting place where God has promised to come to his people with transfiguring power to graft them into his own divine life. It is the vocation of every liturgist to grapple with what that means (liturgical theology), and with what that costs (liturgical asceticism). Liturgical theology is normative for the larger theological enterprise because it alone, of all the activities that make up the family of theological games, is the trysting place where the sources of theology function precisely as sources.

Theology seems to abhor a vacuum as much as nature does. If the meaning is no longer evident in the structure of the rite (liturgical theology), then theological meaning will be assigned to it (theology of/from worship). I do not refuse the name "theology" to other treatments of liturgy, but only when the meaning is read off the structure of the rite itself are we properly talking about liturgical theology. "One of the great contemporary illusions is that one can construct a liturgical theology without a profound knowledge of the liturgical tradition."[3] I am seeking to gain recognition for liturgy as theology, find a home for it in the current taxonomy of the field of theology, and discover its normative quality. Liturgical theology's two defining characteristics are: 1) it is genuine theology, although it is *theologia prima* and not *theologia secunda*, 2) and it is *lex orandi*.

I hope it is clear, then, that liturgical theology has to do with the "what," not merely with the "how." Liturgy is not just the emotional frosting on a theological cake, and it is not just an audio-visual aid for doctrines too sophisticated for simple believers to understand otherwise. Liturgy is an act of theology. Schmemann described the Eucharist as "the *moment of truth* which makes it possible to see the real 'objects' of theology: God, man and the world, in the *true light*, which, in other words, reveals both the *objects* of theology as they really are and gives the necessary *light* for their understanding."[4] The theological task is to see God, ourselves, and our world in their true light, which shines from the eighth-day banquet to which a new humanity is invited in the kingdom's epiphany. That is the milieu in which *theologia prima* is done. It is what Andrew Louth calls "the amniotic fluid in which our knowledge of God takes form."[5] The light makes understanding possible, and to this light *theologia secunda* is obliged. The believer who undergoes the liturgical asceticism required to be capacitated to see by this light merits the title "theologian," even if that person has not been through a graduate studies program. Archimandrite Vasileios, an abbot on Mount Athos, says, "How beautiful it is for a man to become theology. . . . Each of the faithful is called to become a 'theologian soul.'"[6] Liturgical theology looks at existence theologically in the light emanating from liturgy. This requires a considerably more robust vision of liturgy than is usually the case. If liturgical studies is satisfied with nothing more than caring about protocol and rubric for their own sake, then by liturgy's own criterion something has gone vastly wrong with the enterprise.

I do not dispute that something has gone vastly wrong with the enterprise. To many (on both the left and the right) liturgy means exactly no more than this, and it becomes the province of those who get a thrill out of rubrical tidiness, or it becomes the toy of those who use it for ulterior ideological ends. I applaud Prenter, Vajta, Brunner, and Wainwright for having taken liturgy to the theological guild, and I have indicated how each of them tried to nudge liturgy and theology closer together. Unfortunately, applying an academic theology to this impoverished concept of liturgy will not do the trick. A more profound definition of liturgical theology is required, one which sees the theological quality of liturgy and doesn't merely juxtapose the terms.

Liturgy and *Leitourgia*

To the degree that liturgy is understood to be the ontological condition for theology, liturgical theology will be understood to be the ritual, structural expression of that theology epiphanized by the Church. The dictum that comes from Evagrius says, "the true theologian is a person who prays." This does not mean putting an existential spin upon *theologia secunda;* it means theologians are Christians who learn the grammar of faith from the Church's *lex orandi.* "The 'theologian' in this Eastern view is a contemplative whose life is suffused with the *leitourgia* of a cosmos restored to communion with its trinitarian Source."[7] Understanding liturgical theology requires an understanding of *theologia prima* as something that comes at the end of an ascetical journey as an effect of holiness, and it requires an understanding of *leitourgia* as something that is more than the thin business of discovering how to creatively use liturgy, banners, and stoles.

Say it this way: Liturgical theology has less to do with liturgy and more to do with *leitourgia.* Following Schmemann's practice, I can by this distinction tag two tacitly different understandings of the Church's ritual. In the thin sense, liturgy refers to the "how," the order and etiquette, the ceremonial and protocol of worship; in the thick sense, *leitourgia* refers to the deep structures. Liturgy deals with rubrics; *leitourgia* refers to the "what," and brings us back to the *ergeia* (work) that God's people *(laos)* are called to perform on behalf of the many. It deals with what gives rubrics their reason and value.[8]

I do not want to be misunderstood as suggesting that liturgical rubric is unimportant. Anyone who has sat through a liturgical disaster in nave or sanctuary could join me in wishing for greater and more graceful attention to the "how." But one cannot stop at the thin definition of liturgy if one is to come to a thick definition of *leitourgia.* It makes little sense to call liturgy either theological or ascetical if one is only treating the thin definition. And from that starting point, it is thought that someone has to organize this inchoate raw data, so the academic theologian volunteers to make sense of the nontheological, brute experience of believers. *Theologia secunda* undertakes to carefully examine the ideas reflected by the faithful in an unclear and clumsy way, and offers to both clarify the doctrine and critique the expression. We saw our earlier examples of theology of/from liturgy make the claim that dogma "is called upon to bring about a correction" (Vajta), is necessary to establish the correct *usus* (Brunner), and should exercise doctrinal control over *lex orandi* (Wainwright).

To speak of liturgical act as *being* theological act, and not simply a subject or resource for the theological act, will require an understanding of *leitourgia* pitched in a different key than the one more familiar to our ears. To apprehend liturgy as the community's *theologia prima* will require that liturgy be understood as more than mood or style or expression; liturgy must be treated as rite, not merely as protocol. A difficulty presents itself right away. The distinction between liturgy and *leitourgia*, which I am observing in Schmemann and Kavanagh, implies that while nearly all worship services have some sort of liturgy (i.e., function according to a more or less loosely defined protocol), not all worship services could be characterized as *leitourgia*. I do not deny the implication, but does all Christian worship need to be *leitourgia?* The Church has historically appeared to say so, yet *leitourgia's* recent absence seems not to be greatly missed. Kavanagh traces the loss to developments that began before the sixteenth century, but then culminated in that century and continue to leave their mark upon the modern world. He says,

> A sense of rite and symbol in the West was breaking down and under siege. And since it now appears that those who sought to repair the breakdown were its products rather than its masters, they may be said with greater accuracy to have substituted something in its place that was new and, to them, more relevant to the times. It was a new system of worship which would increasingly do without rite, one in which printed texts would increasingly bear the burden formerly borne by richly ambiguous corporate actions done with water, oil, food, and the touch of human hands. . . . *Liturgy had begun to become "worship".* . . . And the primary theological act which the liturgical act had once been now began to be controlled increasingly by practitioners of secondary theology whose concerns lay with correct doctrine in a highly polemical climate.[9]

Why has the substitution of liturgy for *leitourgia* scarcely been noticed? Because of the reductionism of which Schmemann spoke? Because rite has receded, as Kavanagh charges?[10] Yes, to both.

The most troublesome result of this diminished sense of *leitourgia* has been the apparent loss of sensitivity to ecclesial identity and to the deep structure of the liturgy itself. Worship comes to be looked upon as a means to an end, rather than an end in itself, and liturgy comes to be looked upon as one means among many to edify, instruct, stimulate, or exhort the congregation about God, rather than being an encounter that sends shock waves into believers' lives (asceticism) and sight (theology). R. Taylor Scott has given this misunderstanding an interesting name. "As I see it, the chief misunderstanding of liturgy today is *the instrumental error.* This error has it that all these words, vestments, songs, sermons, movements, and so on, which, taken together, constitute the liturgy, exist for one's own spiritual enrichment and nurture. In short, the liturgy becomes an instrument for one's own personal enrichment. There is absolutely nothing problematic to private devotion, but that is not what constitutes liturgy. . . ."[11] To paraphrase in our present jargon, there is nothing problematic to private devotion done in common (thin liturgy), but that is not what constitutes *leitourgia.*[12]

It would be an unacceptable case of overkill to try to defend the importance of liturgical rite by implying that the absence of *leitourgia* meant the absence of God's presence altogether, making the worship service devoid of prayer, praise, grace, and gospel. Such stone-throwing between Christian houses would not be in the Spirit. Although we are indeed charging that liturgical form without *leitourgia* is oxymoronic to Christian tradition, this does not bring us to accuse the worshipers' faith of being inadequate and imperfect. After all, the fire at the burning bush is not confined to the wick of a votive candle, and this Spirit blows where it will. It would be excessive to suggest that only worship done with ritual precision can conjure up God; more than excessive, to suggest such ritualistic control of God would be blasphemous. But this is the whole point! The relationship between liturgy and *leitourgia* is not a sorcerous one. To the contrary, Schmemann thought the relationship was an antinomous one.

In Christianity, liturgical cult does not mean "cultivating the god"; it means creating the Church, the Body of Christ. Even on a sociological level this is true of ritual, as Kavanagh found when he investigated the role of ritual in forming identity:

> The functions of conceiving and enacting the values of the group . . . are what I understand to be cult. The conceiving aspect I take to be myth, and the enactment aspect I take to be ritual. Both myth and ritual thus appear to me as strictly correlative and inseparable functions: their reciprocal union is what I mean by cult. The outcome of cult, so understood, is what I understand as culture . . .[13]

Leitourgia creates a people, a people called Church. The Church might develop liturgy, but *leitourgia* creates Church. It is true that over time the assembly will develop stylistic accoutrements, expressions, symbols, and gestures, but *leitourgia* as encounter with God is the source for the Church's existence and thinking, and thus the ontological condition for any such development. That, and only that, is what is meant by claiming that *lex credendi* rests upon *lex orandi*. The principle does not intend to say that magisterial teaching is to be determined by popular opinion polls. The principle does intend to say that what is taught (theologically, dogmatically, canonically, or magisterially) is not our own invention. Insofar as the Church is birthed and sustained by encounter with the Holy One, the *theologia prima* that occurs here is the source for what is taught.

One indication of having slipped away from *leitourgia* is when we treat worship as the genus, and liturgy as a species within that genus. When worship is understood to be the essential goal, and liturgy is understood to be one of numerous ways of accomplishing that goal, then we are speaking of liturgy in its thin sense. This perspective believes there are many ways to worship, and some people like to do so in a liturgical format, and some people don't. Some people like their worship complex, and some people like it simple, but one may take it or leave it, according to need and disposition. As some people enjoy team sports like bowling and so join a league, while others do not and prefer to go jogging alone, similarly, some people like liturgical community, while others do not and prefer to worship in their own way. Rubrical pomp and protocol might aid some people's worship and faith, but really one's prayer, praise, doxology, service, or thanksgiving might equally be private and personal and spontaneous. The person who has an interest in liturgy would find it difficult to make an apology from within this viewpoint. The theologian with a penchant for liturgy would have to make an argument that liturgical doxology is somehow more inspiring than private doxology, or that liturgical prayer can be as meaningful as extemporaneous prayer, or that liturgical pomp makes worship just a little more exhilarating. Unfortunately, this frequently seems to be the only line along which a defense of "liturgical" versus "nonliturgical" worship is drawn.

The positions are reversed when *leitourgia* is understood as ritual. Liturgy is not one form among many by which to worship; instead worship is one action among the many that take place in *leitourgia*. Kavanagh's list of some of those activities reveals that liturgical place is not a quiet, private place. He calls this trysting place

> a vigorous arena for conducting public business in which petitions are heard, contracts entered into, relationships witnessed, orations declaimed, initiations consummated, vows taken, authority exercised, laws promulgated, images venerated, values affirmed, banquets attended, votes cast, the dead waked, the Word deliberated, and parades cheered. . . . It is not a carpeted bedroom where faith may recline privately with the Sunday papers. . . . [The place of the ekklesia] is the Italian piazza, the Roman forum, the Yankee town green, Red Square moved under roof and used for the business of faith.[14]

Leitourgia includes worship, yes, but much more as well. One petitions for salvation, intercedes in prayer, offers up one's self and the world to the creator, makes anamnesis and eucharist and epiclesis, fortifies one's communal identity for servanthood in the world, and so forth. One does more than worship in *leitourgia;* one does the world as it was meant to be done (Kavanagh) in behavior that is eschatological and cosmological (Schmemann).

Robert Hovda corroborates this theme when he critiques an understanding of Sunday that one sometimes finds. He maintains that contrary to longstanding opinion, the early Church did not believe their Sunday replaced Israel's Sabbath.

> It is clear that the sabbath remained the Sabbath. . . . Among the followers of the way of Jesus, there was a great feeling of fulfillment, a conviction that a new age had dawned. . . . There could not be a "sacred-profane" dichotomy, or even distinction, in this new creation. . . . All places, all days, and all work belong to God in a quite new sense. The preparation for all this was over, the eschaton had dawned, the realization was here.[15]

The Lord's way had been prepared, and while sacred time/space was part of that preparation, for those living in the light of the irruption of God's eschatological rule there was no interest in carving a sacred day out of an allegedly profane week. This explains the early Church's conscious avoidance of cultic terminology for the place, the time, the officiant, and even the action, which was simply called "the assembly." But at some point, Hovda observes, this eschatological sense was surrendered to an institutional sense: Sunday became a sacred day, and the assembly became a people saved from the world rather than being Christ's body for the world. The sacred-profane opposition was restored. It seemed that "God, Christ, our oneness as the body of Christ and as agents of the new age — these are absent everywhere else. I have to 'go to church' to find them."[16] Hovda's point is that this is wrong. Christians do not assemble on Sunday for worship because God is confined to a sacred place on a sacred day. They assemble in order to be the icon of a redeemed world, and then conform the rest of life, politics, family, and social obligation to that very image. The arena in which the life of faith is played is not determined by the boundary of the temple, but by the boundaries of world history.

Then what is the purpose of assembling on Sunday? Not because God is here and not there, but so that in their vocations the baptized can transform what is there by what was ritualized here. Christians proclaim Christ's cross until he comes again by eucharistic memorial and by living a cruciform life. This is the purpose of the rhythm of moving between sacred and profane, and it is the basis of the antinomy Schmemann saw between cult and noncult. "If 'assembling as the Church' presupposes separation from the world, . . . this exodus from the world is accomplished *in the name of the world,* for the sake of its salvation. . . . We separate ourselves from the world in order to bring it, in order to lift it up to the kingdom, to make it once again the way to God and participation in his eternal kingdom."[17] This same point is affirmed by a Russian philosopher named Vladimir Solvoyof when he writes:

> In order to realize the Kingdom of God on earth, it is necessary, first, to recede from earth; in order to manifest the spiritual idea in the material world it is necessary to be free and detached from that world. A slave of the earth cannot possess it and consequently cannot make it the foundation of God's Kingdom. . . .

The highest aim for Christianity is not ascetic detachment from the natural life but its hallowing and purification. But in order to purify it, one must, in the first instance, be pure from it. The purpose of Christianity is not to destroy earthly life, but to raise it towards God who comes down to meet it. . . . Only he who is free from the world can benefit it. A captive spirit is unable to rebuild its prison into a temple of light: he must first of all free himself from it . . . the purpose of Christian asceticism is not to weaken the flesh, but to strengthen the spirit for the transfiguration of the flesh.[18]

Taft's remark may also be taken as prescriptive: "The purpose of all Christian liturgy is to express in a ritual moment that which should be the basic stance of every moment of our lives."[19] It decodes Kavanagh's otherwise cryptic rule of liturgy: "Liturgical ministers should never be seen to do in the liturgy what they are not regularly seen to do outside the liturgy."[20]

Although leitourgia also stimulates and nourishes one's private doxology, that is not its first purpose. "What is really important is that the Christian community celebrate its origin, existence and destiny and thereby build itself up. In other words, it is not primarily the individual Christian's fulfillment of a personal responsibility to worship God that is at stake in regard to Sunday worship, but the responsibility of the Christian community to grow."[21]

In a different context Schmemann inadvertently calls attention to what *leitourgia* involves by describing what its absence would feel like. He describes the Orthodox lenten observance of the Liturgy of the Presanctified Gifts. A normal eucharistic service celebrates the fact that Christ is in the midst of his people, but during Lent a second truth is observed, namely that we are sojourners. We are still on pilgrimage, and this is the great lenten reminder. So during Lent, a Liturgy of Presanctified Gifts is held on Wednesdays and Fridays, not a Divine Liturgy. At this special evening service of communion, the body of Christ consecrated at an earlier liturgy (presanctified) is distributed. Schmemann describes the transfer of the presanctified bread to the Holy Table:

Externally this entrance is similar to the Great Entrance of the Eucharist but its liturgical and spiritual meaning is of course totally different. In the full Eucharistic service, we have here the Offertory procession: the Church brings herself, her life, the life of her members, and indeed that of the entire creation as sacrifice to God, as re-enactment of the one full and perfect sacrifice of Christ. Remembering Christ, she remembers all those whose life He assumed for their redemption and salvation. At the Presanctified Liturgy, there is no offering, no sacrifice, no Eucharist, no Consecration, but the mystery of Christ's presence in the Church is being revealed and manifested![22]

The actions Schmemann enumerates give a small hint of what *leitourgia* involves. This is a description of the work *(ergeia)* that liturgists do, clergy and lay in cooperation. I am not suggesting that Christ is absent in nonliturgical services; but when this work is absent, can the service rendered be called *leitourgia?* When Calvary is understood in such a way that its sacrifice precludes the eucharistic sacrifice, then is it not a communion service at which the ministers distribute a presancti-fied gift of Christ, without liturgical offering, sacrifice, anamnesis, or transubstantiation? What makes a church "liturgical" is neither that a printed prayer book is used, nor that the priest happens to like to sing. A church is "liturgical" when the community brings itself and creation as sacrifice to God in order to be healed by being joined to Christ's self-offering to the Father in a memorial prayer of thanksgiving through which matter is consecrated and lives are transfigured in the Holy Spirit.

A FLAWED QUESTION: THE CHICKEN OR THE EGG?

Since the Church's adjustment to its encounter with God is preserved in the rite's structure, I have argued that *leitourgia* is theological. The body of Christ gathers to be shaped by the Holy One. Theology that is liturgical is the search for meaning by this community after it has been approached by God, and which meaning is preserved in its ritual structures. Those rites do not merely provide data for theological anal-ysis; they are themselves a theological artifact and can be read. "Here the student of liturgy may be of some modest service in aiding the secondary theologian to read the primary body of perceived data in a living tradition of Christian worship. What needs to be read is rite."[23] The meaning preserved and manifested in the structure of the commu-nity's rites is as truly theological as what is contained in the books of the community's dogmaticians, academics, and pastors.

> Liturgy is an object of theological investigation because it is just as much an expression of belief as are the verbal monuments of tradition (patristic

writings, theological treatises, conciliar decrees, even the Bible). To think that a homily of John Chrysostom or John Calvin, or a book by Karl Rahner or Karl Barth, is worthy of the theologian's attention, and fail to understand how the ways and the prayers by which these same gentlemen . . . have worshiped God is worthy of the same, is the prejudice of those so locked into a narrow concept of expression as to think that only words communicate anything theological.[24]

Liturgical theology does not begin with *leitourgia* due to some historical elitism or idealistic repristination. It begins where theology must begin: with God's encounter with his people, where the liturgist is given the capacity of theological speech (in both oral and symbolic form). Liturgical theology is not what happens when an academic prays while thinking, or thinks while praying, or focuses his attention upon some doxological expression of Christian dogma, or examines theological and anthropological dimensions of the liturgy, or leafs through sacramentaries to quarry support for a controlling thesis. Liturgical theology is what comes from taking *lex orandi* seriously. And that's why *lex orandi* establishes *lex credendi*. This is not affirmed out of some vague egalitarianism that rejoices in cases where ordinary worshipers formulate a doctrine before the magisterium does. I reject the very setup of the "chicken-or-the-egg" question. The law of prayer establishing the law of faith is not a matter of antecedence, but it is a matter of priority. *Lex orandi* is not claimed to be chronologically antecedent to every *lex credendi;* rather, the former is claimed to be the foundation for doing the latter. Christians believe what they believe (about Christ, the Trinity, heaven and hell, etc.) in order to account for the verities they encounter liturgically (Jesus is Lord, we prayer to the Father through the Son in the Holy Spirit, beatitude is ours unless we spurn mercy, etc.). *Leitourgia* establishes theology the way tradition establishes icon, and gospel establishes homily. It is not mainly a chronological relationship, but a normative one. Christians believe what they believe, because they know what they know by doing it.

If it were only a matter of antecedence, we need not have looked further than Gregory Dix. His *Shape of the Liturgy* abounds with examples of how changes in liturgical style have reverberated through doctrine and piety, if that was all we needed. Ecclesiology was affected, Dix says, when the priest began to face the altar with his back to the people though the change in position "appears to have begun, almost accidentally . . . due to certain architectural and devotional changes of fashion";[25] "considerable structural variations between Eastern and Western rites" developed out of a "trifling original difference in the treatment of the people's offerings";[26] innovative phrases in the liturgy preceded the doctrine of transubstantiation, they did not follow it;[27] "a 'high' doctrine of the sacrament has always been accompanied by an aroused conscience as to the condition of the poor";[28] Cyril's "theology is based upon his prayer" and the inclusion of such an invocation has "clear and novel doctrinal implications in prayers."[29] Theodore elaborated his scheme of the eucharistic elements as Christ's dead body in order to accommodate the elaborate procession of elements from the sacristy which began as a convenience.[30] One could go on to include examples from how the faith of the Church was impacted by liturgical calendars, vestments, the passivity of the laity at Eucharist, and ocular communion.

The chicken-or-the-egg question is misleading because it treats *lex orandi* as the expression of an idea (a rather poorer expression than *lex credendi* can give, it is thought) and then looks for cases where it appeared first. But *leitourgia* is not an expression; it is an epiphany. *Leitourgia* does not teach simplified lessons to unsophisticated people; it teaches the whole theological grammar to believers willing to undergo the discipline. It creates theologians, and some of them might even read and write books. To be comfortable with this unfamiliar ground requires a thicker definition of liturgy. What caused this gap between the thin and thick senses of liturgy? Schmemann says it is due to a metamorphosis in our liturgical consciousness that overlooks the eschatological dimension; Taft says it is because of a shift from structure to symbolic interpretation in the way we approach liturgical commentary; Kavanagh says it is because of our atrophied sense of rite and the academy's uneasiness with *theologia prima*. Whatever the cause, the result is a difference in understanding that seems so wide that the two sides scarcely engage each other. So liturgy scholars offer an apologetic to their university for the value of studying ancient sacramentaries; academics with a commitment to the church's life say systematic theology should have an existential relevance; historians search for evidence of liturgy's influence upon doctrine, as if to prove occasionally the chicken does come before the egg, or vice versa. All these efforts prod liturgy and theology a bit closer together, but the formula is still written with the dash that dodges commitment to a priority: *"lex orandi – lex credendi."*

Finding historical examples of antecedence does not decide the question. Of course liturgy has influenced doctrine, and of course doctrine has influenced liturgy. If one reads *lex orandi* in its thin sense, this is indisputable. But *leitourgia* is another matter. Then the whole question changes. Kavanagh understands the verb used by Prosper of Aquitaine when discussing *lex supplicandi* (the law of supplication, a special kind of prayer) to mean exactly this.

> That verb was *statuat,* as in *lex supplicandi legem statuat credendi:* The law of worshiping founds the law of believing. So long, I think, as the verb stays in the sentence it is not possible to reverse subject and predicate any more than one can reverse the members of the statement: the foundation supports the house. Having said that, one cannot really say that the house supports the foundation. One must say something different, such as the house puts great stress upon its foundation, or the house influences its foundation in ways different from those by which the foundation influences the house resting upon it. . . . The old maxim means what it says. One thing it does not, however, say or mean is that the *lex credendi* exerts no influence upon the *lex supplicandi:* only that it does not constitute or found the *lex supplicandi.* That is all. But it is a precious, because fundamental, insight. . . .[31]

The way the Church exists is by its *leitourgia,* like the way a society exists is by the language that it speaks.

> An aliturgical Christian church is as much a contradiction in terms as a human society without language. By this I mean something harder and more definite than the general assertion that Christians worship. I mean that *ecclesia* and *leitourgia* are coterminous in origin and very nearly convertible as terms. The community in which my faith is worked out is Christian because the cult it practices is Christian throughout. . . . In this sense a human community does not merely use a language; it *is* the language it speaks. Similarly, a Christian church does not merely use a liturgy; it *is* the liturgy by which it worships.[32]

That is what is being claimed when *lex orandi* is said to be the foundation for *lex credendi. Lex orandi* takes priority because *leitourgia* is formative of the Christian. In class Kavanagh liked to say that we don't go to Mass because we're Catholic; we're Catholic because we go to Mass.

The biggest stumbling block to the definition I am advancing is the claim that the law of prayer establishes *(statuat)* what is believed. I sometimes sense an attempt made by some people to deal with this stumbling block by proposing a look-alike variant of liturgical theology. This variant modifies the explanation just slightly, as follows. Suppose, it says, that rite does not establish theology any more than theology establishes rite, but rather the Church establishes them both. Suppose there is a third thing existing behind the other two, then this metafoundation could avoid the *statuat* question altogether. It is the Church's faith that issues in two formats, one liturgical and the other dogmatic. The faith of the Church could be expressed both academically and devotionally. Consequently, this position would say, the faith of the Church ensconced in devotional form can be translated by some well-meaning theologian to aid the theological task, and, conversely, the faith of the Church rationally outlined in doctrinal contours can be translated by some well-meaning liturgiologist to aid the liturgical task. But the Church itself would be called the source of both faith and theology, devotion and doctrine, liturgy and dogma. If this sounds familiar to the earlier description of theology from worship, it is not by accident; I have only entered it by the back door.

This may sound promising, but now arises the question that distinguishes liturgical theology from this variant: Where do we find this Church? The Church whose faith is, in turn, expressed devotionally and rationally, how do we know it? How do Christians participate in it? It is the distinctive mark of liturgical theology that its ecclesiology is eucharistic. The Eucharist is not one means of grace among others; rather, its celebration both signifies, and causes by signifying (as is a habit of sacraments), the body of Christ. Liturgical theology does not begin with a concept—whether it be of Church, or a notion of revelation, or a dogma in the mind—it begins with the Church in motion. It begins with tradition coming to be. "The very purpose both of the Church and of her worship [is] above all precisely a *liturgy*, an action *(ergon)*, in which the essence of what is taking place is simultaneously revealed and fulfilled."[33]

THE CAPACITY FOR LITURGICAL THEOLOGY

To say liturgy is theological does not mean a leader pronounces a proposition and the congregation antiphonally responds with a passage from the catechism; it is not as though the people are listening for propositions at all. The form this theology takes is not propositional.

Liturgical theology forms a subject, a self. Liturgists do the hard work *(askesis)* of believing, hoping, grieving, rejoicing, repenting, making glad noises, etc. The Word is proclaimed, and the people do this Word; it grips them, and they exercise it. The mouth can speak *"theos-logos"* because the heart is filled with Christ, who is the logos of God. But that heart must be pure.[34] *Leitourgia* doesn't just make the thinker think doxologically or theologize prayerfully; it forms a believer whose life is theological. That is why I suggest calling the formation "liturgical asceticism." Then the person who prays may be called a theologian. Theology occurs because the community has been beckoned to be conformed to the image of Christ, who is the icon of the Father. If liturgy means sharing the life of Christ (being washed in his resurrection, eating his body), and if *askesis* means discipline (in the sense of forming), then liturgical asceticism is the discipline required to become an icon of Christ and make his image visible in our faces.

As much significance as all this gives to the liturgical rite, it also gives as much necessity to extending the liturgy's parameters beyond the rite (and, therefore, beyond the section of the seminary catalogue having to do with merely practical skills of the trade). The liturgy does not exist to stimulate worshipers, but to make them over into new sons or daughters of God. Paul Holmer insists on the point:

> It would be odd to say that Christian worship and liturgy are only stimu- lating or expressive. For worship requires not that one like the liturgy but that one come to abide in God himself. To worship God requires that one really worship him and not get engrossed in the liturgy. The liturgy gets its legitimacy and point from the fact that God requires an offering, enjoins contrition and repentance, promises a pardon, and proffers redemp- tion. But this makes sense only because there is a God whose will is our law, whose pardon is our renewed life, and whose mercy reads our very hearts. . . .[35]

It is true that liturgical form will reflect the community's struggle for meaning, but this is always in the context of tradition. *Leitourgia* is ontological (not just expressive) because it reveals how God sees the world. Seeing with these eyes, learning the grammar of the logos, is what it means to be a theologian. Liturgy should shape and change us to fit God's vision of what a human being is; it should not be a series of snap-on formats that express the ideals of this generation or that, this culture or that. *Leitourgia* is revelation-in-motion: the picture as icon, the Bible as scripture, speech as proclamation, bath and meal as sacrament. To come into the presence of this God is to be deeply changed, to stand in judgment, and being thus changed to practice theology upon the world by speaking God's word—both holiness and mercy—to it. This is how liturgy and theology and asceticism are interwoven. There is nothing deadlier than didactic liturgy, but there is nothing more antithetical to *leitourgia* than one that does not form. Thin liturgy gives information; thick liturgy in-forms the practitioner.

A growing number of authors have addressed the subject of liturgy's influence upon the worshiper. It would be beneficial to note the work of some of them in drawing points of connection between liturgy and the formation of the believer.[36] Don Saliers suggests that a "crisis of liturgical language" has occurred. He is not referring to a linguistic problem that could be solved by developing a new vocabulary or a new set of symbols for our time, but he means that many people do not seem to understand the language of faith. "[M]any people do not understand it, not because they lack the definitions of the words, but because they fail to see the point of speaking the way. . . . To see the point of the language does not mean that we can always comment upon it or theorize about it. No, to see its point is to take it to heart, to act upon it, and to let it shape our life."[37] To speak the language of faith requires formation in the Christian life, he suggests, which could be called liturgical formation. The *lex orandi* of the Church at prayer provides a language of faith that can shape us even if we cannot theorize about it. Considered from this perspective, one's ability to think theologically requires more than just clear-headedness, or logic, learned from other disciplines. Primary theology, by this analysis, aims to do more than provide a lexicon of terms. It aims to allow the thinker to hang concepts together by the logic of theological grammar.

This is a theme that Saliers sounds elsewhere as well. "Worship is something done, not something merely said or merely experienced. It is the work of the people of God, training themselves in the language of faith and using the language to address God. If understood fully, it is linked with doing God's work in the world. We may, if you like, call worship the rule-keeping activity of the language of faith."[38] Elsewhere he expresses the same theme by arguing that prayer and worship are not so much derived from, as generative of, a doctrine of God. Although this does not mean "a simple 'reading off' of a doctrine of God from the surface diction of . . . prayer," nevertheless the logic suggests that prayer is less a consequence of first having believed, than it is constitutive of believing in God in particular ways. If there is an intrinsic relation between theology as language about God and prayer as language addressed to God, then Christian prayer is generative of the doctrine of God in crucial respects. "Christian prayer is a cognitive encounter with God which governs central features of how God is to be conceived and expressed in language. . . . The eucharistic prayers may be said to be 'grammatical' in that they provide rules governing the formulation of doctrines."[39] And in the fifth chapter of *The Soul in Paraphrase* he relates prayer to theology again when he asks, "What has praying *to* God to do with thinking *about* God?" In the context of this book on religious affections he proposes that "the central and decisive Christian affections require concepts, judgments, and thoughts which yield insight into the nature of God."[40]

David Power also asserts a formative connection between liturgy and theology. A common definition of theology, he notes, is faith seeking understanding. On this ground alone "we would have to assert the role of cult in the life and thought of the theologian." As the primary language of faith, liturgy "is a kind of theology, because it is already an attempt to express the movement of the heart towards God in Christ. . . . It is primary, because ritual and symbolic language is the core language of religious reality and faith."[41] He continues by considering what implications this has for transcendental method, i.e., for a secondary theology whose role is to interpret the language of the imagination and analogy, but the point is that this secondary task finds its point of reference in liturgy. If theology's role can be described as mediating cult to culture, then "liturgy is not just another discipline in religious studies. It is in its way foundational to theology. . . . [R]ite and sacrament provide a basis for such disciplines as christology, ecclesiology and God-talk."[42]

Elsewhere Power speaks of two expressions of faith, the symbolic and the theoretical (he identifies them as *theologia prima* and *theologia secunda*) but insists that these are complementary and not competitive or alternative. "To put it very simply: there must be modes of devotional expression which makes it possible for the Christian person to enter fully and personally into the faith-experience of communion with God, but there must also be modes of theological enterprise which guide the devotional and make intelligent inquiry possible without the hazards of self-interest and sentiment."[43] These two expressions of faith must not interfere with each other, but neither may one or the other be sacrificed without peril. It appears to have been the case that the "living experience of spiritual brotherhood . . . [was] not absorbed into the church's institutions or liturgy," the consequences being that as devotional expression waned in the west, the official Church had nothing of the devotional whereby to attract its people or to inspire the theologian to fresh questions. Besides a language of objective study, the Christian community needs "a language which can incite it to respond intersubjectively to God's call and to dispose of itself to God. It is this latter which ought to be the language of liturgy."[44] The liturgy transmits the Christian experience, deeply felt and demanding, in which God makes claims upon us. This will form and influence the alternate expression of faith, theology.

Peter Fink emphasizes the formative influence of the liturgical community by defining liturgical theology as an interaction between three parties: theologians, the praying Church, and liturgists. (Whereas I have resolved to reserve this last word for the people who commit liturgy, and Fink is referring to the specialized discipline of liturgical study, I will instead employ the term *liturgiologist*.) "The problematic to which a liturgical theology must address itself is the all too observable discrepancy between actual liturgical celebrations in the church and the claims which theological reflection makes for those celebrations."[45] Theologians can establish interpretation, liturgiologists can establish one or another past practice, but it is in ritual celebration that the praying Church will answer the question about the credibility of this interpretation or practice. Therefore it is the liturgy director's task "to structure a worship service that will render what the church promises perceptible to the senses. At the same time it is important for the theologian to remember that the ultimate test of his theological model is not its theological correctness, but the ability of the praying church to recognize in its prayer the richness which the model promises."[46]

David Newman challenges the widespread assumption that "if we get our principles right then our liturgy will naturally follow in good order." When he says that liturgical theology is rooted and grounded in the liturgy itself, he means that theology must follow the liturgy. "What does it mean to follow the liturgy?" he asks. "We have been thinking of it in the sense of succeeding rather than preceding. But I want also to think of it as a dynamic category that presupposes liturgy as an action or movement to be followed." Rely less on the metaphor of worship as a shape, and think of it more as a body that has life and movement. "Liturgical theology that follows the liturgy can be described as a hermeneutic of word, symbol and action. Paul Ricoeur has said that 'the symbol gives rise to thought.' This could be a motto for liturgical theology."[47] Insofar as liturgy is an active, dynamic body and not a static shape, theological expressions will be affected when they are played out in practice in liturgy.

Michael Aune also utilizes the concept of hermeneutic. His piece is addressed to a Lutheran audience, asking for a rationale for the why and wherefore of liturgical reform in the Lutheran Church in the United States. Is there any hermeneutic for interpreting liturgy from a Lutheran perspective? He answers yes by arguing that Luther came to see words in a new way, different from the way Western tradition had seen them as signaling or pointing to things out there. Based on his biblical studies, Luther saw words as God's own per-formative utterances. The Word becomes incarnate in words: in hearing the words "you are forgiven," you are forgiven. According to Luther the rite, no less than the Word, communicates the full reality of Christ. Aune states, "What is remarkable about such a liturgical perspective is the recognition that the truth which theology examines and seeks to understand, namely 'Word' as God's visible and verbal communication, happens *somewhere* and looks and sounds like *some-thing*."[48] Although in the centuries following the Reformation this perspective was generally lost, the Lutheran liturgy could be reformed according to a liturgical hermeneutic contained in its own confessions.

Aune says Lutherans have, in their neglect of matters ritual, bifurcated word and rite (or, meaning and communication) and then they wonder why word and rite have not moved the hearer to believe! "Usual Lutheran approaches to the interpretation of worship have restricted meaning to theological intent or content—e.g., forgiveness of sins, grace, righteousness—and have left issues of communication to repristinators of (pick-your-century) ceremonial styles."[49] Aune wants the salvific efficacy of the Word which the Lutheran hermeneutic has recognized for biblical words, and preached words, to be also recognized for ritual words. "Luther's unique notion of the nature of language as performing a certain kind of action moves us from an understanding of liturgical activity and expression as a representation of historical and doctrinal truths to its purpose as an accomplishment or performance of the promise of the Gospel. . . . Such a promise is not an idea to be taught but a reality to be experienced."[50] This is what the Bible and the Reformation call faith, and it is what the liturgy does: "nothing less than the heart moved and hence transformed." Liturgy forms faith; liturgy forms the faithful theologian.

All these authors have, in their various ways, argued the case that liturgy has impact on a theologian. I shall borrow a concept from Paul Holmer in order to loosely summarize the point they are making about liturgy's influence: They say that liturgy capacitates a person.[51] Capacities differ from a skill or activity in that capacities are formed and developed over a long period of time, and must be practiced consistently. They are normally not done by the hour but by the lifetime. A skill or activity has a beginning and an end ("I will read or study from noon 'til three") but it sounds odd to affix temporal parentheses to a capacity ("I will understand from noon 'til three"). The capacity of understanding is different from the skill of reading, or the act of studying. Capacities serve to shape a life; they are not so much the doing of something as the way in which something is done. So it is with capacities such as love, faithfulness, and hope; kindness, tastefulness, and the capacity to understand; gratitude, a sense of obligation, and being joyful.

It is in this sense that I would summarize the above authors as wanting to say that liturgy capacitates a person. They are right in saying worship should be more than an activity, skill, or mood: Liturgy should also capacitate the participant in doxological life (Wainwright), or shape one's faith by learning to pray (Saliers), or move one's heart (Aune), or give vent to the devotional expression of the faith (Power). The concern in all these authors, I take it, is to ground theology in liturgical experience. I do not disagree with this. But I wish to view the matter from yet one more angle, in addition to this. Thinking of theology as a grammar reveals one more verity, also pointed out by Paul Holmer. The grammar of a language is not a personal invention, any more than logic is a personal invention. And if theology does function like a grammar, this would suggest that theology is not a personal invention either.

Theology answers the question: what is Christianity? But it tells us the answer by giving us the order and priorities, the structure and morphology, of the Christian faith. It does this by placing the big words, like *man, God, Jesus, world,* in such a sequence and context that their use become ruled for us. And if we begin to use those words like that, with the appropriate zest and pathos, then we, too, become Godly as those earlier believers were.[52]

Liturgical theology is the ruled use of language, also called Tradition. It teaches us how to use the big words, what company they keep, and what they mean so we can mean something when we use them. Kavanagh says such theology is worked out "not in the modes and terms of secondary theology as practiced in academe, but in the modes and terms of prayer, of life, and of concrete practical reflection."[53]

I think this distinguishes liturgical theology from the simple doxological influence on a theologian. The grammar learned by the liturgical theologian exists in the liturgy's *lex orandi*. That is why Kavanagh says the law of prayer not only influences, but establishes the law of belief. The theological grammar by which doctrine is done at the second order level comes out of the *theologia prima* contained in the Church's rite. However important one thinks it is for theologians to believe while they think, this is not the main thrust of liturgical theology. Liturgical theology's primary reference is to the prior and foundational ritual theologizing of the Church-at-work (the *laos*-at-*ergeia*). In their transaction with God, the assembly speaks the big words according to the grammar of faith as a theological corporation. Although liturgists may not be able to analytically rear back and explain that grammar, they do possess the capacity to employ it. That they don't use the jargon of academic theology does not mean the adjustment they make to their encounter with the Holy One is non-theological, it only means it is non-academic. It's less a matter of using the right words, as using the words rightly. Liturgical theology is not simply *theologia secunda* done devotionally. Liturgical theology is the product of the assembly's ritualized grammar wherein the liturgists do not concoct their own ideas but celebrate what has been revealed. The assembly's product—*lex orandi*—is ordered, structured, disciplined and formed. If one knew this *lex orandi*, one could make "god-talk."

---

1. G. K. Chesterton, *Why I Am a Catholic*, vol. III in *Collected Works* (San Francisco: Ignatius Press, 1990) 132.

2. I am making reference to the constant use of the story of Moses' ascent as a paradigm for the ascetical ascent through purification and illumination to union with God. E.g. Gregory of Nyssa, *The Life of Moses* (New York: Paulist Press, 1978).

3. Robert Taft, "The Liturgical Year: Studies, Prospects, Reflections," *Worship* 55 (1981) 2.

4. Alexander Schmemann, "Theology and Eucharist," 22.

5. Andrew Louth, *Discerning the Mystery: An Essay on the Nature of Theology* (Oxford: Clarendon Press, 1983) 65.

6. Archimandrite Vasileios, *Hymn of Entry: Liturgy and Life in the Orthodox Church* (Crestwood, NY: St. Vladimir's Seminary Press, 1984).

7. Aidan Kavanagh, *On Liturgical Theology*, 124.

8. I have taken liberties with a line from Kavanagh's book, *Elements of Rite* (New York: Pueblo Publishing Co., 1982). He describes the book by saying, "[it] is not about rubrics. It is about what gives rubrics their reason and value. If it cannot avoid occasionally calling attention to them, this is because adequacy of liturgical celebration rests upon them as adequacy of language rests upon rules of grammar" (3). Later he writes that though the book is about liturgical laws and rubrics, he is endeavoring to put them into proper perspective. "Taken together, rubrics and laws constitute a checklist of the factors to be considered in the art of putting a liturgy together and celebrating it" (8). In Schmemann's framework, liturgy deals with the content in the Typicon; *leitourgia* deals with that element of the Typicon that is presupposed by its whole content.

9. Aidan Kavanagh, *On Liturgical Theology*, 108–9; underscoring mine.

10. "Once rite receded, so did the need for that kind assembly whose common burden was the enactment of rite rather than attendance upon didactic exposition of set texts. . . . Liturgical hypertrophy and the invention of printing by movable type were not, of course, the only factors involved in the reform movements of Catholics and Protestants during the sixteenth century and after. But when one tries to account for the fate of rite and symbol in Reformation and counter-Reformation churches, the combined effects of liturgical hypertrophy and printing technology cannot be ignored safely." Ibid., 104–5.

11. R. Taylor Scott, "The Likelihood of Liturgy: Reflection Upon Prayer Book Revision and Its Liturgical Implications," *Anglican Theological Review*, 57:2 (April 1980) 106.

12. For the relationship between private devotion and the liturgy, see the 2001 "Directory on Popular Piety and the Liturgy: Principles and Guidelines" from the Congregation for Divine Worship and the Discipline of the Sacraments.

13. Aidan Kavanagh, "The Role of Ritual in Personal Development" in *The Roots of Ritual,* ed. James D. Shaughnessy, (Grand Rapids: William Eerdmans Publishing) 148–49.

14. Aidan Kavanagh, *The Elements of Rite,* 16–17. Hence his sixth rule of liturgical usage which states, "The church building is both shelter and setting for the liturgical assembly. Nothing more, but nothing less" (14).

15. Robert Hovda, "Sunday Assembly in the Tradition," in *Sunday Morning: A Time for Worship,* ed. Mark Searle (Collegeville: The Liturgical Press, 1982) 35. On the theological point see Schmemann, *Introduction to Liturgical Theology,* 55–67 and *Great Lent,* 67–76; on the development of Sunday see Willy Rordorf, *Sunday* (London: SCM Press, 1968); Thomas J. Talley, *The Origins of the Liturgical Year* (New York: Pueblo Press, 1986); and the essay preceding Hovda's in the same book by Eugene Laverdiere, "The Origins of Sunday in the New Testament."

16. _____, 39.

17. Alexander Schmemann, *The Eucharist,* 53. See also chapter 2 of *For the Life of the World* (Crestwood, NY: St. Vladimir's Seminary Press, 1963) in which he describes the liturgy under the metaphor of journey, speaking of departure from and return to the world.

18. Vladimir Solovyof, "The Jews and the Christian Problem," *A Solovyof Anthology,* arranged by S. L. Frank (London: SCM Press, 1950) 119–20.

19. Robert Taft, "Sunday in the Eastern Tradition," *Beyond East and West: Problems in Liturgical Understanding* (Washington, DC: The Pastoral Press, 1984) 32.

20. Aidan Kavanagh, *Elements of Rite,* 12.

21. Christopher Kiesling, *The Future of the Christian Sunday* (New York: Sheed and Ward, 1970) 33.

22. Alexander Schmemann, *Great Lent,* 58.

23. Aidan Kavanagh, *On Liturgical Theology,* 147.

24. Robert Taft, "Liturgy as Theology," *Worship* 56:2 (March 1982) 114.

25. Gregory Dix, *The Shape of the Liturgy* (London: Dacre Press, 1945) 30 and 591.

26. _____, 123.

27. _____, 199.

28. _____, 251.

29. _____, 280.

30. _____, 290.

31. Aidan Kavanagh, "Response: Primary Theology and Liturgical Act," *Worship,* (vol. 57, 1983) 323–24.

32. ____, *On Liturgical Theology*, 97. Anthony Ugolnik seeks to make the same point when he writes, "Theology, like language, is a communal act. The theologian cannot work in a white lab coat, nor can he or she make a scientific treatise of the Gospel. A theologian who does not speak from or for a community has forgotten the reason for speaking." *The Illuminating Icon*, 141.

33. Alexander Schmemann, *The Eucharist*, 165.

34. Evagrius called freedom from distorting passions *apatheia*. John Cassian substituted the phrase *puritas cordis:* purity of heart.

35. Paul Holmer, "About Liturgy and Its Logic," 21, 23.

36. In retaining the original content of this chapter, I am including only the examples that were in the first edition at the time of its writing. A number of significant works have appeared since. The reader should note Kevin Irwin, *Context and Text: Method in Liturgical Theology* (Collegeville: The Liturgical Press, 1994); Don Saliers, *Worship as Theology: Foretaste of Glory Divine* (Nashville: Abingdon Press, 1994); Don Saliers, *Worship and Spirituality* (Akron: Order of St. Luke Publications, 1996); Gordon Lathrop, *Holy Things: A Liturgical Theology* (Minneapolis: Fortress Press, 1998); Gordon Lathrop, *Holy People: A Liturgical Ecclesiology* (Minneapolis: Fortress Press, 2003); and a collection of essays on the liturgical theology have been collected by Dwight Vogel as *Primary Sources of Liturgical Theology: a Reader* (Collegeville: The Liturgical Press, 2000). I continue to see some difference between the understanding represented in these works and the specific definition of liturgical theology I am attempting, but these works contribute significantly to the recognition of liturgy's theological and spiritual component.

37. Don Saliers, "On the 'Crisis' of Liturgical Language," *Worship* 44:7 (August–September, 1970) 405.

38. ____ , "Prayer and Emotion," in *Christians at Prayer*, ed. John Gallen, (Notre Dame: University of Notre Dame Press, 1977) 58.

39. "Prayer and the Doctrine of God in Contemporary Theology," *Interpretation* 30 (1980) 265–78.

40. Don Saliers, *The Soul in Paraphrase: Prayer and the Religious Affections* (New York: Seabury, 1980) 77.

41. David N. Power, "Cult to Culture: The Liturgical Foundation of Theology," *Worship* 54:6 (Nov. 1980) 482.

42. ____ , 494.

43. ____ , "Two Expressions of Faith: Worship and Theology," *Concilium: Liturgical Experience of Faith* (New York: Herder & Herder, 1973) 99.

44. ____ , 101.

45. Peter Fink, "Towards a Liturgical Theology," *Worship* 47:10 (Dec. 1973) 602.

46. _____, 603.

47. David R. Newman, "Observations on Method in Liturgical Theology," *Worship* 57:4 (July 1983) 379.

48. Michael B. Aune, " 'To Move the Heart': Word and Rite in Contemporary American Lutheranism," *Currents in Theology and Mission,* 10:4 (August 1983) 212.

49. _____, 217.

50. _____, 221.

51. I do not mean the Augustinian sense of capacity: *sensus mentis.* I do not mean to argue the Western question of grace and nature at all, but for an Orthodox critique of it see John Meyendorff, "The Significance of the Reformation," *Catholicity and the Church* (Crestwood, NY: St. Vladimir's Seminary Press, 1987) 66ff. Holmer employs the concept "capacity" to wed Wittgenstein's remarks about grammar and Kierkegaard's studies on existential passion. For example, he believes the liberal arts education should capacitate a student, but alas, "Becoming wise would be almost as surprising and as embarrassing — certainly as unexpected — an outcome of the academic study of philosophy as becoming a believer would be out of the academic study of theology." *The Grammar of Faith* (New York: Harper & Row, 1978) 4.

52. _____, 20.

53. Aidan Kavanagh, "Response: Primary Theology and Liturgical Act," *Worship,* (vol. 57, 1983) 322.

Chapter 5

Introducing Mrs. Murphy

The definition of liturgical theology I am proposing not only acknowledges the theologian as believer, it further asserts the believer as theologian. It does help to establish a sort of connection between liturgy and theology if we say *theologia secunda* should be done in light of the liturgy, but it does not yet treat liturgy itself as *theologia prima*. Academic theologians can be influenced by liturgy, but I want to assert that *leitourgia* capacitates primary theologians, collectively named "Mrs. Murphy" by Kavanagh.

Kavanagh produced a provocative symbol by his creation of Mrs. Murphy. Exactly who she is — that is, what she represents for Kavanagh — needs to be carefully defined because she has been used by people to symbolize all sorts of things, ranging from deeply held opinions ("Mrs. Murphy will not abide . . .") to widespread practices ("the Mrs. Murphy in the pew still wants . . .") to personal causes ("Mrs. Murphy demands that the clergy not . . .") to projected abstractions ("Mrs. Murphy's attitude toward Vatican II is . . ."). What Kavanagh himself meant is revealed when he says:

> The language of the primary theologian . . . more often consists in symbolic, metaphorical, sacramental words and actions which throw flashes of light upon chasms of rich ambiguity. As such, Mrs. Murphy's language illuminates the chaotic landscape through which I must pick my professional way with the narrow laser-like beam of precise words and concepts — which is why what she does is primary and what I do is secondary; which is why, also, what she does is so much harder to do than what I do. My admiration for her and her colleagues is profound, and it deepens daily.[1]

I think Kavanagh uses Mrs. Murphy to name someone who has been capacitated by liturgical rite in the language of primary theology.

Allow a momentary detour in order to pick up a couple of helpful concepts again from Wittgenstein, and also from a student of his named Friedrich Waismann. The latter observes that there is language that can be called "complete" and language that can be called "incomplete." We can thus distinguish perfectly *formalized* languages constructed by logicians from *natural* languages as used in describing reality. In a formalized system the use of each symbol is governed by a definite number of rules, and further, all the rules of inference and procedure can be stated completely."[2] Mathematics is a very formalized language, while the language games of ordinary speech are more incomplete. I propose that Mrs. Murphy's liturgical language is like what Waismann calls a natural language: open-ended and not tightly screwed down. *Theologia secunda* is a formalized language, created for a particular purpose and therefore tighter. Its functions vary—to fine-tune a definition and combat a heresy, to exclude one option in the face of another, to interface with a philosophical tenet—but its rules may be taught to initiates and stated more or less completely. (Hence the numerous courses in theological method!) One would be hard pressed, however, to state completely and formally the rules by which liturgical theology works. This does not mean it lacks rules. It only means its grammar is "incomplete" in Waissman's sense of being more capacious and flexible.

Wittgenstein provides an allegorical picture of the difference between natural and formalized language when he compares the former to the center of a city and the latter to the suburbs. "Our language can be seen as an ancient city: a maze of little streets and squares, of old and new houses, and of houses with additions from various periods; and this is surrounded by a multitude of new boroughs with straight regular streets and uniform houses."[3] Liturgical language spoken naturally by believers according to the grammar of faith consists of affirmations that wind, maze-like, through their lives. Second-order theology is laid out according to straight, regular rules of inference, and is cast in vocabulary that struggles to be uniform. Both neighborhoods use ruled speech, but of different kinds. Talk of God made by the worshiper can be just as ruled and disciplined as talk about God made by the systematician, but you cannot judge the former by the latter.

Mrs. Murphy represents the person who speaks the natural language of theology, even though she doesn't know the formalized language of theology. This means that when Kavanagh makes reference to her, it is not to name idiosyncratic opinions or popular causes. He uses Mrs. Murphy to put a name to the tradition of the Church as it is learned by constant and regular exposure to the proletarian, quotidian, and communitarian *theologia prima*. Mrs. Murphy is a liturgist. And she is under theological discipline because she cannot think any way she pleases: That's the force of the *lex* in *lex orandi*. If theology is the search for words appropriate to God, as Schmemann put it, then the liturgist who wants to speak about God, of God, and even to God, is under the discipline of theology, too. Mrs. Murphy's theology is disciplined, even if the complete set of inferences cannot be worked out by academic convention. She knows more than they can say.

Two-Tiered Religion

Why has Mrs. Murphy's mode of theology been ignored and even denigrated? Peter Brown makes some intriguing suggestions in the course of his study on the origin of the cult of saints in Latin Christianity. Brown suggests that this subject, and others like it, have been treated suspiciously at best and contemptuously at worst because of an attitude held during the last three centuries, an attitude which pits enlightened religion against superstitious popular religion.

> In modern scholarship, these attitudes take the form of a "two-tiered" model. The views of the potentially enlightened few are thought of as being subject to continuous upward pressure from habitual ways of thinking current among "the vulgar." . . . When applied to the nature of religious change in late antiquity, the "two-tiered" model encourages the historian to assume that a change in the piety of late-antique men, of the kind associated with the rise of the cult of saints, must have been the result of the capitulation by the enlightened elites of the Christian church to modes of thought previously current only among the "vulgar."[4]

In other words, modern scholarship has assumed an upper tier for the few, consisting of enlightened, spiritual religion, and a lower tier for the many, consisting of quasi-superstitious popular religion. The formalized language has no time for the natural language.

Whence arose this two-tiered model? Brown suggests that the religious history of late antiquity and the early Middle Ages "still owes more than we realize to attitudes summed up so persuasively, in the 1750s, by the philosopher David Hume, in his essay *The Natural History of Religion.*"[5] Hume's argument against his religious contemporaries was that human beings were not natural monotheists, and never had been. But the unnaturalness of monotheism was caused less by sin and more by the intellectual limitations of the average human mind. Monotheism was rare because it depended upon social and cultural preconditions and upon a coherent, rational view of the universe, which was not easily attained by the vulgar mind. In Hume's own words: "The vulgar, that is, indeed, all mankind a few excepted, being ignorant and uninstructed, never elevate their contemplation to the heavens . . . so far as to discern a supreme mind or original providence."[6]

In this description of the vulgar, Hume exemplified the then prevailing attitude. Progress in religion was thought to consist of the top tier suppressing superstitious popular religion, and regress in religion consisted of vulgar practices corrupting enlightened religion. "The religious history of mankind, for Hume, is not a simple history of decline from an original monotheism; it is marked by a constant tension between theistic and polytheistic ways of thinking."[7] Brown suggests that this attitude was mainstreamed into modern scholarship by Edward Gibbon, who expanded on the theme when he described the early Christian cult of the saints as if the vulgar merely pasted a Christian facade over pagan practices,[8] and by nineteenth-century religious revival which "hardened the outlines of Hume's model and made a variant and of it part of many modern interpretations of early medieval Christianity."[9] Rationalists would cringe at the words of John Cardinal Newman: "The religion of the multitude is ever vulgar and abnormal; it will ever be tinctured with fanaticism and superstition, while men are what they are."[10]

We must pick our way through this material carefully. In the face of this overwhelming denigration of the lower tier, the reader might respond by romantically lionizing whatever originates from the vulgar. In my opinion, popular religion is often defended in this way, and sometimes (incorrectly) in the name of Mrs. Murphy. Certain pieties, theologies, or practices are portrayed as invulnerable to criticism by virtue of the fact that they originated from and belong to her. I disagree. I do not want to fall victim to this pendulum swing, as if because modern scholarship has said for three centuries that vulgar expressions of religion can contain nothing good, we should now assume they can contain nothing wrong. This would be an uncritical, roman- ticized view of popular religion. I do not think a liturgical practice or a theological doctrine is beyond criticism by virtue of belonging to the lower tier. Were this the case, then liturgical theology would be as guilty as Hume was of blind prejudice regarding the lower tier, this time pro instead of con. Scholarship's neglect of popular religion may need to be rectified, but it is not done at the expense of dismissing our critical faculties. What I am proposing is a third option. Not 1) there can be no theological critique of popular religion, nor 2) only *theologia secunda* can critique popular religion; rather 3) it is possible for *theologia prima* to critique popular religion.

Brown seems to advocate this position as well, when he points out a problem in the two-tiered model. He does not offer a blind defense of popular religion, of the sort just described above, but he does claim that this two-tiered model has a weakness because it overlooks a crucial fact. "The basic weakness of the two-tiered model is that it is rarely if ever, concerned to explain religious change other than among the elite. The religion of 'the vulgar' is assumed to be uniform. It is timeless and faceless. It can cause changes by imposing its modes of thought on the elite; but in itself it does not change."[11] This perception of popular religion does not match the facts, Brown concludes, at least from his research into the cult of saints. It is a tenacious perception, however. Modern scholarship suffers the prejudice that vulgar religious expression is a monotonous continuity. Therefore scholarship observes distinctions within the upper tier, and between the upper and lower tier, but never within the lower tier itself. Practices regarded as superstitious are an embarrassment, and so scholarship assumes that the uneducated (read: "nontheological") Christian lay person mimicked pagan practices without differentiation or transformation.

In this two-tiered model, liturgical cult would be reckoned atheological. "Up to the present, it is still normal to assume that the average *homo religiosus* of the Mediterranean, and more especially, the average woman, is, like Winnie the Pooh, 'a bear of very little brain.'"[12] Mrs. Murphy, as a resident of the lower tier, is assumed to be a bear of very little theological brain, indeed. Because her theological language is not formalized, her language is thought to be non-theological. Because her theological language is natural, it is assumed to be unruled opinion. But these assumptions are wrong. In point of fact, liturgical theology, of which Mrs. Murphy is a personified holder, is stringently theological, both linguistically and symbolically, even if that rule formation comes from inside the assembly and not from the ivory tower above it. Mrs. Murphy may not have been able to *speak about theology* before taking a university course, but she was able to *speak theologically about* God, world, and herself according to the grammar of faith imparted by liturgical theology.

We must pick our way carefully through yet one more issue. I have claimed that a crucial difference between Mrs. Murphy and a secondary theologian is that the latter analyzes the grammar and the former speaks by the grammar. All would now be lost if someone concluded that although the lower-tier in which Mrs. Murphy lives is theological, she cannot understand it, or tell about it. If this were true, then she really would be engaged in mindless activity, and the difference between liturgical religion and superstition would be indistinguishable, and the two tiers would be justified. If Mrs. Murphy did the liturgical act without knowing why, then it would be mindless ritualism, and could hardly be called theology.

Liturgical theology is, first of all, transacted under *leitourgia's* ritual logistics, and, second of all, liturgical theology is the elucidation of the meaning of worship. Mrs. Murphy does both (although the latter not necessarily in propositional form). One should take care not to confuse *lex credendi* with secondary theology. Rather, *lex orandi* is the ground for the Church's *lex credendi*, which can then be expressed either in natural language, or in formal and secondary language.

> This means that *lex credendi* is at root not merely something which is done exclusively by secondary theologians in their studies, as opposed to *lex supplicandi* done by nontheologians indulging in religious worship elsewhere. On the contrary, *lex credendi* is constantly being worked out, sustained, and established as the faithful in assembly are constantly working out, sustaining, and establishing their *lex supplicandi* from one festive, ordered, aesthetic, canonical, and eschatological liturgical act to the next under grace.[13]

This point, illustrated by Kavanagh, is completely baffling if the communal act is not a festive, ordered, aesthetic, canonical, and eschatological *leitourgia*—i.e. if it has plenty of *orandi* but not enough *lex*. Worship done at our whim cannot very convincingly be argued to be the root of any theology, whether primary or secondary, natural, or formalized. But I am interpreting Kavanagh to mean that Mrs. Murphy is the personification of someone who has been formed by a normative grammar, one at play in the Church's *leitourgia* even before it is reflected propositionally. *Lex orandi* is a theological enterprise, and that's why a simple survey of the lower tier by the upper tier will not discover it. One cannot arrive at *lex orandi* by sheer phenomenology or historical survey (the latter simply a case of phenomenology done diachronically instead of synchronically).

Brown identifies tremendously imaginative changes effected by the liturgical theology of the vulgar Christian, changes that transformed pagan reverence of the dead into a Christian cult of saints.[14] He concludes that while certainly some people possessed the ability to articulate this in more abstract terms, there is no evidence to suggest that they felt themselves to be elite. True, understanding all the ramifications of Christianity

> assumed a level of culture which the majority of the members of the Christian congregations were known not to share with their leaders. Yet it is remarkable that men who were acutely aware of elaborating dogmas, such as the nature of the Trinity, whose contents were difficult of access to the "unlettered," felt themselves so little isolated for so much of the time from these same "unlettered" when it came to the shared religious practices of their community and to the assumptions about the relation of man to supernatural beings which these practices condensed.[15]

This quote must not be taken in the context of the modern bifurcation between theology and faith, for then it would be mistaken to mean that the lettered person who lived above the masses most of the time, in the rational world of clear thought, occasionally forsook theology to condescend to the irrational world of nontheological religious practice. No, not this opposition between theology and faith (or theologians and believers). There was indeed an expression of beliefs in a tightly formalized linguistic style, whose full understanding and accurate formulation assumed a level of culture the majority of congregations did not share, yet what these lettered persons elaborated in the secondary order was what all Christians celebrated in the primary order. In fact, Brown writes, differences of class and education played no significant role in the area of life covered by religious practice. He concludes by making the words of Arnaldo Momigliano his own: "Thus my inquest into popular beliefs in the Late Roman historians ends in reporting that there were no such beliefs. In the fourth and fifth centuries there were of course plenty of beliefs which we historians of the twentieth century would gladly call popular, but the historians of the fourth and fifth centuries never treated any belief as characteristic of the masses and consequently discredited among the elite." [16] Gregory Dix commented upon the matter nicely half a century ago: "The people have a certain right to be vulgar; and the liturgy, even while it must teach them, has never a right to be academic, because it is their prayer." [17]

Mrs. Murphy knows a natural language that is less tidy, but no less disciplined. There are reasons to use formalized language, with the rules of inference clearly articulated to purge ambiguity and equivocation, but this is not the only language by which theology is done. Mrs. Murphy does not rear back and reflect upon the speech (second-order theology) or upon the rite (liturgiology) but, then, that is the obligation of academicians anyway. Her theological understanding of the intersection of world and kingdom is accomplished and preserved as liturgical rite.

Celebrating Theology

The deep rift between theologian and believer in modern discourse makes this difficult to understand. As Schmemann charged, on the one hand, the laity today are scarcely interested in the theological curriculum of the university or seminary (indeed they grumble when a young priest, newly hatched and knowing no better, fills the homily with old class notes); on the other hand, many theologians avoid discussing the Church's life and do not even dream about influencing it. But it was not always so. Kallistos Ware comments that "today, in an untheological age, it is all but impossible to realize how burning an interest was felt in religious questions by every part of society, by laity as well as clergy, by the poor and uneducated as well as the Court and the scholars." [18] Theological questions were not kept behind a door which required an academic degree to unlock. So Gregory of Nyssa describes the unending theological arguments in Constantinople at the time of the second Council:

> The whole city is full of it, the squares, the market places, the cross-roads, the alleyways; old-clothes men, money changers, food sellers: they are all busy arguing. If you ask someone to give you change, he philosophizes about the Begotten and the Unbegotten; if you inquire about the price of a loaf, you are told by way of reply that the Father is greater and the Son inferior; if you ask "Is my bath ready?" the attendant answers that the Son was made out of nothing. [19]

Gregory's words only bring a smile to our lips, for we can hardly take them as anything but hyperbole. Why should the old-clothes men, the money changers, and Mrs. Murphy care a whit about Arianism or subordinationism? Why, indeed, unless christology is not only about Jesus' metaphysical makeup, but also about how we might become by grace what he is by nature? Why, indeed, unless the doctrine of the Trinity is not philosophical speculation about the makeup of God, but reveals the way to salvation? Theology should be a window to see through, and our attention should not be diverted to our own cleverness reflected in the pane of glass itself.

Imagine doctrines to be chapters in the story. In that case, liturgical theology includes them all because in the Divine Liturgy the entire story is celebrated. The liturgical theologian can know the story of salvation in an open-ended language because Mrs. Murphy knows the entire story. Liturgical theology involves ecclesiology, for this identifies the assembly that celebrates; ecclesiology involves christology, for this confesses whose body the Church is; christology involves soteriology because this reveals the (functional) identity of the incarnate one into whose paschal mystery we are grafted; and how can a soteriology be done without a doctrine of sin? and how can one understand what sin is without a doctrine of creation that reveals what humanity was meant to be? These doctrines are each facets on a single diamond, chapters in a real and unfolding story put into song by tradition and sung by the Church in anaphora and incense, speech and symbol, kerygma and icon. Theology is enacted and proclaimed at each liturgical celebration, symbolically and completely. "Liturgy consists of the various means whereby the church makes it possible for the faithful to experience through their senses the mysteries of religion, that is, the sweetness of the kingdom of God."[20] The adjustment to the experience of these mysteries may be called theology because theology is a ruled attempt to understand what God's love in Christ entails. Liturgical asceticism is the discipline required to capacitate a liturgist for this knowledge. To know, we must love; to love, grace must discipline the passions; asceticism is *ordo amoris*. Those whose lives are hid in Christ know this paschal grammar.

If liturgical theology is the elucidation of the meaning of worship, the laity will not show their grasp of its meaning by articulating propositions; rather, they will show their grasp by the grammar they use to understand the world and to shape their own lives. A life is put in concord with the deep structure of the liturgy. The meaning of baptism will be elucidated when one lives a regenerate life, of Eucharist when one becomes a *eucharistos* (thankful one),[21] of liturgy when the rite becomes a joyful summons home to God.

Unfortunately, at some point *leitourgia* was replaced by "a new system of worship which would increasingly do without rite."[22] Schmemann spoke of the metamorphosis of liturgical consciousness such that something besides *leitourgia* now occupies the assembly in its gathering. Symptomatic of this metamorphosis is the reduction of *leitourgia* to one of two anemic forms.

> Our approach to worship is either rational or sentimental. The rational approach consists of reducing the liturgical celebration to ideas. [For such an approach] liturgy is at best a raw material for neat intellectual definitions and propositions. . . . As to the sentimental approach, it is the result of an individualistic and self-centered piety. . . . For that kind of piety worship is above everything else a useful framework for personal prayer, an inspiring background whose aim is to "warm up" our heart and direct it toward God. The content and meaning of services, liturgical texts, rites, and actions is here of secondary importance; they are useful and adequate as long as they make me pray.[23]

In the example of fasting, one can see either reduction at work. The purpose of Lent is to recover our Christian sense that sin is alien so that we are roused to begin the spiritual journey toward Easter, and not be content in our fallen state. For this purpose, people fast during Lent. There is no Lent without fasting. Fasting is how one means Lent, like words are how one means. The meaning of Lent is to fast. But with the loss of liturgical consciousness, this theological meaning is attenuated to either side. On the one hand, the rationalist fasts for half a day until he can declare, "Now I get it! Now I see the point!" and stops. On the other hand, the sentimentalist makes a symbolic fast to create an excitation in the heart rather than a hunger in the stomach. But fasting is not an expression (of thought or sentiment); it is an act. Doing it theologically declares something about the world and one's relationship to it. When Mrs. Murphy does primary theology, she actually fasts and knows the reason why. If, as Schmemann says, liturgical theology elucidates the fundamental meaning of worship, then the goal here is neither to elucidate the idea of Lent (and once the idea comes through, the fasting is no longer necessary), nor to stimulate the feeling of Lent (and once the feeling comes through, a symbolic fasting will do). Practitioners of lower tier popular religion did not have a thought about Lent, they did not have a feeling about Lent, they did Lent by fasting. They struggled for, expressed, preserved, and experienced the meaning of Lent by fasting, and their theology can be read off the liturgical rubrics and canon law regarding the lenten fast.

Leitourgia is ordered, logical, grammatical, canonical, mean-ingful, deeply structured, and it functions according to tradition. As such, it is itself theological. Kavanagh writes, "What emerges most directly from an assembly's liturgical act is not a new species of theol-ogy among others. It is *theologia* itself."[24] The shop keeper of whom Gregory of Nyssa wrote may not have understood the lettered form of the doctrine, but if someone had explained it to him he would have recognized it from the Divine Liturgy because there he would have witnessed it in word and symbol, in ritual and icon. Liturgical theology and secondary theology are not in competition, but they are two dif-ferent tasks for two different callings. *Leitourgia* is not a substitute for secondary theology; how could it be a substitute for analyzation when it is not analytic? In *leitourgia* the content of *lex credendi* is beheld by the people week after week in their *lex orandi*. Speaking of liturgy in the Orthodox rhythm, Taft writes,

> Worshiping in this atmosphere of profuse symbolism through which the supernatural splendor of the inaccessible divine majesty is approached, Eastern Christians witness the exaltation and sanctification of creation, the majestic appearance of God who enters us, sanctifies us, divinizes us through the transfiguring light of his heavenly grace. It is not only a matter of receiving the sacraments, but also one of living habitually within a liturgical atmosphere which stirs us in body and soul in order to transform us before a vision of spiritual beauty and joy.[25]

Taft is describing liturgy as divine epiphany. Were it not so—if the Spirit inspired an idea only, and the subsequent liturgical form and theology were both only human creations—then liturgy would merely be the assembly's corporate opinion, and would carry no more weight than a solitary opinion.

Liturgy celebrates a reality (liturgy is doing the world) by bring-ing to ritual moment what is steadfastly and pervasively true. To "cele-brate" means to accomplish or repeat. In a celebration the pervading reality is focused and consciously remembered, as when birthdays or anniversaries celebrate the life or relationship in which one constantly lives. It is not true only on the anniversary day, as if someone is not married the rest of the year, but on the day of celebration what is always true is made explicit for experience. The celebration enables one to express in specific moments what is constantly real. In the words of Godfrey Diekmann,

> the world is our means of worship, and our use of these means . . . reveals the inherent and ultimate meaning of the world, the fulfillment of its destiny. . . . Water, all water, can be called holy because it is a sacrament, a sign of God's power and beauty and love. Blessing water, or using it in liturgy, simply reveals more convincingly the fulfillment of water's intrinsic sacramentality. Liturgical word and sacrament are, so to speak, the intensification, the visible concentration of what is already incipiently present.[26]

Liturgy does not suppose God is conjured into this world by cultic snatches of transcendence. God is in the world already, and human beings need ritual moments to celebrate this in reality. The Divine Liturgy is primarily a celebration of resurrection. In a world dominated by death, Schmemann says, "there appeared one morning someone who is beyond death and yet *in* our time. . . . Christianity is first of all the proclamation in this world of Christ's Resurrection."[27] The Divine Liturgy is a celebration of Christ's ongoing heavenly liturgy. The resurrecting power of God is celebrated, accomplished, made present in a moment, and it is realized, displayed, and epiphanized for us. Jean Corbon reminds us that this is the purpose and necessity of the Christian liturgical celebration:

> A celebration can now be seen as a "moment" in which the Lord comes with power and his coming becomes the sole concern of those who answer to his call.
>
> That concern should pervade every other concern of Christian life. Every celebration of the liturgy is geared to that lived liturgy in which each instant of life should become a "moment" of grace. The liturgy cannot be lived at each moment, however, unless it is celebrated at certain moments. Furthermore, the celebration contains an irreducible newness which is an argument for its necessity; for it is in the celebration that the event of Christ becomes the event of the Church assembled here and now. The celebrating Church welcomes the heavenly liturgy and takes part in it. The Church is thereby shown to be the body of Christ and becomes that body more fully. . . .[28]

Church celebrations are moments when we are taken up to the Father by Christ's eternal, heavenly sacrifice. Our whole life is to become a liturgy to the Father, but we cannot live this each moment if we do not do it some moments. These realities are ritually as I am bodily. The loss of ritual that Kavanagh bemoans therefore involves more than the loss of a certain formal style. The celebration of family rituals like Thanksgiving, suppertime, a birthday, and a bedtime backrub are the ways a family is family. The Church is Church by ritually celebrating *leitourgia*.

The people of God participate in the work of Christ. Those who are of the Lord (*kyriakos*—Christian) participate in his heavenly liturgy and perpetually present his sacrifice on the Lord's day (*he kyriake hemera*—Sunday).[29] Schmemann said the fundamental task of liturgical theology is to uncover the meaning and essence of this unity. The liturgy should be an icon of this, to be witnessed by Mrs. Murphy and Gregory of Nyssa's shop keeper. If it is not understood meaningfully, then more theologians are called for at the assembly—but by now it should be clear that I do not mean more professors, pastors, and graduate students. The liturgical renewal should be the renewal of liturgists. That renewal should be a theological and ascetical renewal, not just a stylistic one.

Men and women were created to be liturgists. *Anthropos* is *homo adorans*. When in Christ eucharistic life was restored to humanity, God was only completing what had been undertaken from the beginning. Vladimir Lossky contends that "After the Fall, human history is a long shipwreck awaiting rescue: but the port of salvation is not the goal; it is the possibility for the shipwrecked to resume his journey whose sole goal is union with God."[30] The Divine Liturgy is a cosmological event because what humanity was meant to be comes to fruition in the Eucharist, and earth rejoices. This is resurrection at work in our lives, and well-articulated by Jean Corbon, "Only when the life that burst from the tomb had become liturgy could the liturgy finally be *celebrated*—only when the river returned to its fountainhead, the Father. The liturgy begins in this movement of return."[31] The Divine Liturgy is the ongoing epiphany of God's kingdom, brought to perfection in Christ even though it is hidden except to faith. Because the mystery is seen in the temple, it can be known in the world. Because the mystery is celebrated here, it can be lived there. Christian liturgy is the end of cult because God's kingdom has come, yet the mode of *leitourgia* in this world is cult. Schmemann puts it this way:

> In this world, the *eschaton*— the holy, the sacred, the "otherness"— can be expressed and manifested only as "cult." Not only in relation to the world, but in relation to itself as dwelling in the world, the Church must use the forms and language of the cult, in order eternally to transcend the cult, to "become what it is." And it is this "transition" of the cult— the cult which itself fulfills the *reality* to which it can only point, which it can announce, but which is the consummation of its function as cult— that we call sacrament. . . .
>
> Theology is *possible* only within the Church, i.e. as a fruit of this new life in Christ, granted in the sacramental *leitourgia,* as a witness to the eschatological fullness of the Church.[32]

If my gait has seemed somewhat ungainly, it is because I have had one foot in each of two worlds. With one foot I have marched through methodological observations about theology, while with the other I have sought clarity about liturgy itself. I have migrated back and forth between methodological comment and trying to dilate the concept of liturgy. Where *leitourgia* has been replaced with other prejudices (puritanism, biblicism, pietism, rationalism), liturgical theology as I understand it cannot exist.

I hope that liturgy's definition has been sufficiently enlarged to make it clear that the adjective *liturgical* means more than style or format. When we call worship, time, assembly, sacrifice, symbol, person, gesture, procession, icon, food, or oil or water "liturgical," we do so not because someone is using them with pontificating flair. We do so because they are used in a rite that is the celebration of the kingdom, a symbol (joining together) of heaven and earth, an icon of the transaction in Christ between God and his people. Where liturgy is understood as a more or less elaborate format for worshiping, it is rarely felt to be the fructification of that new life begun in the waters of baptism.[33]

This sense of *leitourgia* has frayed at the edges, if not unraveled right up the middle. I have sought a way to discern liturgy's theology— the theology worked out, preserved and manifested in ritual acts of that assembly called Church. To agree that liturgy is theological, one must admit that liturgical rite is ruled, shaped, traditional. The upper tier may find it difficult to make such an admission. The tier

that looks upon multisensate ritual as vulgar, and therefore untheological, finds it difficult to suppose that Mrs. Murphy is speaking faith
by a grammar which merits the name theology. That is why one
consequence of dilating the definition of liturgy to *leitourgia* was the
complementary widening of the usual definition of theology. The
theology worked out and preserved in ritual logistics does not take
the same form as academic theology, that is quite true, but this only
means it is not academic, not that it is not theological.

It was Wittgenstein's conviction that philosophical problems
arise when language goes "on holiday," and it was his aim to bring
words back from their metaphysical use to their everyday use. One
example he uses is the concept of certainty. Tongue in cheek, he
describes the puzzlement of a philosopher's companion who is eluded
by the deep brooding over the problem of certainty. "I am sitting with
a philosopher in the garden; he says again and again, 'I know that
that's a tree,' pointing to a tree that is near us. Someone else arrives and
hears this, and I tell him: 'This fellow isn't insane. We are only doing
philosophy.'"[34] Schmemann accused school theology of extracting
sacramentology from liturgy when it asked questions of the eucharistic
species without regard to the liturgical event. Then the species were
no longer considered within the context of their use, and the language
had gone on holiday. The theologian said again and again, "I know
that that is transubstantiated," and when someone overhears this,
we tell him, "We are only doing theology." If theological discourse
about worship is not to become language on holiday, it must take the
surrounding rite into account, the "liturgical coefficient" as Schmemann
called it.

A theology of prayer is not the same as a prayer's liturgical
theology because the former does not take into consideration where
that prayer lies in the rite, by whom it is prayed, and for what purpose.
One can make some general remarks about prayer, as one can make
some general remarks about games, but the difference between the
Great Litany and the anaphora is as great as the rules between the game
of chess and the game of football. Or, take another example: Why use
incense? Carolingian allegory said it is a symbol of our prayer rising
to God, mimicking Old Testament themes. Prior to that time, the
incense also had an honorific use (it preceded the bishop's entrance as it
did the emperor). Prior to that, it had a sacrificial meaning, one which
precluded it from Christian use until that pagan connection wore out.

So which is it—honorific, sacrificial, or symbolic of prayer rising? The incense does not possess a naked theological meaning; its meaning is discovered by its liturgical coefficient, by what ritual language game it plays in. Its significance is acquired as a result of its symbolic use in the worship. Burning incense before the altar feels different from censing the congregation, or leading in the presider. Knowing when, where, how, before whom, and why something is censed will disclose meaning, which is why the structure of the rite must be investigated. Precisely such a range of questions occupies liturgical theology, distinguishing it from theology of worship, on the one hand, and from liturgiology, on the other, despite the latter's usefulness in uncovering a rite's historical origin and trajectory.

Here's still one more example. In his study on the origins of confirmation, Kavanagh hypothesizes that confirmation originated in a dismissal rite that completed the preceding rite only in the sense of formally concluding it. Such dismissal prayers did not at the outset take the form of an epiclesis of the Holy Sprit. In other words, this dismissal rite was not what we know as confirmation. Kavanagh explains, "The purpose of the *missa* rite [rite of dismissal] was to conclude and formally 'seal' a unit of public worship or instruction by dismissing the assembly either in whole or part with prayer and by physical contact between the dismissed and its chief minister— bishop, catechist, abbot or, by concession, ordained monastic."[35] But when that rite's liturgical structure was obscured and its blessing and dismissing role was forgotten, then theologians filled in a new meaning. Theology can't stand a vacuum, and so in a letter written near 416, Pope Innocent I interpreted the rite in terms of the eighth chapter of Acts (where the apostles bestowed the Holy Spirit by a rite of hand-laying), and concluded that confirmation belongs solely to the episcopal office, and that it consists of bestowing the Holy Spirit. Kavanagh's examination of the evidence suggests that the original dismissal prayer had already been altered to include an epiclesis of the Holy Spirit, giving Innocent the opportunity to interpret the customary episcopal *missa* as an episcopal confirmation of the Spirit through hand-laying.

> Given all this in its historical setting, one must conclude that Innocent's letter . . . is propaganda rather than a serene and objective articulation of doctrine—well meaning, understandable in the circumstances, and for high motives, but propaganda nonetheless. Based on a selective biblical

appeal, it seeks to justify a new understanding of an old post-chrismational structure in Roman baptismal procedure.[36]

If by confirmation one means a bestowal of the Holy Spirit, then Kavanagh concludes that the earliest dismissal prayers were no confirmation rite. They were an episcopal *missa* of neophytes from their baptism into their first eucharist, but "this is something that will be reiterated each time they commune sacramentally for the rest of their lives in the *ecclesia*, where the Spirit flourishes."[37] To appeal to this time period in an attempt to ground a later understanding of confirmation is pure anachronism. Worse, it is a case of liturgy being bent to serve theology and pastoral needs. "Innocent is not doing mystagogy here. He is theologically enhancing one element in the old *missa*, the episcopal signation *in frontem*, in such a way that it eventually will alter people's perception of the structure as a whole and even alter the structure itself."[38]

If Kavanagh is correct about the development of confirmation, it serves as a striking example of what happens when a rite's structure or *ordo* loses its force. If the deep structure fades from attention then its liturgical purpose becomes invisible; if liturgical purpose becomes invisible then the theological adjustment is not made; if the theological adjustment is not made then the subject matter of liturgical theology is gone. The solution is not for some second order theologians to teach doctrine to the unthinking ritualists; the solution is for the rite's structure to be sufficiently discernible that the whole community can adjust theologically to it. The questions that liturgical theology puts to liturgy are about theology, not liturgics, said Schmemann. Some historical knowledge may shed light on what this action or that symbol does, but liturgical theology is primarily theology, not history. The liturgy symbolizes the kingdom, but when liturgy's symbolic intelligibility is lost then liturgy has no theological muscle and it is replaced by flabby sentimentalism or rationalism.

Traditional Theology

The theological grammar learned in liturgy from God's own speaking patterns can also properly be called Tradition. Tradition continues as a present force. As Taft says, "Tradition is not the past; it is the Church's self-consciousness *now* of that which has been handed on to her not as an inert treasure but as a dynamic inner life. Theology must be reflection on the whole of that reality. . . . Tradition is not the past, but the present understood genetically, in continuity with that which produced it."[39] The reason for leafing through the pages of history, Taft continues, is to understand the present, not the past, like a psychiatrist investigates a childhood in order to understand the adult.

The Orthodox lay theologian, Vladimir Lossky, uses a spatial image to describe Tradition. The vertical line of Tradition unpacks itself on a horizontal line. It is projected onto a public horizontal line (proclaimed and written), namely scripture, icon, liturgy, dogma, or exegesis. Though these belong to the world of *logoi* (words), by His Holy Spirit God's own *logos* (word) is projected onto this horizontal plane.

> If the Scriptures and all that the Church can produce in words written or pronounced, in images or in symbols liturgical or otherwise, represent the differing modes of expression of the Truth, Tradition is the unique mode of receiving it. . . . [Tradition] is not the content of Revelation, but the light that reveals it; it is not the word, but the living breath which makes the word heard at the same time as the silence from which it came.[40]

Tradition is the Holy Spirit living in the church, giving to each the faculty of hearing, receiving, and knowing. Tradition is not the expression itself, the *logoi* of scripture, icon, dogma, exegesis, liturgical rite, yet in these horizontal projections the inexpressible is expressed. I have been trying to refer to this by the concept of grammar: Grammar is not the words, but it is what holds the words together rightly, meaningfully, and intelligibly. One speaks according to a grammar, as one paints an icon, interprets scripture, or formulates dogma according to Tradition. A dogma is "an intelligible instrument which makes for adherence to the Tradition of the church. A doctrine is traitor to Tradition when it seeks to take its place. . . ."[41] Development of dogma is not the augmentation of Tradition but a means for adherence to it.

We might compare the role of Tradition in intellectual form (dogma, exegesis, and creed) with its presence in pictorial form (icon), and in ritual form (liturgy). In every case, the content of the horizontal line must be interpreted in light of the vertical. In the case of icons, this means that completely excluded is "any possibility of painting icons of Christ or of the saints according to the painter's imagination. . . ."[42] I would apply the thought in this way: Artists could no more paint an icon according to their painters' imagination than story tellers could tell the life of Jesus according to their poetic imagination, or preachers preach the gospel according to their ideology, or theologians theologize according to their philosophical imagination. All icon, catechesis, homily, and doctrine must be traditional, composed according to a grammar which derives from the Holy Spirit. Ouspensky argues in his study of icons that a priest, in order to be a priest to a people, should be capable of distinguishing between icon and secular image. To know if it is orthodox, "a priest should simply know how to 'read' an icon as well as the liturgy,"[43] and Mrs. Murphy knows the grammar by which to read icon and liturgy, too.

It is the Holy Spirit who capacitates the primary theologian. To distinguish icon from secular art, symbol from sign, mystagogy from allegory, or liturgical gesture from pontifical showmanship is more than a science, it is pneumatic art. If so, it is not true that the first of the terms in the above pairings (icon, symbol, mystagogy, and gesture) can be recognized only by the educated upper tier, while the second term (art, sign, allegory, and showmanship) are embraced uncritically by the vulgar lower tier. Mrs. Murphy also becomes capable of "reading" an icon, a liturgy, a scriptural exegesis, and even a doctrine (if it is taken out of the elite jargon in which doctrines are normally cast and made intelligible to her) because she hears the Christian grammar and sees the Christian mystery epiphanized every eighth day. Tradition, Lossky said, is the unique mode of receiving the scriptures and all that the Church has produced in words, images, and symbols (liturgical or iconic); liturgy capacitates Mrs. Murphy for such reception because it is precisely here that sources function as sources. She becomes theologian when she is capacitated to read an icon and distinguish it from secular image; scripture and distinguish exegesis from ideology; liturgical rite and distinguish it from sentimentality or pontificalism; theology and distinguish it from religious kitsch. Liturgical theology is not corporate devotional opinion. Not anything and everything floats just because it is popular devotion, but it is possible that the lower tier can itself identify that which deserves to be sunk without the help of the upper tier.

A liturgical theologian exercises another obligation as well, a macrocosmic task: The Christian is capacitated to "read" the world. In liturgical confrontation with the kingdom, one discovers what it means to "stand aright," or what a "good place" would be like, or how the world was meant to be done. One learns a grammar in order to say something, and Christians learn God's grammar in the liturgy in order to tell the world the truth about itself. Theology used for Church business alone becomes the rational version of the kind of cult that is perpetuated in isolation from an allegedly profane world. The body of Christ does not assemble to do a cultic Church, but it assembles to do the world, redeemed. The objective is for the hearer to become godly in order to draw the world back to its source.

This indirectly leads to a potential of liturgical theology for ecumenism. It is important to immediately clarify that I do not mean advancing ecumenical relations by letting theology become fuzzy. Liturgical theology's contribution to the ecumenical dialogue does not consist of descending from an upper tier, where thinking is sharp and disciplined, to a lower tier where there is none at all, as though one can sidestep hard theological issues if one deals with them in inchoate form at the level of faith feelings (allegedly liturgy).

Nevertheless, liturgical theology does provide a way of thinking about how Tradition establishes a theology that is not dead-ended in propositional categories. By way of illustration, consider Ouspensky's description of what makes an icon orthodox. It is not by virtue of copying a particular historical style. "An Orthodox iconographer faithful to Tradition always speaks the language of his time, expressing himself in his own manner, following his own way. . . . In the Church there is only one criterion: Orthodoxy. Is an image Orthodox or not? Does it correspond to the teaching of the Church or not? Style as such is never an issue in worship."[44] Similarly, doctrinal formulation will speak the language of its time, be expressed in its own manner, follow its own way, but nevertheless can be subject to the criterion of Tradition: Orthodoxy. Lossky says that preserving "the 'dogmatic tradition' does not mean to be attached to doctrinal formulae: to be within the Tradition is to keep the living truth in the Light of the Holy Spirit, or rather—it is to be kept in the Truth by the vivifying power of Tradition."[45] Tradition is inwardly changeless, but constantly assumes new forms that supplement the old without superseding them.[46] To renew does not mean to replace ancient expressions with new ones, and when dogma develops it expands, it does not add. As is often the case, Chesterton makes the point all the more vividly by means of an image:

> There seems to be a queer ignorance, not only about the technical, but the natural meaning of the word Development. The critics of Catholic

theology seem to suppose that it is not so much an evolution as an evasion; that it is at best an adaptation. . . . But that is not the natural meaning of the word Development. When we talk of a child being well-developed, we mean that he has grown bigger and stronger with his own strength; not that he is padded with borrowed pillows or walks on stilts to make him look taller. When we say that a puppy develops into a dog, we do not mean that his growth is a gradual compromise with a cat; we mean that he becomes more doggy and not less. Development is the expansion of all the possibilities and implications of a doctrine, as there is time to distinguish them and draw them out. . . .[47]

Taft said the theological craft is practiced at the intersection of tradition and contemporary culture. The new forms of tradition result from the application of the changeless mystery and meaning of Christ to new circumstances.

When George Lindbeck reflects upon the nature of doctrine from his position as a historical theologian, he comes to similar sounding conclusions. I find friendly the categories he created. Lindbeck acknowledges that ecumenical agreement is often greeted with suspicion due to either of two inadequate assumptions. On the one hand, somebody assumes that one doctrine must be right and the other wrong, and therefore agreement can be achieved only when someone admits error. This perspective Lindbeck identifies as a propositional theory of religion; i.e., doctrine is essentially cognitive content. On the other hand, somebody assumes that doctrines don't really matter anyway, since they're only peepholes from various perspectives upon the same shared reality; these people propose we can ignore theological discussion in favor of ecumenical shared experiences. This perspective Lindbeck identifies as an expressive-experiential theory of religion; i.e., doctrine is essentially only an idiosyncratic expression, a sort of style peculiar to a group but not incumbent on all.

Lindbeck's aim is to steer a middle course between these unacceptable alternatives with a third option, namely, what he calls a cultural-linguistic theory of religion. According to this understanding, religion does not find its significance in propositionally formulated statements alone, or in inner experiences alone. Rather, religion's abiding and doctrinally significant aspect is located "in the story it tells and in the grammar which informs the way the story is told and used."[48] There is, in other words, an underlying shape to a doctrine which is more important for understanding the point of the doctrine than is the particular formulation. "On this view, doctrines acquire their force from their relation to the grammar of a religion. . . . Faithfulness to such doctrines does not necessarily mean repeating them, but rather requires adherence to the same directives which were involved in their formulation in the making of any new formulations."[49] In its own way, the cultural-linguistic theory accommodates the strengths of both the propositional and the experiential theory, while correcting their weaknesses. Like the propositional theory, the cultural-linguistic theory considers the external beliefs primary. The "givenness" of the religion is significant, and not just any feeling will meet the established criteria. But, correcting the propositional theory, these are known in the form of story, not in propositions that can be stated. Like the experiential theory, the cultural-linguistic theory does justice to the unreflective dimension of human existence. The aesthetic and nondiscursive elements in theology are not taken as mere ornamentation. Yet due to its external grounding it can discriminate between objectifications of religion.

This tightrope may be difficult to walk at first, Lindbeck admits.

> It may be more difficult to grasp the notion that it is the framework and the medium within which Christians know and experience, rather than what they experience or think they know, which retains continuity and unity down through the centuries. Yet this seems to make more empirical, historical, and doctrinal sense. . . . The permanence and unity of doctrines . . . is more easily accounted for if they are taken to resemble grammatical rules rather than propositions or expressive symbols.[50]

In one sense, we are dealing with a less tangible factor here in the framework, viz. the grammar, the rules of doctrine. Yet it is the more common factor. The grammar of faith establishes itself in a life by its weekly exercise in liturgical rhythms. A Christian's life will there become steeped in the Christian lexicon, formed by the Christian story, and capacitated to exercise the Christian grammar.

To use another phrase from Lindbeck, one can understand the *code* even if one does not know the details and history of how it has been *encoded*: "This stress on the code rather than the (e.g. propositionally) encoded, enables a cultural linguistic approach to accommodate the experiential-expressive concern for the unreflective dimensions of human existence far better than is possible in a cognitivist outlook."[51] The meaning of the liturgy, its *lex orandi*, is ultimately the Church's faith enacted, i.e., symbolized. Vertical, pneumatic Tradition projects itself onto the horizontal historical line and is manifested in scripture, liturgies, icons, and dogmas, where these sources function precisely as sources. Liturgical theology searches for the code presupposed by the whole content of what is encoded in liturgy. It searches for the *lex orandi* code which establishes *lex credendi* encodements.

Under the propositional model, liturgy looks like soft experience, of little help to the hard-headed discipline of theology; the experiential-expressivist model doesn't mind, because that is its preferred milieu anyway. But the cultural-linguistic theory takes liturgy seriously as a locus for theology.

> To become religious—no less than to become culturally or linguistically competent—is to interiorize a set of skills by practice and training. One learns how to feel, act, and think in conformity with a religious tradition which is in its inner structure far richer and more subtle than can be explicitly articulated. The primary knowledge is not *about* the religion, nor *that* the religion teaches such and such, but rather *how* to be religious in such and such ways. Sometimes explicitly formulated statements of the beliefs or behavioral norms of a religion may be helpful in the learning process, but by no means always. Ritual, prayer, and example are normatively much more important.[52]

As I have argued all along, liturgy has a more significant role to play regarding doctrine than just being mystical ornamentation of a concept. The structure, the code, the grammar is not invented; it is learned. The Church's *leitourgia*, said Schmemann, is the full and adequate epiphany of what the Church believes. If this is true, then all theology ought to be liturgical (not in the sense that theology should only study liturgy). If liturgy is *ruled activity*, not just a fuzzy experiential exercise, then it is wrong to cast as opposites the terms in the couplets prayer-belief, faith-doctrine, liturgist-theologian. These are not opposite actions for the very reason that the former term in the pairing also names ruled activities, and their ruled grammar is the womb from which the latter activities arise. Liturgical theology is the attempt to grasp liturgy's theology in that womb, so to speak.

Mrs. Murphy's language illuminates the landscape through which Kavanagh said he picks his professional way. That is why what she does is primary, and what he does is secondary. Liturgical theology is therefore primarily what transpires in the rite. But this can occasionally be written down. I would call that written account "liturgical theology" so long as it is understood in a derivative sense. It is not an individual's theology; it is a record of the theology transacted by a liturgical community. I will turn to two such examples of derivative liturgical theology next: commentaries on the Eucharist by Germanus and Schmemann.

---

1. Aidan Kavanagh, "Response: Primary Theology and Liturgical Act," 323.

2. Friedrich Waismann, "Verifiability," in *Essays on Logic and Language,* ed. Antony Flew (Oxford: Basil Blackwell, 1955) 129.

3. Ludwig Wittgenstein, *Philosophical Investigations,* par. 18.

4. Peter Brown, *The Cult of the Saints: Its Rise and Function in Latin Christianity* (Chicago: University of Chicago Press, 1981) 17.

5. Hume drew on evidence in classical authors and "placed this evidence together with such deftness and good sense that the *Natural History of Religion* seems to carry the irresistible weight of a clear and judicious statement of the obvious" making it virtually "impossible to challenge . . . the accuracy of his portrayal of the nature and causes of superstition in the ancient world. . . ." Ibid., 13.

6. _____, 14.

7. _____.

8. "The imagination . . . eagerly embraced such inferior objects of adoration as were more proportioned to its gross conceptions and imperfect faculties. The sublime and simple theology of the primitive Christians was gradually corrupted. . . ." From ch. 28 of Edward Gibbon's *Decline and Fall,* quoted by Brown, ibid., 15.

9. _____, 15. Brown cites Dean Milman's *History of Latin Christianity,* which contains the observation, "As Christianity worked downwards into the lower classes of society, as it received the crude and ignorant barbarians within its pale, the general effect could not but be that the age would drag down the religion to its level, rather than the religion elevate the age to its own lofty standards."

10. _____, 16.

11. _____, 18.

12. _____, 20. The passage is an acknowledgment that in this two-tiered model, the vulgar was a class "to which all women were treated as automatically belonging, as members of 'that timorous and pious sex.' "

13. Aidan Kavanagh, *On Liturgical Theology,* 150.

14. ". . . the rise of the cult of saints was sensed by contemporaries, in no uncertain manner, to have broken most of the imaginative boundaries which ancient men had placed between heaven and earth, the divine and the human, the living and the dead, the town and its antithesis. I wonder whether it is any longer possible to treat the explicit breaking of barriers associated with the rise and the public articulation of the cult of saints as no more than foam on the surface of the lazy ocean of 'popular belief.' " Brown, *Cult of the Saints*, 21.

15. ____, 19.

16. ____, quoting A. D. Momigliano, "Popular Religious Beliefs and Late Roman Historians," *Studies in Church History*, vol. 8 (Cambridge: At the University Press, 1971).

17. Gregory Dix, *The Shape of the Liturgy*, 586.

18. Timothy Ware, *The Orthodox Church* (New York: Penguin Books, 1964) 43. Timothy Ware became Father Kallistos Ware upon his ordination.

19. *On the Deity of the Son* by Gregory Nyssa, quoted in Ware, 43–44.

20. Fotis Kontoglous, *Byzantine Sacred Art*, selected writings translated by Constantine Cavarnos, (Massachusetts: Institute for Byzantine and Morn Greek Studies, 1985) 127.

21. "Clearly, the one idea predominating from the end of the first century is that what the Lord established at the Last Supper and what the Church has since been celebrating is an *eucharistia*. The word was suggested already by the *eucharistesas* of the New Testament accounts. In the linguistic usage of that time it means to consider and conduct oneself as *eucharistos*, that is, as one richly overwhelmed with gifts and graces—an attitude that found expression in words but did not exclude expression in the form of a gift." Joseph Jungmann, *The Mass* (Collegeville: The Liturgical Press, 1974) 33.

22. Aidan Kavanagh, *On Liturgical Theology*, 108.

23. Alexander Schmemann, *Great Lent*, 80. It was my idea to use the example of fasting as an illustration of primary theology in action; Schmemann is quoted because his categories of "rational" and "sentimental" inspired it.

24. Aidan Kavanagh, *On Liturgical Theology*, 75.

25. Robert Taft, "Sunday in the Eastern Tradition," 69.

26. Godfrey Diekmann, "Celebrating the Word," *Celebrating the Word: The Third Symposium of the Canadian Liturgical Society* (Toronto: The Anglican Book Centre, 1977) 19.

27. Alexander Schmemann, *Liturgy and Life*, 76.

28. Jean Corbon, *The Wellspring of Worship*, 79.

29. See Eugene Laverdiere, "Origins of Sunday in New Testament" *Sunday Morning: A Time for Worship,* 17ff. The simple designation *he kyriake* ("the Lord's") even without the noun *hemera* ("day") was understood by early Christians to mean Sunday, the eighth day, the day on which resurrection is encountered. Thus Ignatius refers to "the Lord's of the Lord" *(kata kyriaken de kyriou)* an expression that appears tautological but refers both to the day and to the people: the Lord's [day] of the Lord.

30. Vladimir Lossky, *Orthodoxy Theology, An Introduction* (Crestwood, NY: St. Vladimir's Seminary Press, 1978) 84. Or, in Kavanagh's words, "a Church is the central workshop of the human City, a City which under grace has already begun to mutate by fits and starts into the City-of-God-in-the-making. . . . This is because it is not fundamentally the Church which has been redeemed in Christ but the World itself." Kavanagh, *On Liturgical Theology,* 43.

31. Jean Corbon, *Wellspring of Worship,* 39.

32. Alexander Schmemann, "Theology and Liturgy Tradition," 174–75.

33. Kavanagh says that "baptism and all it presupposes is the way the eucharist begins, and . . . the eucharist and all it causes is the way baptism is sustained," in "Christian Initiation: Tactics and Strategy," *Made, Not Born,* (Notre Dame: University of Notre Dame Press, 1976) 4. And G. W. H. Lampe retells the remark, not his own, that had Saint Paul heard the phrase "the Blessed Sacrament" he would have thought it meant baptism. Lampe then goes on to describe baptism as "the initiation of which the subsequent course of the convert's entire life in the Church was a fulfillment and working out." "The Eucharist in the Thought of the Early Church," *Eucharistic Theology Then and Now,* Theological Collections 9 (London: SPCK, 1968).

34. Ludwig Wittgenstein, *On Certainty* (New York: Harper Torchbooks, 1969) 61, par. 467.

35. Aidan Kavanagh, *Confirmation: Origins and Reform* (New York: Pueblo Publishing Co., 1987) 39.

36. _____, 58. Kavanagh conjectures about conditions that might have urged such a change: heightened pneumatological debate, plus the association of the Holy Spirit with hand laying, plus episcopal jealousy over presbyteral consignation, plus a dismissal rite with hand laying at the close of the baptismal rite equaled a shift from a *missa* prayer to an epicletic prayer. See 60ff.

37. _____, 70.

38. _____, 63.

39. Robert Taft, "The Liturgical Year: Studies, Prospects, Reflections," *Worship* 55 (1981) 2–3.

40. Vladimir Lossky, "Tradition and Traditions," in *The Meaning of Icons,* eds. Lossky and Ouspensky (Crestwood, NY: St. Vladimir's Press, 1983) 15.

41. _____, 19.

42. Leonid Ouspensky, *Theology of the Icon* (Crestwood, NY: St. Vladimir's Press, 1978) 165.

43. _____, 18.

44. Leonid Ouspensky, *Theology of the Icon,* 14–15.

45. Vladimir Lossky, "Tradition and Traditions," 19.

46. Timothy Ware, *The Orthodox Church,* 260.

47. G. K. Chesterton, *St. Thomas Aquinas,* vol. 2 of the Collected Works (San Francisco: Ignatius Press, 1986) 427.

48. George Lindbeck, *The Nature of Doctrine* (Philadelphia: Westminster Press, 1984) 80.

49. _____, 81.

50. _____, 84.

51. _____, 35.

52. _____.

Part III

Two Examples of Liturgical Theology

Chapter 6

An Ancient Example: Germanus of Constantinople

Liturgical theology is fundamentally the rule in motion. It is contained in the structures of the rite unfolded over time. But sometimes this is written down. Sometimes, someone gives voice to what transpires in the *leitourgia* by writing it down. Such a person is neither formulating a theology of worship in general, nor looking to the liturgy for data. This person is trying to enunciate what the structure expresses, communicates, and preserves. Such a task could be called liturgical theology in a derivative sense. In its fundamental sense, liturgical theology is the rite itself (in action), and is transacted with procession and incense and sacrament. A book is not a rite. Rites are events; books are paper and ink. One would look for liturgical theology in naves and sanctuaries, not inscribed on pages in books. Nevertheless, sometimes someone records the tracks of liturgical theology, and I propose that certain liturgical commentary would fit this derivative definition, though not all.[1] If that commentary is not a rumination upon why people pray (theology of worship), nor a theological treatise illustrated by examples from ritual practice (theology from worship), then it would seem to be liturgical theology in a derivative sense. It is an account of the liturgical theology that takes place. Written liturgical commentary would direct the reader to the theology transacted by generations of Christians who assemble, encounter God, and are theologically exercised.

I have selected two examples of liturgical theology written down. One is modern, and one is ancient. The modern example will sound more familiar to our contemporary ear, and the other will sound more foreign. The contemporary example is *The Eucharist* by

Alexander Schmemann and will be treated in the next chapter. The ancient example is the *Ecclesiastical History and Mystical Contemplation* by Germanus, patriarch of Constantinople in the eighth century.

THE BACKGROUND: ANTIOCH AND ALEXANDRIA

Liturgical commentary has its origin in fourth-century mystagogical catecheses. These originally oral instructions were intended to explain the Christian mysteries, particularly baptism and eucharist, to the surging number of people joining the Church in the fourth century. The mystagogies were recorded and expanded, and continued to be useful in written form. As Paul Meyendorff describes them, "The goal of the commentary was to make its recipients understand the meaning of what they were supposed to experience in the liturgy, as well as to inspire in them a feeling of awe and fear."[2] Two ancient strands of tradition can be identified in liturgical commentary—one from Antioch and one from Alexandria. These two traditions are some-times complementary but often divergent, as is familiar from their contribution to the christological debates.[3] The Alexandrian focus is almost exclusively eschatological, scarcely mentioning Christ's earthly ministry, death, and resurrection, and so the liturgy is perceived as an ascent from the material to the spiritual realm. The Antiochene tradition emphasizes a typological approach, which, when applied to liturgy, stresses connection of the rites with the historical Jesus, focusing "on Christ's earthly ministry and the historical events of his life which are reenacted and made present in the rites, *as well as* the high priesthood which Christ now exercises in heaven."[4]

The Alexandrian tradition receives its talent for anagogical allegory from Origen, and is systematized by Dionysius, who in the third chapter of his *Ecclesiastical Hierarchy* gives an interpretation of the liturgy that becomes a primary model for later Byzantine commentators (notably Maximus the Confessor and Symeon of Thessalonica). The Antiochene approach is first seen in the writings of Isidore of Pelusa and John Chrysostom. It is eventually synthesized by Theodore of Mopsuestia in a different direction, and continued in the liturgical commentaries of our exemplar, Germanus, and then in Nicholas and Theodore of Andida, and Nicholas Cabasilas. Later Byzantine theology will balance and integrate these two traditions.[5] To understand what is distinctive in Germanus' commentary, therefore, it would help to understand the Antiochene tradition by comparing it to its Alexandrian counterpart. After that we can come to terms with the general root and purpose of allegorical interpretation as it explains the liturgical action by reference to the mystery made present.

Dionysius can serve as representative of the Alexandrian school.[6] He places his explanation of the liturgy after a meditation on two hierarchies, one heavenly and one ecclesiastical. Hans-Joachim Schulz explains that, "According to Dionysius, the function of both the heavenly and the earthly hierarchies is to mediate the divine illumination that radiates from the Most Holy Trinity, the source of all hierarchies, and descends through the ranks of the angelic world and the ordained priesthood to the believing people, and by means of this communication to lead the people to the knowledge of God."[7] The illumination communicated in a spiritual manner in the angelic sphere "is repeated in the Church in symbols, sacraments and images, that is, in half-spiritual, half-visible forms which at once copy and conceal the spiritual process occurring in the higher sphere."[8] The earthly liturgy presents the concurrent heavenly liturgy in symbolic forms, so that the participant can ascend from material to spiritual realities. A typical example can be seen in Dionysius' interpretation of the opening action in the synaxis, in which he compares the incensation of the church by the bishop with a divine action: "[He] walks from the altar to the farthest reaches of the church with the fragrance rising from the censer and, having completed his round, returns again to the altar. Inspired by his own goodness, the blessed God who is supreme above all beings, comes forth from himself to enter into communion with those who share in his holy gifts; and yet he does not abandon his essential and immutable repose and immobility."[9] What God enacts in the mystery of heaven is unfolded in a varied fullness of symbolic ceremonies. The liturgical symbols are the figurative representation of the divinity as the liturgy mediates the supratemporal saving action of God.

The great church in Constantinople, the Hagia Sophia, will be the paradigmatic expression of this view. Schulz notes, "The star of Dionysius will be in the ascendent in the now beginning age of Justinian, whose most brilliant creation, Hagia Sophia, bears witness to the same view of the world."[10] Under the influence of this Alexandrian perspective, both Byzantine liturgy and architecture reflect a hierarchical view of spirit and matter, the angelic and the human. As place of worship, the Temple is a world controlled by heaven, an earthly place filled with heavenly reality. The church structure itself, as well as the use of images within it, manifests the celestial vision of Dionysius (and that of his disciple, Maximus).[11] "By reason of the images that adorn it the church itself henceforth becomes a liturgy, as it were, because it depicts the liturgico-sacramental presence of Christ, the angels, and the saints, and by depicting it shares in bringing it about. The iconography of the church also shows it to be the place in which the mysteries of the life of Christ are made present."[12] For Dionysius, the great mystery of redemption is revealed in all the liturgical realities: the church structure, icons, the priest, sacraments, rites, and symbols. Taft adds, "The liturgy is an allegory of the soul's progress from the divisiveness of sin to the divine communion, through a process of purification, illumination, perfection imaged forth in the rites."[13]

We will see how different this allegorical interpretation is from the Antiochene tradition that Germanus inherits, but first something more should be said about allegorization. Both the traditions employ allegorization, but it does not mean for Dionysius (Alexandrian), or Theodore and Germanus (Antiochene), what it seems to mean today. In modern usage, allegory connotes an interpreter arbitrarily fixing to an object any meaning he wishes (like fitting a square peg in a round hole). It feels like free-floating pedagogy, by which any allegorical meaning that even roughly suits the interpreter's needs can be applied. Schulz explicitly denies that this could account for Dionysius' method. The explanation of the ceremonies is not arbitrary; "on the contrary, in his system every 'allegoresis' (relating of one thing to another) is kept within bounds because in every case the meaning of the rite emerges from a 'higher' and never from 'another' irrelevant reality."[14]

Such an argument will sound like liturgical legerdemain, both here and when we read Germanus, unless it is taken within the context from which it arose: early Christian scriptural exegesis. Taft devotes some effort to explaining the purpose of liturgical allegorization. It simply applies an interpretive process to the liturgy that had already been applied to scripture.

> All healthy liturgical interpretation depends on a ritual symbolism determined not arbitrarily, but by the testimony of tradition rooted in the Bible. Like the scriptures, the rites of the Church await an exegesis and a hermeneutic and a homiletic to expound, interpret, and apply their multiple levels of meaning in each age. Mystagogy is to liturgy what exegesis is to scripture.

It is no wonder, then, that the commentators on the liturgy used a method inherited from the older tradition of biblical exegesis.[15]

Sacred Scripture presents more than history, holy or otherwise. In addition to its literal (historical) meaning, scripture is also reckoned to contain a higher meaning, variously labeled as "spiritual" or "mystical" or "allegorical." Whatever it is called, this higher meaning has traditionally been divided into three classifications. First, scripture's allegorical meaning (dogmatic aspect) refers to the mystery of Christ and the Church; second, its tropological meaning (moral aspect) relates the text to an individual's life; third, its anagogical meaning (eschatological aspect) directs us to the kingdom to come.[16] In other words, when the historical event is contemplated in faith it is "perceived as containing a higher truth . . . as well as a practical application for here and now, and a sign that points to what is to come."[17]

This threefold spiritual meaning of scripture is its allegorical meaning. In classical rhetoric, allegory is an extended metaphor. Allegorization is a helpful and necessary tool for understanding; what is condemned is arbitrary application of allegory. Taft explains:

> Christian exegetes borrowed this figure of *speech* and applied it not to *language*, but to event, as when the passage of the Red Sea is seen as a figure of Christ's baptism. . . . It is not a question of the hidden sense of the text, or of the relation between visible and invisible realities, but of the relation between two historical events of different epochs in salvation history, such as the passover of the Jews and that of Jesus. But in addition to this *allegoria facti* there was also the *allegoria dicti,* which sought hidden meanings, often contrived, in the biblical text. As we have seen it is the application of this arbitrarily extended metaphorical interpretation to liturgical rites in the Middle Ages that contemporary liturgists generally refer to pejoratively, as allegory.[18]

When this method of allegory worked out for scripture was applied to the liturgy in the fourth century, the genre of Christian mystagogy was born. It was entirely natural for the composers of the mystagogies to interpret liturgy in this way, since "they understood the liturgy, like scripture, to be a channel leading to God, a means of experiencing divine life here and now, explains Meyendorff. "This exegetical method was thus a most appropriate tool to present all these different levels and to keep them in dynamic tension."[19] At stake was the ability to understand and integrate the historical unfolding of the mystery of salvation. What the Old Testament foreshadowed by prophetic type was fulfilled in Christ; therefore the Divine Liturgy can be perceived as already the banquet of the anticipated kingdom.

We have seen that the Alexandrian tradition employed allegorical meaning to direct the liturgy toward heaven, under the influence of Dionysius. The Antiochene tradition will employ allegory in another way. It will use allegorical interpretation to include attention upon the historical Jesus.

This is already evident in Theodore of Mopsuestia three centuries before Germanus. Schulz describes Theodore as

> the most typically Antiochene representative of the new, anti-Arian emphasis on the high priesthood of Christ. He sees Christ as the heavenly high priest. . . . Therefore this priestly activity must also be imaged forth in the liturgy. Just as the priest is an image (eikon) of Christ, so too must the liturgical actions become images of the historical work of redemption and in particular of the resurrection.[20]

For Theodore, the liturgy not only images an individual's internal spiritual journey, as suggested by the Alexandrians, it also images forth Christ's priestly activity. And where does Christ function as priest? In heaven, to be sure, and so "we are taught to perform in this world the symbols and signs of the blessings to come";[21] but the economy of salvation was accomplished by the High Priest as a human being. Therefore the liturgy not only images Christ's priestly activity in heaven, but in the liturgy we can also see Christ as he is led away to his passion, and as he is stretched out on the altar to be immolated for us. Theodore explains that the deacons spread cloths on the altar to remind us of burial sheets, while others stand on either side and fan the air above the sacred body. Theodore focuses dually upon the high priesthood that Christ exercises in heaven, and the historical events of his life, which are reenacted and made present. In this type of allegorical mystagogy, specific rites and objects naturally begin to take on specific meanings. Theodore synchronizes individual rites of the liturgy with stages in the life of Christ, that is to say, phases in the work of redemption. For example, the offering procession images Christ being led to his passion; the deacons standing round the bishop image the angels; the linen spread on the altar represents the liturgical service of Joseph of Arimathea; and the epiclesis and subsequent liturgical actions correspond to the resurrection. Even though Theodore was no longer a direct authority for the Church after the year 533, "by then his approach to the liturgy had become so much a part of ecclesiastical tradition that his interpretative motifs are interwoven inextricably with the later Byzantine explanation of the liturgy." [22]

In exegesis of scripture, observes Taft, Antioch was more prone than its Alexandrian counterpart to interpret the Old Testament in terms of typology; "this same bias is manifest in their mystagogy, with its strong emphasis on the relation between the liturgical rites and the saving acts of Christ's life." [23] What was prefigured in the Old Testament and fulfilled in Christ has passed into the sacrament in expectation of its eschatological fulfillment. These four phases of salvation—Old Testament foreshadow, fulfillment in Christ, ecclesial celebration, and eschatological parousia—are to be integrated. To be sure, Theodore does not ignore the heavenly, mystical element of the liturgy ("[e]very time, then, there is performed the liturgy of this awesome sacrifice, which is the clear image of the heavenly realities, we should imagine that we are in heaven . . ." [24]) but what is new in Theodore is his systematic interpretation of the liturgy as a dramatic reenactment of the passion of Christ. As noted, the actions of priest and deacon, the vestments and table linens, the altar and bread represent to us the economy of salvation by dramatic reenactment of the passion of Christ.

To summarize, a systematic Christian liturgical theology appeared in fourth-century catechetical homilies, and was worked out from two perspectives. Both observed the eschatological dimension of liturgy, but each in its own way.

> Among the Antiochenes the emphasis shifts rather to a cultic, "realised eschatology" of the presence of the Risen One among His own as proleptic experience of the Pasch of the final days. Among the Alexandrians a moral, individual eschatology is stressed: the true Christian does not wait for the Pasch of the parousia, but is "passing continuously from the things of this life to God, hastening towards His city." [25]

Whence arose this Antiochene perspective? Taft suggests at least a couple influences: Arianism and Jerusalem.

The struggle against Arianism "shifted attention from Christ's second coming at the parousia to His first coming in the incarnation" [26] and emphasized Christ's pre-existent divinity and equality with the Father. Arius thought that in order to protect monotheism it was

necessary to say that the Son was not equal to the Father. Arius'
reputed code phrase was "there was a time when he was not," meaning
that the Son was the first and foremost creature God made, but
could not be considered divine, or else bitheism would ensue. The
Council of Nicea repudiated Arianism by affirming the Son's equality
with the Father (he is of the same substance: *homoousios*, and was
"begotten, not made"). The Son is not subordinate to the Father in
heaven, as Arius thought, but functions as mediator between God
and *anthropos* in the economy of salvation. If the Son is equal to the
Father, then the Son would serve as mediator only as human being,
not as Son. This is intended to directly contradict the Arian agenda
of proof-texting from scripture Christ's heavenly subordination, as
Joseph Jungmann explains in his classic study:

> In order to support their heresy, the Arians zealously collected all texts
> in which a "humbling" was attributed to Christ, especially a subordination
> to the Father. They particularly favoured the texts of scripture in which
> there was a mention of the praying of Jesus. On the tacit assumption that
> the Logos took the place of the human soul, they concluded triumphantly:
> therefore the Son himself is subordinate to the Father; consequently,
> he is only a creature.[27]

Limiting subordinational phrases to the earthly Jesus, and relating
them solely to his humanity, was the Church's anti-Arian reaction.
Therefore, Christ's role as mediator of our prayers and sacrifices
was decreasingly described in the present, even as his priestly activity
was increasingly described in the past as a historical work of redemption. There was increased stress upon the general anamnetic (memorial) character of the eucharistic celebration.

> In Alexandrian theology, this resulted in a weakening of Christ's medi-
> atorship. Among the Antiochenes it provoked greater stress on Christ's
> high priesthood as pertaining to His humanity. . . . What happened is
> that the middle fell out . . . and we are left with the two, unbridged poles
> of the dilemma: God and the historical Jesus.[28]

The second influence upon the Antiochene tradition mentioned
by Taft came from Palestine. It was there, in Jerusalem, that we first
hear of "the topographical system of church symbolism" in which
various parts of the building are interpreted to symbolically represent

places hallowed during Holy Week, and also there that the city's liturgy revolved around its sacred topography.[29] In Taft's opinion,

> What was spread across the map of Jerusalem's holy history came to be written small in the humbler churches of eastern Christendom. . . . Thus the sanctuary apse becomes the cave of the sepulcher, and the altar the tomb from which salvation comes forth to the world. . . . Its application to the eucharist was so congruous as to be inevitable. The next step, or perhaps a concomitant one . . . was the burial cortege symbolism at the transfer and deposition of the gifts.[30]

The rise of a sense of historicism in the fourth century is more complicated than the impression given by Gregory Dix when he suggested that Jerusalem's new historical consciousness transformed or even displaced the more primitive eschatological outlook. Thomas Talley argues that Jerusalem was in fact conservative in such matters, and it is more likely that it was the expectations of pilgrims coming to Jerusalem which led to the association of liturgical celebrations and historical events, nurturing the rise of historicism.

> Jerusalem was much more conservative and resisted such partition of the paschal season into the fifth century. We shall be concerned to argue later that many fourth-century observances that have been considered innovations at Jerusalem are better accounted for as responses to the expectations of pilgrims who had learned in their home churches to associate certain events in the life or Christ with particular days in the liturgical year.[31]

According to Talley, the situation seems to be more complicated than smaller churches simply copying Jerusalem; the expectations held by visiting pilgrims was conditioning the Jerusalem liturgy too. However, it is true "that the recovery of the tomb of Christ following the Council of Nicea and the Constantinian building program in Jerusalem and environs did much to the way in which liturgical events were celebrated."[32] The symbol-system that sees tomb and resurrection reenacted in the liturgy was given a substantial boost by Jerusalem's historical concreteness, but it depended also upon Antiochene typological exegesis. And this exegesis, applied by Theodore in the early fourth century, inaugurated a tradition of interpretation that eventually spread throughout the whole of Christendom.

All of this—Antiochene exegesis of scripture, its application by Theodore to liturgy, the anti-Arian reaction, and the vividness of Palestine geography — feeds the anamnetic quality found within the New Testament itself. Christ did say, "Do this as my memorial." What was memorialized was simply expanded in two directions. First, the content of the memorial was expanded to include his entire human economy of salvation, as well as the Passion,[33] and second, the synchrony between the liturgy and the historical Jesus was worked out not only in the anaphora but throughout the entire rite. It would be misleading to therefore suggest the fourth-century Fathers of the Antiochene school invented salvation-history symbolism; it is more accurate to say they chose to emphasize and synthesize it. It was Theodore's accomplishment to systematize this, but in Taft's opinion, "he was developing a trend present in eucharistic thought from the start."[34]

THE PATRIARCH

It is in this context, then, that we meet Germanus. Born probably in the early 640s, he was patriarch of Constantinople from 715 until 730. He thus overlaps by several years the first iconoclastic attack (726–780) begun by Leo III. He was deposed for resisting this threat, and died three years later in 733. He was anathematized by the iconoclastic Council of 754, but after the later restoration of icons (what came to be called the triumph of Orthodoxy) he was eventually canonized in 787. Through him, Theodore's Antiochene interpretation from the early fifth century enters the Byzantine tradition in the eighth. The two leitmotivs in Theodore, the historical self-offering of Christ and the heavenly liturgy, become a permanent basis of the later Byzantine synthesis through the popular influence of Germanus' commentary. Taft acknowledges that Maximus Confessor is a more significant author and that his is the first extant Byzantine commentary, and that Nicholas Cabasilas represents the final synthesis of liturgical symbolism, but Germanus' patriarchate from 715 to 730 overlooks the beginning of a watershed period in Byzantine tradition. His work, observes Taft, is therefore "our earliest witness to the new synthesis in popular liturgical piety," and is thus not to be judged as fanciful allegory but as "a viable, consistent eucharistic theology, suited to the mentality of his times and in continuity with the patristic tradition to which he was heir."[35]

Germanus writes this liturgical commentary at a period when piety was changing profoundly on two fronts: First, there was a large rank of Christians who attended Eucharist but did not commune, and second, a new estimate of the liturgy was required in the face of icono-clasm. Germanus' synthesis of the "new" historical emphasis with the anagogical emphasis, which had hitherto marked Byzantine identity and tradition, can be considered a new liturgical theology, one which remained faithful to tradition and yet spoke to a new *circumstance*. For this reason Taft defends him as being "what every theologian must be: a man of tradition and a man of his times," and suggests that we ask of Germanus no more than what we would ask of theology today, namely,

> that his "model" of the eucharist present a valid expression of the common tradition so as to make it alive for the genius of his age. For it is at that intersection of tradition and contemporary culture that the theological craft is exercised, and in Byzantine liturgical explanation at the start of the eighth century this crossroad was occupied by Germanus.[36]

In the first place, a new liturgical piety was developing as a result of the increasing number of noncommunicants at the Eucharist. Due to a number of factors (including the massive influx of new members, returning apostates undergoing an extended period of peni-tence, and catechumens who postponed their own baptism indefinitely) the community was fractured "into a communicating minority and a majority who were in church only as observers. . . . In the same century came the development of a spirituality of fear and awe with regard to the eucharist, and this only encouraged the flight from the eucharistic banquet."[37] It was as if the community was arranging into concentric circles of degrees of participation. In the Hagia Sophia, for example, new and old social divisions in the church (clergy, laity, catechumens, the faithful, men and women, the common folk and the imperial court) were coordinated with symbolic reflection upon the physical divisions in the church building (atrium, narthex, nave aisles, and galleries). One account of the social and physical ranks is found in a letter by Gregory Thaumaturgus who distinguishes five degrees of participation in the liturgy,

> based on the individual's standing in the community: "weeping," which was done outside the door where one asked the prayers of the faithful who entered; "listening," which was done in the narthex where one heard the scripture and preaching, but left before the prayers and before the catechu-mens had gone out; "falling down," which was done within the doors of the church before one left with the catechumens; "standing by," which

meant remaining with the faithful throughout the liturgy but abstaining from Communion; and finally "communicating."[38]

The new approach to the liturgy took these new divisions into account. Communion was decreasingly a common sharing of gifts that instantiated *koinonia* [communion], and increasingly an act of personal devotion. "Under such conditions the eucharist could no longer sustain its former ideology as a rite of *koinonia*, and Antiochene liturgical explanation begins to elaborate a symbolism of the presence of the saving work of Christ in the ritual itself, even apart from participation in the communion of the gifts."[39]

In the second place, liturgical piety was rocked by a challenge that had just begun to arise during Germanus' patriarchate, and would rend the Eastern Church for the next century. Iconoclasts (literally, "icon smashers") objected to portraying Christ in icon, and to the veneration icons received. This also presented a new circumstance, one for which Meyendorff thinks

> the traditional Byzantine approach was no longer fully adequate: more attention had to be paid to the historical man, Jesus. The danger no longer came from the Arians, who had denied Christ's divinity, but from the iconoclasts, who now challenged the dogma of Christ's full humanity, and who in consequence saw the eucharist only as a symbol. . . . This shift is clearly reflected in Germanus' commentary.[40]

Patriarch Germanus was deposed because of his public defense of images. In 726 the iconoclast Emperor Leo III openly took a position against the veneration of icons and insisted that the patriarch of Constantinople sign a decree to this effect.[41] Germanus categorically refused. He was the first to see that this threatened the incarnation, and the first leader of the Orthodox opposition to the iconoclasts. He wrote a letter in which he already expounds the argument that John of Damascus or Theodore the Studite will use: "We make no icon or representation of the invisible divinity. . . . But since the only Son himself, Who is in the bosom of the Father, deigned to become man . . . we draw the image of His human aspect according to the flesh. . . ."[42]

In consideration of the iconoclast challenge, the place of emphasis found in Dionysius or Maximus had to be recast. But by no means is their anagogical emphasis eliminated. It is evident that Germanus is building upon the commentary by Maximus, even as he adds representational references to salvation's historical economy. The foundation of Byzantine liturgy was laid in the age of Justinian, but this newly developing representational perspective exercised no less a lasting influence. An adjustment in meaning was being made to fit the new circumstances of iconoclasm and fewer communicants. This was a theological adjustment, one worked out liturgically and iconographically.

The parallel change in the iconography of this period can be charted both in the choice of images and their arrangement within the church space. Icons became more representational. Moved to greater realism, the iconodules ("icon reverencers") invoked the Trullan Synod of 692 that defined that although the Church "lovingly accepts the ancient shadows and images that have been handed down to the Church as symbols and hints of the truth," she gives preference to grace and truth themselves. The Church therefore prescribed "that from now on, in place of the lamb of old, Christ our God, the Lamb who takes away the sins of the world, is to be portrayed in human form in the icons, so that in his state of abasement the majesty of God the Word may be seen and we may be reminded of his life in the body, his suffering, his saving death and the redemption of the world which his death accomplished."[43] The focus in iconography shifted to a more realistic representation of Christ, particularly to the details of his earthly life. Icons depicted Christ, angels, saints, prophets, and not scenes, because historical facts have little place in this kind of iconography. The same principle is at work regarding the arrangement of the icons within the Church. "It is no longer the historical course of Christ's life but the salvific importance and continuing efficacy of what is represented that primarily determines the rank of images."[44]

Just as iconography became more representational, so did the liturgy. Liturgical symbols were conceived after the manner of sacred images, and as many new symbolic elements as possible were introduced into the liturgy. Schulz points out that given the traditional and sacrosanct organization of the liturgy, there was limited possibility to introduce these new symbols within the liturgy proper, and they occurred primarily at the *prothesis* (the beginning preparation of the elements), which was freer for elaboration. At hand lay the Antiochene scriptural exegesis as a model of allegory by which to relate two historical events of different epochs in salvation history. "The command that the commemoration of redemption be proclaimed in a perspicuously visible way was applied not only in iconography but also and especially in the development of the liturgy."[45]

Germanus knows of the eschatological tradition inscribed by Maximus and embodied in the Hagia Sophia, but his commentary registers, like a Richter scale, a shift in the Byzantine perception of the Eucharist, a shift which took place to deal with a swelling number of Christians who attended the Divine Liturgy without communing, and to refute the growing iconoclastic movement. This is indicated in the very title of the work that registers it: *Ecclesiastical History and Mystical Contemplation*.

> In Maximus and in Dionysius before him, the focus had been on *theoria*, that is, on the understanding of the realities which lie *behind* or *over* that which is visible. Contemplation thus becomes an ascent from the image to its archetype. . . . In contrast to *theoria*, but not opposed to it, is *historia*: this too is contemplation, but a contemplation which seeks to clarify the spiritual dimension of an event, of a rite. Here, the outer forms are taken very seriously and are not secondary.[46]

Theoria leads the spiritual seeker to the reality which is God, while *historia* focuses on God's self-revealing incarnation; the former struggles to ascend from image to archetype, while the latter takes the outer form more seriously; in the former, contemplation means to understand realities which are behind the visible, while in the latter, contemplation means to discern the spiritual dimension of the visible rite. Still, *historia* is not arbitrary or imposed. Its purpose is to draw the observer into salvation history, to make the observer a participant in it by anamnetically portraying the unified salvation event.

Schulz concludes that iconoclasm provoked a change in iconography that was paralleled in the liturgy: "Symbolic representation is replaced by portrait-like image in which the higher reality becomes accessible to direct vision." However, Schulz renders a negative judgment on this process, while Taft takes a different view. Schulz thinks that when liturgical explanation transforms symbols into images (as he thinks Germanus has done) it risks losing sight of the real human community doing the activity of praying, offering, sacrificing, or thanking. "This community can hardly be given its due place in a liturgy that is interpreted in a purely pictorial way, whereas this is not difficult when the liturgy is understood as symbolic."[47] Taft, on the other hand, characterizes Germanus' struggle with iconoclasm more favorably as "the victory of a more literalist popular and monastic piety, precisely in favor of a less abstractly symbolic and more representational, figurative religious art."[48] He agrees that symbolism was replaced by representational portrayal—both in art (where Orthodoxy defended a move from the symbolical portrayal of Christ as a lamb to the image of the human Christ) and in liturgy (where the rite symbolizing the soul's spiritual ascension into heaven was recast to also representatively portray the earthly economy, which makes such an ascent possible). The abuses of iconoclasm forced a reevaluation of the spiritualized symbolism contained in Maximus, and the shift in both icon and liturgy was toward pictorial image and pictorial rite. Just as art changed from abstractly symbolic to representational, so liturgy became less abstractly spiritual and more anamnetically connected to historical event.

Taft points out, "Now symbolism and portrayal are not at all the same thing either in art or in liturgy, and the effect of this popular mentality on liturgical theology can be observed in the condemnation of the iconoclastic view that the eucharist is the only valid symbol of Christ. Orthodoxy responded that the eucharist is not a symbol of Christ, but indeed Christ Himself."[49] Leonid Ouspensky characterizes the argument as pure equivocation: The two parties differed in their definition of icon. Iconoclasts called the Eucharist the only true icon, while the Orthodox responded that only icons are icons, and the Eucharist is Christ himself. Iconoclasts believed that an icon is an object that shares the same nature as its prototype (it is consubstantial with its model), and therefore they could only accept an image when this image was identical in nature to that which it represented. Under this definition, a painted image simply cannot be an icon of Christ. If the painted image was called an icon, one of two blasphemies would be committed. Either the icon would represent both the human and divine nature of Christ, in which case the natures are confused (the Monophysite heresy), or the icon would represent only the human nature of Christ, in which case the natures are separated (the Nestorian heresy). The iconoclasts sought to overcome the essential difference between the image and its prototype because they thought iconic image had to be of the same nature as the person it represented. Ouspensky thinks that by "[b]asing themselves on this principle, the iconoclasts came to the inevitable conclusion that the only icon of Christ is the Eucharist."[50] Christ chose bread as the image of his incarnation because bread has no human likeness and thus idolatry can be avoided.

The Orthodox understanding was completely different. The Orthodox defined an icon as that which represents the person, not the nature. The icon is an image not of Christ's divine nature or human nature but of the divine person (incarnate). This meant, for them, that "the Holy Gifts are *not* an icon precisely because they are identical to their prototype."[51] Because the Eucharist is consubstantial with Christ, it cannot be an icon (the very opposite of the conclusion reached by the iconoclasts). John of Damascus argued that there must be an essential difference between the image and its prototype, and the Orthodox party, fully aware of the distinction between nature and person, maintained that the icon does not represent the nature, but the person. "When we represent our Lord, we do not represent His divinity or His humanity, but His Person which inconceivably unites in itself these two natures without confusion and without division, as the Chalcedonian dogma defines it."[52]

If there is no difference between the image and its prototype, as the iconoclasts said, then the only way something earthly can symbolize the divine is if the earthly thing is changed into an immaterial, spiritual thing. But such an idea exactly contradicts the incarnation, and here is what was at stake in the controversy. Icons are not only permissible, they are necessary because icons safeguard a full and proper doctrine of the incarnation. Ware thinks the fault of iconoclasm is a kind of dualism. Regarding matter as a defilement, iconoclasm wants a religion freed from contact with what is material: to be spiritual is to be nonmaterial. But the doctrine of incarnation is precisely the affirmation that matter can be, and has been, redeemed. The body as well as the soul is to be transfigured. "The Incarnation has made a representational religious art possible: God can be depicted because He became man and took flesh."[53]

The incarnation has also made possible representational liturgy, as Meyendorff explains:

> In its perception of the liturgy, the Antiochene approach of Theodore of Mopsuestia, with its greater attention to the historical Jesus and to his humanity, was clearly more suited to this new, more realistic approach of the Orthodox. It supported the Orthodox polemic against the iconoclasts far better than the older, more spiritualizing approach of the Alexandrians. . . . In fact, the iconoclastic position was heavily dependent precisely upon [this] Origenistic approach. . . . It was probably from Dionysius that the iconoclasts derived their notion of the eucharist as the only valid "image" and "symbol" of Christ, because only here is the image consubstantial with its prototype. . . .[54]

Liturgical outer forms are not secondary, existing only to be transcended as the soul makes its ascent; they are taken seriously. This is *historia*. God enfleshed is dramatically represented in the liturgical rite. This is a new liturgical theology at work.

Though dealing with a liturgy essentially unchanged, each author of liturgical commentary reflects a different element that is being worked out by the community's differing social conditions and theological reactions. Schulz says Dionysius allegorized the liturgy anagogically, highlighting deification through ethical imitation of the incarnate Logos; Theodore reflected a reenactment typology, influenced by anti-Arian themes and Palestinian topographical symbolism; Saint Maximus the Confessor wished to show the importance of the liturgy for monastic life, thereby correcting a trend which had little use for eucharistic piety; in Nicholas and Theodore of Andida the comparison between present liturgy and the historical Jesus was worked out superlatively, while in Nicholas Cabasilas the same sacramental actualization was reflected without requiring an unbroken sequence of rites representing historical details. Each commentator reflects a theological emphasis made by the assembly in *leitourgia*—their liturgical theology. "Underlying all these commentaries," says Meyendorff, "is a sense that the liturgy is itself a source of theology. Just like Scripture, the liturgy is a revelation, which implies a multiplicity of meanings, and indeed offers the possibility for participation in divine life."[55]

For his part, Germanus registers the fundamental liturgical theology being worked out by a community during a time that saw a decline of participation at communion, and a threat to iconography's affirmation of the incarnation. As Taft says, "A theology is not *the* theology; *his* times are not *all* times. But studies in the history of theology always show the fatuousness of seeking anything more."[56] Germanus' commentary develops by pastoral necessity. By applying the representational symbolism of Antioch, Germanus' commentary presents a liturgy absorbed into "mystical contemporaneity" with events in the life of Jesus, yet without dissecting the mystery. In addition to the liturgy's anagogical character, a typological character of the rite is emphasized without splintering the unified mystery. A single mystery is celebrated, even if this mystery was unfolded over the course of several historical events which are represented in several liturgical acts.

The Commentary

Germanus' synthetic flexibility is promptly demonstrated in the first ten chapters of his work. In chapter one he describes the church as "the temple of God, a holy place, . . . an earthly heaven in which the supercelestial God dwells and walks about," and immediately after, in the next sentence, adds, "It represents the crucifixion, burial, and resurrection of Christ. . . ." In the next nine chapters he gives allegorical interpretation of the physical details of the church. The simandron represents the trumpets of the angels (ch. 2); the apse corresponds to the cave in Bethlehem and the tomb (ch. 3); the holy table corresponds to the spot in the tomb where Christ was placed (ch. 4); the ciborium represents here the place where Christ was crucified (ch. 5); the altar corresponds to the holy tomb of Christ (ch. 6); the ambo manifests the shape of the stone at the Holy Sepulchre (ch. 10).

Germanus continues in this manner throughout 43 chapters of the commentary, ending with an interpretation of the anaphora (eucharistic prayer), which in length is approximately one quarter of the commentary. Chapters 1–10 allegorize the structure and furnishings of the church; chapters 11–13 explain prayer action (facing east and why one doesn't kneel); chapters 14–19 allegorize vestments worn by the priest (stole, embroidery on the sleeves, why the phelonia is unbelted, the representation of presbyters and deacons); chapters 20–22 deal with the sacramental elements (the bread's symbolism, the lancing of the bread, and wine mixed with water); chapters 23–33 allegorize mainly the Liturgy of the Word (antiphons, Little Entrance, Trisagion, ascent of bishop to throne, prokeimenon, alleluia, censor, gospel and people's blessing) and chapters 34–41 allegorize the liturgy of the Eucharist (eiliton cloth on altar, catechumens' departure, proskomede, Great Entrance, the discos and chalice and veil).

What is to be observed, however, and what is badly represented by such a list, is that the same object or action can receive layered interpretation. This is especially striking when Germanus refers an act or object to both Jerusalem and heaven within the same chapter. Here are some examples. In chapter 4 the holy table "corresponds to the spot in the tomb where Christ was placed," and it "is also the throne of God, on which, borne by the cherubim, He rested in the body;" furthermore, it is the table at which Christ sat among his disciples, and that prefigured by the table of the Old Law upon which the manna was placed in the tabernacle (the bread descended from heaven is obviously Christ). In chapter 6 "the altar corresponds to the holy tomb of Christ," and "the altar is and is called the heavenly and spiritual altar." In chapter 30 "the censer demonstrates the humanity of Christ, and the fire, His divinity" (even more graphically, the interior of the censer is the womb of the Theotokos who bore the divine coal, Christ) and also the sweet-smelling smoke reveals the fragrance of the Holy Spirit. Immediately following this the censor is compared to the font of holy baptism, which issues forth sweetness through the operation of the Holy Spirit. In chapter 38 "The discos represents the hands of Joseph and Nicodemus, who buried Christ. The discos on which Christ is carried is also interpreted as the sphere of heaven, manifesting to us in miniature the spiritual sun, Christ, and containing Him visibly in the bread."

In most cases Germanus makes connection with the historical Jesus. Sometimes he only makes connection with Christ Pantocrator (the presbyters are compared in chapter 16 to seraphic powers "covered, as if by wings, with stoles," and the deacons as images of the angelic powers, "go around thin wings of linen oraria as ministering spirits sent out for service"). And sometimes the allegory includes not only Jerusalem and heaven, but the Temple of Israel, too.

Such an allowance of multiple meanings is frequently looked upon as a sign of ancient carelessness. Ascribing multiple allegorical meanings to the same object is misunderstood to be a sign of imprecision or thoughtlessness, and it confirms the modern suspicion that the allegorist can impose any interpretation he likes, and as many as he likes. But there is a difference, Taft explains.

> This misses the point, I think, because it fails to grasp Germanus' methodology, the whole basis of his symbol-system. For the problem of later medieval liturgical allegory consists not in the multiplicity of systematically layered symbols, such as we find here and in patristic exegesis. The later one-symbol-per-object correspondence results not from the tidying up of an earlier incoherent primitiveness, but from the decomposition of the earlier patristic mystery-theology into a historicizing system of dramatic narrative allegory.[57]

As just witnessed, Germanus lets multiple meanings of a symbol stand, and he does not feel the need for unequivocal coherency as do those who insist on assigning single meanings (whether rational or allegorical). Because symbol can, in fact, entertain several layers of meaning simultaneously, allegory theologizes several layers of the liturgy simultaneously.

The allegory invoked by Germanus is biblical and traditional and multivalent. He does not share the modern conviction that communication of meaning depends upon suppression of equivocation. For speakers of formalized languages (Waissman), the end is reached when we can say "It means this, not that." But in Germanus, it is not as though the table symbolizes where Jesus was laid, but not the throne of God; neither is it the case that the discos means the hands of Joseph, but not the sphere of heaven. The natural grammar at work in liturgical theology can issue in multiple allegories because the liturgy, like scripture, is revelation on more than one level. Taft adds, "It is not the multiplicity of meanings but the attempt to parcel them out that can lead to an artificial literalism destructive of symbol and metaphor, and this is precisely what Germanus refuses to do. . . . He rejects the later temptation of the historicizing decomposition of the unitary mystery into the component parts of its actual historical enactment."[58]

The Antiochene tradition gave pictorial representation to a particular facet of the mystery, or to a particular phase in Jesus' life. Once this happened, could it again become integral to the mystery? If a liturgical commentary has lifted out a facet, allegorically, for theological appreciation, then must that ritual action be forever delimited by that allegorical meaning?

> Even though many interpreters of the liturgy in fact succumbed to this danger, the developing liturgy itself did not yield to it in an excessive degree. Theodore of Mopsuestia did not pave the way for this kind of deterioration. . . . [And Orthodox] life and piety is accustomed even today to looking upon its faith as articulated less in doctrinal definitions than in its liturgical tradition, which is indeed respectful of the old and yet possessed of ever new vitality.[59]

Germanus did not succumb to this temptation, either. The liturgy is the source for his theology (a *locus theologicus*) because his commentary exegetes the natural language of liturgical theology. It does not fix predetermined principles onto liturgical actions by means of allegory. The reader—or, better, the worshiper—is simultaneously directed to Sinai, Bethlehem, Jerusalem, and heaven. Says Taft, "All levels— Old Testament preparation, Last Supper, accomplishment on Calvary, eternal heavenly offering, present liturgical event—must be held in dynamic unity by any interpretation of the Eucharist. To separate these levels, then parcel out the elements bit by bit according to some chronologically consecutive narrative sequence, is to turn ritual into drama, symbol into allegory, mystery into history." [60]

After chapter 41, where Germanus treats the anaphora, it is Schulz's opinion [61] that the synthesis of the new Anitochene tradition with the established Alexandrian tradition diminishes, but at least in the opening lines their interweaving still seems evident when Germanus writes:

> Thus Christ is crucified, life is buried, the tomb is secured, the stone is sealed. In the company of the angelic powers, the priest approaches, standing no longer as on earth, but attending at the heavenly altar, before the altar of the throne of God, and he contemplates the great, ineffable, and unsearchable mystery of God. He gives thanks, proclaims the resurrection, and confirms the faith in the Holy Trinity. The angel wearing white approaches the stone of the tomb and rolls it away with his hand, pointing with his garment and exclaiming with an awed voice through the deacon, who proclaims the resurrection on the third day, raising the veil and saying: "Let us stand aright"—behold, the first day! "Let us stand in fear"—behold, the second day!—"Let us offer in peace"—behold, the third day! The people proclaim thanks for the resurrection of Christ. . . . [62]

The earthly economy of salvation has been completed, the stone is sealed, and we await the resurrection. The angel exclaims it, with awed voice, through the deacon. Where is this resurrected Christ? At Jerusalem? at table with the disciples behind locked doors? at table with the faithful behind the open-doored iconostasis? at the right hand of the Father? Yes. He was, and is, and shall be.

Germanus lets the symbol play according to multiple grammars, in multiple language games. In doing this, he is being faithful to the type of Christian liturgical signification that is rooted in biblical typology, not in medieval allegorization. The allegory that the patristic period applied to the Old Testament was based upon a typology which, by pneumatic revelation, discerned in Jesus of Nazareth the inauguration of a new phase of salvation history still connected with God's first covenant: Old Testament prototype, historical Jesus, and coming *parousia.* The liturgical theology of Germanus understands the present sacramental and ecclesial reality as a temporal phase by which God's eternal salvific mystery is manifested. Liturgy epiphanizes in sacramental form the same mystery that was prefigured in the Old Testament, accomplished historically in the earthly life of Christ, lived mystically in souls, accomplished socially in the Church and will be consummated eschatologically in the heavenly kingdom.[63] Insofar as liturgy epiphanizes this mystery, and insofar as theology is reflection upon the mystery revealed, liturgy is the ontological condition for theology.

The liturgical theology that Germanus offers is not a formalized language seeking to impose an allegorical system, but a natural language seeking to express the tradition in a new way needed by his day. It thus avoids two misunderstandings of contemporary allegory. As Taft explains,

> Christian liturgical signification is rooted in biblical typology . . . but it is the whole sacramental rite, not its individual details, that bears this signification. "Allegory" violates these presuppositions either by overstepping the bounds of objective biblical typology, seeing in the rites meanings that are personal to the allegorist and have no warrant in the biblical interpretation of salvation history; or by fragmenting the integrity of symbol and signified, assigning to individual details of a sacramental action separate aspects of the signified reality. In both cases, symbol is stretched to the breaking point. . . . This is not, however, the traditional sense of "allegory" in Christian tradition.[64]

Germanus' commentary manifests the first mark by which I have been identifying liturgical theology: It is the community's *theologia prima*. His commentary gives voice to a meaning of the liturgy which his community was forging and to which they apparently resonated. "The proof of the success of Germanus' synthesis is its viability," says Taft: "for over six hundred years it reigned with undisputed primacy over the field of Byzantine liturgical explanation."[65] In the face of new social circumstances, and the iconoclast challenge to incarnational theology, the divine word worked a novel adjustment in the Byzantine liturgy. A liturgical theology grasped the tradition in new ways. Germanus' commentary also manifests the second mark by which I have been identifying liturgical theology: It comes from the rite, and it is not imposed upon the rite from without. This means that liturgical theology is communal and not personal to the commentator (or theologian). The meaning must be read off the rite in its entirety, and not off pieces, which in their splintered isolation might fail to communicate the *lex orandi*.

---

1. For an overview of the liturgical commentaries of Maximus, Germanus, Nicholas and Theodore of Andida, Symeon and Cabasilas, see Hans-Joachim Schulz, *The Byzantine Liturgy, Symbolic Structure and Faith Expression* (New York: Pueblo Publishing Co., 1986). Though it does not fit our tight definition of liturgical commentary, a reader might find interesting the inter-weaving of liturgy and catechesis in the eastern catechism entitled *The Living God: A Catechism for the Christian Faith* (Crestwood, NY: St. Vladimir's Press, 1989). A group effort by persons within the Orthodox Fraternity of Western Europe, this catechism illustrates God's saving covenants by using "certain elements within the life of the Church—hymns, icons, sacraments—which express them, render them present, and enable us to participate in them." They maintain that scripture or theology "studied apart from the life of the Church is nothing more than a history of past events rather than the New Covenant, the encounter between man and the living God. The aim of this book is to help our readers in achieving that very encounter" (xvi). This catechism is not liturgical commentary *per se*, but it surely is a long way from a theology of worship.

2. Germanus of Constantinople, *On the Divine Liturgy*, introduction, translation, and commentary by Paul Meyendorff (Crestwood, NY: St. Vladimir's Seminary Press, 1984) 24. On mystagogy in general see Hugh M. Riley, *Christian Initiation* (Washington: Catholic University Press, 1974). He distinguishes theology and mystagogy by claiming the former offers a meaning of the event while the latter offers a meaning of a given liturgical ceremony (215). His thesis in the rough is that mystagogy must include three factors: the liturgy itself, the world of consciousness of the candidate, and materials employed to give exposition (220). Thus his is a study of what *materials* were adopted to explain to *these neophytes* what had happened in *these rites*.

3. E.g., Alloys Grillmeier, *Christ in Christian Tradition*, vol. 1 (Atlanta: John Knox Press, 1975) comparing 133ff. with 421ff.; P. Smulders, *The Fathers on Christology* (DePere, WI: St. Norbert Abbey Press, 1968); or note studies on the development of Christian doctrine such as J. N. D. Kelly, *Early Christian Doctrines* (New York: Harper & Row, 1960); or Jaroslav Pelikan, *The Christian Tradition*, vol. 1: The Emergence of the Catholic Tradition (100–600) (Chicago: University of Chicago Press, 1971) ch. 5. On specific exegetical differences between Alexandria and Antioch see James Wood, *The Interpretation of the Bible* (London: The Camelot Press, 1958) ch. 5 "Alexandria and Antioch." A summary of their respective spiritualities is contained in Louis Bouyer, *The Spirituality of the New Testament and the Fathers* (New York: Seabury Press, 1960).

4. The terms of the comparison are from Meyendorff, "Introduction," 26–33; the quote is from 29 (underscoring mine).

5. Even if Schulz claims they are fundamentally opposed in orientation: "Dionysius' explanation of the liturgy is thus opposed diametrically to that of Theodore of Mopsuestia. The later Byzantine explanation of the liturgy will strike a balance between these two basic possibilities." *The Byzantine Liturgy*, 28.

6. I call the reader's attention once more to the study of Dionysius made by Alexander Golitzin. Its relevance here lies in his thesis that Dionysius did stand within the Orthodox tradition, despite the failure by more recent scholarship to appreciate that fact.

7. Hans-Joachim Schulz, *The Byzantine Liturgy*, 25.

8. _____.

9. _____, 26.

10. _____, 28. Another sign of its potency is that while Theodore's Antiochene tradition eventually takes firm root also, "it was possible for the ideas of Theodore to enter the Byzantine liturgy of the sixth century only through the transposing medium . . . of the Dionysian vision of the world" (36).

11. The *Mystagogy* by Maximus begins with a meditation on the church and relates it symbolically to the heavenly-earthly bipolarity. "The holy church of God presents itself as an image and likeness of the entire cosmos, which encompasses visible and invisible beings. . . ." (Schulz, *The Byzantine Liturgy*, 43–49 on Maximus). Thomas Mathews points out that Maximus' divisions are not structural but functional, i.e., liturgical. "The division is made to carry a variety of symbolic interpretations: It represents the whole created universe divided into the invisible angelic world and the corporeal world of men, or the visible world divided into heaven and earth, or man himself in his twofold nature of soul and body, or the soul of man in its division between higher and lower faculties." *The Early Churches of Constantinople: Architecture and Liturgy* (University Park: Pennsylvania State University Press, 1971) 121. For a very useful review of Maximus' commentary, see Andrew Louth, "Apophatic Theology and the Liturgy in St. Maximos the Confessor," *Wisdom of the Byzantine Church*, 1997 Paine Lectures in Religion, University of Missouri, ed. Jill Raitt (Curators of the University of Missouri: 1998).

12. Hans-Joachim Schulz, *The Byzantine Liturgy*, 51.

13. Robert Taft, "The Liturgy of the Great Church," *Dumbarton Oaks Papers*, nn. 34 and 35 (1980–81) 61.

14. Hans-Joachim Schulz, *The Byzantine Liturgy*, 27.

15. Robert Taft, "The Liturgy of the Great Church," 59.

16. A medieval ditty was created in the West as a memory tool: "The Letter shows us what God and our fathers did; the allegory shows us where our faith is hid; the moral meaning gives us rules of daily life; the anagoge shows us

where we end our strife." Steven Ozment, *The Age of Reform* (New Haven: Yale University Press, 1980) 66ff.

17. _____, "The Liturgy of the Great Church," 59. Scripture is read within the realms of history, faith, charity, and hope (60). For a positive estimate of this allegorical reading of scripture see also Louis Bouyer, *The Meaning of the Monastic Life* (London: Burns & Oates, 1955) Part Two, ch. 5, "Lectio Divina."

18. _____, 60, footnote 72.

19. Paul Meyendorff, "Introduction," 24. Taft: "It is part of a much larger problem manifested in all areas of patristic theology, not just in liturgy" ("Historicism Revisited," 106).

20. Hans-Joachim Schulz, *The Byzantine Liturgy*, 17.

21. Theodore of Mopsuestia, Homily 15, cited in Meyendorff, "Introduction," 30. See otherwise Edward Yarnold's translation in *The Awe Inspiring Rites of Initiation* (England: St. Paul Publication, 1971).

22. Hans-Joachim Schulz, *The Byzantine Liturgy*, 20.

23. Robert Taft, "The Liturgy of the Great Church," 62.

24. Paragraph 20 of Baptismal Homily IV, quoted in Taft, 63; also Yarnold, 224.

25. Robert Taft, "Historicism Revisited," 102.

26. _____.

27. Joseph Jungmann, *The Place of Christ in Liturgical Prayer* (London: Geoffrey Chapman, 1965) 172.

28. Robert Taft, "Historicism Revisited," 102.

29. Such as described by Egeria's Diary. Cf. *Egeria: Diary of a Pilgrimage*, trans. George Gingras (New York: Newman Press, 1970).

30. Robert Taft, "The Liturgy of the Great Church," 66.

31. Thomas Talley, *The Origins of the Liturgical Year*, 39–40. Thus his judgment: "If at the end of the fourth century in much of the Church the individual moments of that redemptive *transitus* were celebrated as distinct festivals, it would be wrong to suppose that this was because they were looked upon only as events in a departed past, to be recalled in our now distant present" (70).

32. _____.

33. Hans-Joachim Schulz notes that the anaphora of Hippolytus simply says "Mindful of his death and resurrection we offer . . ." but in the Byzantine anaphora texts the object of remembrance becomes the passion, cross, burial, resurrection, ascent into heaven, session at the right hand of the Father, and second coming in glory. *The Byzantine Liturgy*, 11.

34. Robert Taft, "The Liturgy of the Great Church," 67–68.

35. _____, 46.

36. _____, 72 and 47.

37. Paul Meyendorff, "Introduction," 40.

38. Thomas Mathews, *The Early Churches of Constantinople,* 126.

39. Robert Taft, "The Liturgy of the Great Church," 69.

40. Paul Meyendorff, "Introduction," 51.

41. For the history of iconoclasm, see Leonid Ouspensky, *Theology of the Icon* (Crestwood, NY: St. Vladimir's Press, 1978); George Ostrogorsky, *History of the Byzantine State* (New Jersey: Rutgers University Press, 1969); John Meyendorff, *Christ in Eastern Christian Thought* (Crestwood, NY: St. Vladimir's Press, 1975); or A. A. Vasiliev, *History of the Byzantine Empire,* vol. 1 (Madison: University of Wisconsin Press, 1952).

42. Germanus' letter to John of Synades, quoted Meyendorff, "Introduction," 49. Compare with Theodore's argument: "In so far as [Christ] proceeded from a Father who could not be represented, Christ, not being representable, cannot have an image made by art. . . . But from the moment Christ was born of a representable Mother, he clearly has representation. If he had no image made by art, it would mean that he was not born of a represent-able mother." Ouspensky & Lossky, *The Meaning of Icons* (Crestwood, NY: St. Vladimir's Press, 1983) 31.

43. Hans-Joachim Schulz, *The Byzantine Liturgy,* 57. For a discussion of early iconography in its evocative and not representative stage, see Andre Grabar, *Christian Iconography: A Study of Its Origins* (New Jersey: Princeton University Press, 1968).

44. _____, 55. He goes on to make this intriguing comparison: "The images of this period seem comparable in function, therefore, to the liturgical *procla-mation* of the gospels according to the liturgical cycle rather than to the *account* as found continuously in the gospels themselves."

45. _____, 64.

46. Paul Meyendorff, "Introduction," 48.

47. Hans-Joachim Schulz, *The Byzantine Liturgy,* 69–70. At the end of his book, Schulz therefore gives a brief pitch for a methodology which he finds more palatable, that of Nicholas Cabasilas. He affirms that Cabasilas stands in the Antiochene tradition with Germanus and the Andidans, but thinks the former turns the mind to the event without reducing the rite to a sequence of pictorially represented historical details (190).

48. Robert Taft, "The Liturgy of the Great Church," 72.

49. _____ .

50. Leonid Ouspensky, *Theology of the Icon* (Crestwood, NY: St. Vladimir's Press, 1978) 149.

51. G. Ostogorsky, cited in Ouspensky, Ibid., 149. Underscoring mine.

52. _____ , 152.

53. Timothy Ware, *The Orthodox Church*, 41.

54. Paul Meyendorff, "Introduction," 50–51.

55. _____ , 41.

56. Robert Taft, "The Liturgy of the Great Church," 46.

57. _____ , 73.

58. _____ , 74.

59. Hans-Joachim Schulz, *The Byzantine Liturgy,* 157–58.

60. Robert Taft, "The Liturgy of the Great Church," 73.

61. He remarks that in the earlier part of the commentary "the symbolism based on the life of Christ was to some extent combined harmoniously with a symbolism based on the heavenly liturgy. . . . From this point on, however, the symbolism of the heavenly liturgy takes over completely" (74).

62. Germanus, ch. 41, p. 89 in Meyendorff, "Introduction."

63. The list is Jean Daniélou's, "Le symbolisme des rites baptismaux," *Dieu Vivant,* found in Robert Taft, "The Liturgical Year: Studies, Prospects, Reflection," *Worship* 55 (1981) 23.

64. Robert Taft, "The Liturgy of the Great Church," 55, footnote 62. Regarding the influence this typological method had upon Western sacramentology, see Enrico Mazza, *Mystagogy* (New York: Pueblo, 1989).

65. _____ , 74.

Chapter 7

A Modern Example: Alexander Schmemann

As noted in chapter three, Schmemann frequently addressed the question of what liturgical theology is, where it is found, and why it is important to both theology and liturgy. The articles we surveyed there addressed liturgical theology as an apologetic. In the last years of his life he approached liturgical theology in a different capacity, though. He describes his book, *The Eucharist*, thus:

> This book is neither a manual of liturgics nor a scholarly investigation. I wrote it during rare moments of leisure, in the midst of many interruptions. Now, putting together these chapters into one book, I do not pretend that they provide a complete or systematic study of the divine liturgy. Rather, this book represents a series of reflections on the Eucharist. These reflections, however, do not come from scientific analysis but from my own experience, limited though it may be.[1]

If this book is not a systematic study of the Divine Liturgy, neither is it simply Schmemann's personal viewpoint. I offer the book as a modern example of a derivative liturgical theology, one Schmemann read off the Divine Liturgy of his own Orthodox tradition. As far as possible, here I will faithfully present Schmemann's own account of Orthodox liturgical theology, without entertaining the ecumenical question of how Eastern and Western perspectives can be brought into harmony. Schmemann had completed the Russian version of this book, but his death in 1983 interrupted the English version beyond oversight of the translation of the first two chapters and the preparation in English of some scattered sections. Having looked in chapter three at Schmemann's abstract apologetic for liturgical theology, we will complete our acquaintance with his position by looking at this example of what liturgical theology comprises.

LITURGY OF THE WORD

The work consists of 12 chapters, already striking the academic eye as more familiar than was Germanus. Still, there is an oddity to the chapter titles. They all begin "The Sacrament of . . .": The Sacrament of the Assembly, the Kingdom, Entrance, the Word, the Faithful, Offering, Unity, Anaphora, Thanksgiving, Remembrance, the Holy Spirit, and Communion. Schmemann's reason for doing this is not explained until 160 pages later, in the chapter on the anaphora (eucharistic prayer) where the chief part of the liturgy begins. There he quickly points out that "chief" is opposed to "nonchief"; it is not opposed to "unessential." He thinks scholasticism erred when it tended in the direction of this latter meaning.

> I categorically reject this meaning. . . . Therefore it was not to sound more solemn but perfectly consciously and responsibly that I have entitled each of the chapters . . . with the word *sacrament*. For I see the entire task at hand in demonstrating as fully as possible that the divine liturgy is a single, though also "multifaceted," sacred rite, a single sacrament, in which all its "parts," their entire sequence and structure, their coordination with each other, the necessity of each for all and all for each, manifests to us the inexhaustible, eternal, universal and truly divine meaning of what has been and what is being accomplished.[2]

One must not isolate a theology of the Eucharist from the entire liturgical act. Liturgical theology is not sacramentology; its subject matter is larger.

Therefore, this book does not begin with historical overviews, theories of real presence, comparative religion studies, or philosophical symbol theory; it begins by discussing the sacrament of the assembly. A liturgical theology of the Eucharist must begin with the first liturgical act, the *Sacrament of Assembly*. The fundamental task is to uncover the meaning and essence of the triunity of assembly, eucharist, and the Church. Scholastic dogmatics, that method which isolates sacrament from the Divine Liturgy to be a separate topic of investigation, "is simply unaware of the ecclesiological meaning of the eucharist, and at the same time it has forgotten the eucharistic dimension of ecclesiology,

i.e., the doctrine of the Church."[3] The gathering is eucharistic, and
the Eucharist is constitutive of the assembly as Church. The Eucharist
is not one of seven sacraments, in the sense of being one means of
grace among others; it is the premiere sacrament because it is how the
Church exists. The liturgical theology contained in Schmemann's book
will not be the dissection of a static rite, because the Eucharist is not
static and the mystery is indivisible. He will not rummage through
a list of meanings, or pick from a pile of interpretations to accomplish
theological explanation. "The first principle of liturgical theology is
that, in explaining the liturgical tradition of the Church, one must
proceed not from abstract, purely intellectual schemata cast randomly
over the services, but from the services themselves — and this means,
first of all, from their ordo."[4]

   Who gathers at this assembly? The Church, consisting of
clergy and laity. Neither the clergy alone, nor the laity alone is the
Church in its entirety. Rather, the apostolic priesthood and the universal
priesthood together make up Church in mutual dependence. This
principle of correlation is expressed in various ways in the ordo ("Every
prayer is 'sealed' by the gathering with one of the key words of Christian
worship, 'amen,' thus binding the celebrant and the people of God at
whose head he stands into one organic whole"[5]), and it is expressed to
greater or lesser degrees in each individual rite (antiphons, preaching,
gift offering, the kiss of peace, etc). The celebrant and the people work
in true synergy. They act in concert, collaboratively. "Each word and
each act continues to express the concelebration of all with each other,
with everyone in his proper place and proper ministry in the single
leitourgia of the Church."[6]

   For what reason does the Church assemble? To experience and
perceive the Temple as "the gathering together of heaven and earth
and all creation in Christ — which constitutes the essence and purpose
of the Church."[7] This is called sobor in the Russian Orthodox tradition.
Sobornicity is symbolized liturgically in the dialogic structure of the
rite, iconographically in the images of Christ, the saints, and the angels,
and structurally in the visible quality of the Temple. This translates the
dialogic structure of the liturgy (priest–people) into a physical structure of the Temple. "The nave is directed toward the altar, in which we
find its end and purpose; but the 'altar' necessarily entails the nave and
exists only in relation to it."[8] Such dialogic unity was also the original purpose of the iconostasis (a screen of icons between the sanctuary

and nave). The icon is a witness to, or better still, a consequence of the unification of the divine and the human, of heaven and earth, standing as interface between sanctuary and nave.

The liturgy is a *Sacrament of the Kingdom* because it symbolizes the divine kingdom, only how shall we understand this word *symbolize?* In the ancient understanding, a symbol meant the epiphany of reality, the way a rose manifests love. The symbol communicated the reality it symbolized because it participated in it. In the modern understanding, however, a symbol seems to mean the absence of reality, like there is not real water in the chemical symbol for water. Symbols are now taken to resemble a reality slightly, illustrate that reality and call it to mind for us, but the reality itself is assumed to be missing. This modern understanding therefore looks upon the Little Entrance (with the Gospel book) or the Great Entrance (of the eucharistic elements) as illustrating a past event in the life of Jesus by symbolizing it. Symbol is treated not only as distinct from reality but even contrary to it.[9]

When Schmemann says that the liturgy symbolizes the kingdom, it is crucial to remember that he is using *symbol* in the ancient, and not the modern sense. The kingdom is symbolized because it is made manifest, made present, joined together (sym + baleo), and given to us in this sacrament. At the eucharistic table, the Church *symbolizes* the kingdom—the verb here being used as an active verb. The Church does not represent or illustrate the kingdom by calling it to mind for edification; rather the Church epiphanizes the kingdom, as a handshake epiphanizes friendship or a kiss manifests love. The kingdom is symbolized by the Church at Eucharist because the kingdom is where the Father's reign is mediated through the Son in the Spirit. The central message of Jesus was that this reign of God has already come. The kingdom is unity with God, reconciliation between a world and its loving creator. Christ's atonement reestablished fellowship with the Father, and for those who have believed it and accepted it, the kingdom is already here and now.

> Returning now to what we said above about the symbolism of Christian worship, we can now affirm that the Church's worship was born and, in its external structure, "took shape" primarily as a *symbol of the kingdom,* of the Church's ascent to it and, in this ascent, of her fulfilment as the body of Christ and the temple of the Holy Spirit. The whole newness, the uniqueness of the Christian *leitourgia* was in its eschatological nature as

the presence here and now of the future *parousia,* as the epiphany of that which is to come. . . . [10]

To forget this and change eschatology into a "then" would profoundly change liturgy. From this fully realized symbol, the whole of the Christian *lex orandi* was born and developed.[11]

The *Sacrament of Entrance* was originally the first act of the liturgy after the assembly of the faithful. A preliminary, pre-entry rite has since grown up. The expression "Little Entrance" originally meant the entrance of clergy and people into the church nave, but by and by, the entrance came to be understood as the priest's entrance through the iconostasis into the holy place of the altar. Schmemann calls this an application of "illustrative symbolism" that "weakened the perception and experience of the 'assembly as the Church' itself as the entrance and ascent of the Church, the people of God, to the heavenly sanctuary."[12] These clerical entrances performed at the altar were later rigged with historicized or allegorized interpretation (e.g., the entrance with the Gospel book was seen as a sacred dramatization of Christ going out to preach).

Today's pre-entry rites consist of the Great Litany, three antiphons, and three prayers. Schmemann provides a brief liturgiological background to the growth of these pre-entry rites[13] but admits this would be of mere historical and archeological interest if it did not emphasize that the beginning of Eucharist is the dynamic ceremony of entering. The Eucharist is movement; it is the Church moving from this fallen world toward the kingdom of God. Such a movement is the evangelical service of the body of Christ.

> If "assembling as the Church" presupposes separation from the world . . . this exodus from the world is accomplished *in the name of the world,* for the sake of its salvation. For we are flesh of the flesh and blood of the blood of this world. We are a part of it, and only by us and through us does it ascend to its Creator, Savior and Lord, to its goal and fulfilment. We separate ourselves from the world in order to bring it, in order to lift it up to the kingdom, to make it once again the way to God and participation in his eternal kingdom. . . . For this [the Church] was left in the world, as part of it, as a symbol of its salvation. And this symbol we fulfil, we "make real" in the eucharist.[14]

The first of these pre-entry rites, the Great Litany, makes this clear. The Church detaches itself from the world in order to know what to pray for on the world's behalf; it ascends from the dusty whirlwind in order to see more clearly. The prayers of the Church cannot be said to be simply those of an individual or a group of people, when the Church prays the prayer of Christ himself. Christ's prayer for the world is entrusted to the liturgical assembly. So in the Great Litany, the Church makes intercession and mediation for peace and the salvation of souls, for the peace of the whole world, for the holy churches of God, for the union of all, for a particular holy house and those therein, for the hierarchy, for world and nature and humankind, and finally the Church commends itself with the saints and the Theotokos (Mary) to Christ. Life is returned to God.

When the Church has assembled and stands before the Holy One, then the *Sacrament of the Word* is celebrated. As we have already noted, Schmemann insists that just because some part of the rite is not the chief part does not mean that it is unessential. He pauses a moment to register the consequences that have accrued from ignoring the sacrament of the Word. In the first place, scripture and Church have become two competing authorities, two sources of the faith, creating the bogus question about which interprets which. In the second place, scripture and sacrament have been ruptured. The sacrament ceases to be biblical and evangelical, and scripture remains locked in history. "In separation from the word the sacrament is in danger of being perceived as magic, and without the sacrament the word is in danger of being 'reduced' to 'doctrine'." [15]

Scripture and homily were originally read and preached from a raised platform called a bema in the midst of the nave. Approach to the altar was restricted exclusively to the liturgy of the faithful, i.e., by making offering and by consecration of the holy gifts. The entire liturgy thus originally consisted of three entrances or processions: ascent into the Temple for assembly, ascent to the bema for the Liturgy of the Word, and ascent into the sanctuary for offering and consecration. This trifold pattern was disrupted by the disappearance of the first entrance and the correlative development of pre-entry rites, by the gradual disappearance of the bema, and by keeping the Gospel book on the altar. Schmemann says the Little Entrance should be the transport of the Gospel book through the iconostasis, culminating in the proclamation of scripture because "the Gospel book is a verbal icon of Christ's manifestation to and presence among us.

Above all, it is an icon of his resurrection."[16] As such, it is accompanied by alleluia verses, censing, and an epicletic prayer.

Organically connected to the reading of scripture, and not extraneous to it, is the homily. The homily should not be a sermon about the Gospel, but a preaching of the Gospel. In other words, it should not be an explanation of what was read, nor a class in theology, nor a meditation on the Gospel theme, because all these depend on the preacher's own gifts and talents. What feeds the congregation is not the preacher's rhetorical or theological or devotional skills, but the Gospel itself. "Here we see why all church theology, all tradition, grows precisely out of the 'assembly as the Church,' out of this sacrament of proclamation of the good news. . . . Tradition is the interpretation of the word of God as the source of life itself, and not of any 'constructions' or 'deductions'."[17] This places a participatory activity upon the laity during the homily. If preaching were theological elaboration on a text, then only the one making the elaboration could be considered active. But because the Gospel has been entrusted to the whole people of God, therefore the laity is active during the homily, too. Schmemann says the ministry of the celebrant is preaching and teaching, and the ministry of the people is in accepting this teaching. One can neither proclaim nor accept the truth without the gift of the Holy Spirit, and the Holy Spirit has been given to the entire assembly, not just the preacher. Only the entire Church has the mind of Christ.

At this juncture the liturgy begins to change from its outward, kerygmatic, intercessory mode to its inner, eucharistic, individual mode. The first half of the Divine Liturgy consisted of assembly as Church, the entrance, and the sacrament of the Word; that is now completed in the *Sacrament of the Faithful*. The identity of the Church has two poles: on the one hand, the Church is directed to the whole world, to the cosmos, to all humanity, and on the other hand, Christ's love is directed to each unique and unrepeatable individual. Religious thought must not polarize these truths in either liturgy, piety, or theology. We must not construe Christianity as only a cosmic and universal calling, but neither construe it as a religion of personal salvation above all. The two poles must be held in tension. Christ sacrificed himself for all, and because the Church is his body, it is directed to the world and commanded to lay down its life for the world. But Christ also turned to each human being uniquely and distinctly.

From here stems the antinomy that lies at the foundation of Christian life. The Christian is called to deny himself, to "lay down his life for his friends"; and the same Christian is summoned to "despise the flesh, for it passes away, but to care instead for the soul, for it is immortal." In order to save "one of the least of these" the shepherd left the ninety-nine, but the same Church—for the sake of her purity and fullness—cuts off sinners from herself.[18]

Therefore, after this point in the liturgy, only the faithful may remain. The Eucharist is a closed assembly of the Church. The Church that does this liturgical action is constituted and made manifest in all fullness by everyone together, baptized and ordained.

Schmemann believes that one can understand what it means to be a royal priesthood only if one contrasts Church with world, not if one contrasts laity with priest. The whole Church, including laity, are to serve a priestly vocation in the world, and therefore a false dilemma of either clericalism or pseudodemocracy results if one sees clergy and laity in opposition. "A false dilemma arises: either the laity are a 'passive' element and all activity in the Church belongs to the clergy, or else some share of the clergy's functions can, and therefore must, be transferred to the laity."[19] All the faithful at the eucharistic liturgy—whether priest by ordination or *laos* by baptism—are Church. Because everything was done by Christ and no one needs to add anything to his work, the Church is not a religious society ruled by God through clerics. The Church is the body of Christ, which means

> no one submits to another, but all together submit to each other in the unity of the divine-human life. In the Church the authority of the hierarchy is indeed "absolute"—but not because this authority is granted to them by Christ. Rather, it is because it is the authority of Christ himself, just as the obedience of the laity is itself the obedience of Christ. For Christ is not *outside* the Church, he is not *above* the Church, but he is in her and she is in him, as his body.[20]

The entire assembly constitutes a single body, realizing the priesthood of Christ. Schmemann thinks both Protestant congregationalism and Roman centralism have missed this point. The Church's first service to the world is to proclaim the death of Christ, to confess his resurrection, and to await his coming, and everyone who was joined with Christ in baptism participates in this ministry.

LITURGY OF THE EUCHARIST

After the catechumens have been dismissed, and the doors have been closed, the first act done by the liturgical people is the *Sacrament of Offering*. Schmemann devotes extended time to this subject in chapter six (the lengthiest in the book) because the issue of sacrifice has been so confused and confusing. This is because the theologians normally treat the issue exclusive of liturgical action, and liturgical scholars usually give a rubrical instead of theological explanation of the proskomide, which is the preparation of the bread and wine that will be taken to the holy table. The word *proskomide* itself means the carrying or conveying of something to a certain place. Originally the deacons carried elements brought by the people to the altar just before the anaphora, but the rite has long since been performed in much more elaborate detail by the ministers alone, before the people assemble and the Liturgy of the Word even begins. A portion of bread is lanced out from the loaf and placed in symbolic order upon the plate. Confusion reigns over the sacrament of offering. The most common question asked is whether it is a preliminary sacrifice, or does it already constitute the essence of the Eucharist? Schmemann says this is an important question for understanding the liturgy, and yet the Orthodox who have adopted the school theology method ignore the question, and liturgy professors give answers consisting entirely of references to a symbolism that explains precisely nothing. The confusion is an indication that symbol and reality are being contraposed.

Before one can understand the symbolism of the proskomide *per se*, a theological context of sacrifice is necessary. In bringing bread and wine the Church performs "that most ancient, primordial rite that from the first day of human history constituted the core of every religion: we offer a sacrifice to God."[21] From whatever angle this rite is explained—theological, historical, sociological, psychological— it remains indubitable that whenever human beings turn to God they sense the need to offer God the most precious thing they have as gift and sacrifice.

> From the time of Cain and Abel, the blood of sacrifices had daily covered the earth and the smoke of burnt offerings has unceasingly risen to heaven.
> Our "refined" sensibilities are horrified by these blood sacrifices. . . .
> In our horror, however, do we not forget and lose something very basic, very primary, without which in essence there is no religion? For in its

ultimate depths religion is nothing other than *thirst of God* . . . and often
"primitive" people know this thirst better, they sense it more deeply . . .
than contemporary man does, with all his "spiritualized" religion, abstract
"moralism" and dried-up intellectualism.[22]

To thirst for God is the beginning of love for God. Ultimately, there
is only one sin: not to want God, and to in fact seek separation from
him. In sacrifice, a person acknowledges his or her dependence on
God and gives expression to a yearning for union with God. Unfortunately, sacrifices have been impotent to achieve this. They cannot
accomplish unity with God because they are powerless by themselves
to destroy sin and restore the desired fellowship with the deity. All
human sacrifice remains under the law of sin, and sin is above all

the rupture from God of life itself. That is why this fallen life . . . does
not, and cannot, have the power to heal and revive itself, to fill itself
with life again, to make itself sanctified once more . . . just as one who
is falling into an abyss cannot turn back upward, one who is buried alive
cannot dig himself up, a dead man cannot raise himself. . . . Only [God]
can fulfil that concerning which all sacrifices remain an impotent plea.[23]

What sacrifice meant to do, it could not do, because it flowed from an
egocentric heart and remained under the law of sin.

The law of sin was broken in Christ, and as mediator between
God and humanity his sacrifice resounds both in heaven and on earth.
In heaven, the Lamb's sacrifice reconciles us to the Father, bringing
forgiveness of all sins and fullness of sanctification. For that reason new
sacrifices are both unnecessary and impossible — unnecessary because
in Christ we have access to the Father, and impossible because through
the sacrifice on the cross our very life was restored and regenerated
as offering and sacrifice. And on earth, sacrifice is restored to those
who in Christ's spirit offer themselves to God. "In [Christ's] sacrifice
everything is fulfilled and accomplished. In it, above all, sacrifice is
cleansed, restored and manifested in all its essence and fullness, in its
preeternal meaning as perfect love and thus perfect life, consisting
of perfect self-sacrifice: in Christ 'God so loved the world that he gave
his only Son,' and in Christ man so loved God that he gave himself
totally. . . ."[24] What sacrifice was meant to accomplish, but could
not, was thereby brought to pass. If sacrifice means perfect love and
total self-giving, then Christ in his unswerving love for the Father
was the perfect sacrifice, and our life in Christ, indeed the whole life

of the Church, is offering and sacrifice. At the Divine Liturgy, the world, including ourselves, is offered to the Father "in a sacrifice of love and unity, praise and thanksgiving, forgiveness and healing, communion and unity."

The Eucharist proper begins with a solemn rite called the Great Entrance. This name was applied, however, only after the inherent meaning (bringing the sacrifice to the table) had become obscured, and the allegory of Christ entering Jerusalem for his passion became predominant. The eucharistic offering did not begin as an illustrative allegory of the Lord's entrance into Jerusalem, or his burial by Joseph, but such an understanding developed due to the gradual detachment of the preparation of the eucharistic gifts from the liturgy itself, and its isolation in the proskomide rite. The logic (or theo-logic) of the proskomide can be uncovered in its liturgical ordo, if one has a little knowledge of the historical development of the offering.

> In the consciousness, in the experience and in the practice of the early Church, the eucharistic sacrifice was offered not only on behalf of all and for all, but *by all,* and therefore the real offering by each of his own gift, his own sacrifice, was a basic condition of it. Each person who came into the gathering of the Church brought with him everything that . . . he could spare for the needs of the Church, and this meant for the sustenance of the clergy, widows and orphans, for helping the poor, for all the "good works" in which the Church realizes herself as the love of Christ. . . .[25]

The eucharistic offering, then, is rooted precisely in a sacrifice of love. The origin of the offering is an expression of love. The elements brought by each Christian were received by the deacons, whose task it was to sort out the gifts they received and prepare a portion of these love-offerings to constitute the eucharistic sacrifice. The other gifts were distributed to the poor during the week. As agents for the Church's exercise of charity, deacons in the Church were charged with a ministry of love and to them fell the duty of the ritual preparation of these gifts of charity. This duty continued well into the fourteenth century, even though it was attenuated after the conversion of the empire in the fourth century. Once most of the populace was Christian, the means of the Church's philanthropy was modified. "Not only was she recognized by the government, but with all 'charitable' activity being gradually concentrated in her hands, the Church could not but have been transformed into a complex organization, overcome by

an 'apparatus'."[26] Other more efficient means were developed to gather
the Church's resources, and they were administered along with the
State's resources. Yet the ancient connection between the Eucharist
and the Church's self-sacrifice to the world through material gifts
was not forgotten. The preparation of the gifts remained as a rite,
even though it was strictly no longer required because the deacon no
longer selected the eucharistic offering from out of the charitable gifts.
Schmemann sees this as an "example of that law of liturgical 'development' according to which changes in outward *form* are frequently
determined by the necessity of preserving inner *content*. . . ."[27] The
development of an organized charitable apparatus uncoupled the sacrifice of love from the eucharistic sacrifice, but a liturgical rite remained
as a witness to this original inner link. No longer a functional necessity, the preparation of the gifts remains nonetheless as rite.

Even in its present position before the Divine Liturgy begins,
while the people assemble in the Church, the proskomide possesses a
theological meaning. There are not two offerings, bread in the proskomide and Christ at the altar (as though the former is a preliminary set-up
for the latter). If the bread and wine that have not yet been blessed are
referred to as "offering" or "sacrifice" or "Body of Christ" in the proskomide, it is because this matter has been sanctified by the incarnation
and is set aside for eucharistic fulfillment. Christ restored creation's
potential to be sacrifice, and humanity's vocation to be
homo adorans.

> Precisely because the sacrifice of Christ, which includes all things in itself
> and was offered *once*, occurred *before* all our offerings . . . likewise the
> proskomide, the preparation of the gifts, takes place *before* the liturgy. For
> the essence of this preparation lies in referring the bread and wine, i.e., our
> very selves and our whole life, to the sacrifice of Christ, their conversion
> precisely into *gift* and *offering*. Here is precisely the reality of the prosko-
> mide — the identification of the bread and wine as the sacrifice
> of Christ. . . .[28]

The proskomide commemorates the whole Church, living and
dead, saints and martyrs, Mary and the angels. The connection between
the eucharistic sacrifice and the self-offering of the Church remains
in charity. At the time of the Great Entrance, the elements are brought
out from the room in which they were earlier prepared and placed
upon the altar. In order to reveal that the entire Church is making an

offering, Schmemann recommends "regenerating in every way possible" each member's inclusion in this act of offering, which in a day of monetary donations could mean joining the people's collection basket to this offering.

The act is accompanied by words, the commemoration. To commemorate is the verbal fulfillment of offering in which we give ourselves and each other to God. This is not yet the Eucharist, but the commemoration does refer everything to the memory of God by praying that God will remember. In scripture, divine memory means God's attentiveness to creation. To live is to abide in the memory of God, and to die is to fall out of God's memory. Human beings have a gift of memory unequaled in any other creature. Out of all the ways of being, only human beings can remember God and truly live through this remembrance. Schmemann summarizes sacrament and sacrifice when he writes that God's remembrance of humanity is the gift of life, and humanity's remembrance of God is the reception of life. "Man forgot God because he turned his love, and consequently his memory and his very life, to something else, and above all to himself. . . . He forgot God, and God ceased to exist for him."[29]

The salvation history of Israel is "the gradually disclosed recognition of Christ, the 'creation' of this memory before his coming in time;" and Christ is both the incarnation of God's remembrance, and the regeneration of human remembrance. "Faith is Christ's memory realized in us through our memory of Christ."[30] Faith does not mean having Jesus as an object of historical memory, any more than it means having doctrine as an object of rational understanding. Faith is Christ's memory, love, obedience, and confidence in the Father being realized in us. Faith means having by grace the relationship with the Father that Christ had by nature. The sacramental memorial of Christ imparts this to faith. To believe in Christ means to remember him, to keep him always in mind (which is the goal of the ascetical practice of the Jesus Prayer). This kind of remembrance is the essence of *leitourgia*—not in order to recollect Jesus but so that through our memory of him, his memory of the Father may be realized in us. Jesus is not remembered as a historical figure; rather, the resurrected Jesus gives us memory, which is life. Because Christ is the incarnate icon of the Father, the Christian is anointed with God's own Holy Spirit when Christ's image is imprinted upon the Christian in baptism. To realize divinization and unity with God is the end purpose of faith.

The new life for which the baptized are destined, and for which they ascetically struggle, is celebrated, actualized, received, accomplished — symbolized! — in *leitourgia*.

This love, which is Christ's and not our own, is symbolized in the *Sacrament of Unity*. Love is the sign by which the body of Christ will be known, for love is the essence of the Church's holiness (the Holy Spirit is its source), unity (the community is built up in love), and its apostolicity and catholicity (for the Church everywhere is joined with the yoke of love). The Church is commanded to be a union of love. But doesn't this sound odd? How can love be commanded? Because "Christianity is not only the commandment but also the *revelation* and the *gift* of love. . . . In this is the staggering *newness* of Christian love — that in the New Testament man is called to love with the divine love, which has become the divine-human love, the love of Christ. The newness of Christianity lies not in the commandment to love, but in the fact that it has become possible to fulfill the commandment."[31] The kiss of peace shared by the Church at this liturgical point is therefore neither a personal gesture of good will, nor a pining for post-parousia love. It is the love of Christ made manifest (as all parts of the liturgy manifest Christ in his kingdom) and so the kiss of peace can be called "a sacred rite of love," a sacramental gift of love. This liturgical symbol vests each member of the body of Christ with the love of Christ, which transforms the stranger into a brother or sister. This love is the fundamental reality of the liturgy. The kiss of peace manifests love sacramentally, and waits to be manifested actually.

The Eucharist is the sacrament of unity because we are united to one another by being united with Christ in one bread and cup. It was for such unity that man and woman were created, and this cannot be eradicated. "The devil could turn man, and in him, the world away from God, he could poison and enfeeble life through sin, permeate it with mortality and death. One thing he could not and cannot do: change the very essence of life as unity."[32] We are made for unity, but sin can turn the instinct to devilish purposes. The work of the devil is diabolical: literally, to "throw in two," from *dia* (two) and *baleo* (to throw). The unity of the Church in Christ, by redemptive contrast, is symbolical: Things separated are thrown together. Until that ascetical healing takes place, unity will often be an occasion for division. The world is divided up into "us and them," and love for one's own kind creates enmity toward the alien. Unity is corrupted if the Church makes this kind of division between itself and the world. This must not happen. Christians must not confuse salvation of the world with salvation from the world. The Church remains and sojourns on earth to beckon a world wracked with divisions and hostilities back to a love for which it was created, but has abandoned. The kingdom of God is manifest when the Church assembles in a unity of love that only the Holy Spirit can inspire. This is the Church's *leitourgia* and the task of each baptized initiate therein. The community's ritual *leitourgia* and the individual's lived *leitourgia* are oriented toward enacting love.

After the brothers and sisters of Christ have symbolized this eschatological love (for truly, it is of heaven and not earth), they are summoned to a new act. "Let us stand aright! Let us stand with fear! Let us attend, that we may offer the Holy Oblation in peace." Schmemann suggests that this summons clearly indicates that something has been completed and a new thing is beginning, the *Sacrament of Anaphora.* This is the "chief part" of the Divine Liturgy, but we have already seen that other parts are not thereby denigrated. The other parts reach their climax here, and their true character. The anaphora contains the answer to the question, what is accomplished in the Eucharist?[33]

Schmemann discusses the sacrament of anaphora here in chapter eight, but has yet a ninth chapter entitled the *Sacrament of Thanksgiving.* This tips the reader off that he means something more specific by "anaphora" than simply a title for the thanksgiving prayer. The deacon summons us to "stand aright," to "stand straight," or even to "be good." What would it mean for humanity to stand aright? or for the creation to be declared good and said to stand straight? In our corruption, we do not know. To really understand what this means, and what is therefore being manifested here at the beginning of the eucharistic prayer, one must see in double vision: first in the light of creation where God saw that what had been created corresponded to his own conception and was therefore right and good, and second in the light of redeemed creation where the disciples saw the Lord transfigured and declared, "Lord, it is good that we are here." This vision of what is good constitutes the Church and defines it. Such a reception of the divine good is humanity's calling. "The divine liturgy—the continual ascent, the lifting up of the Church to *heaven,* to the throne of glory, to the unfading light and joy of the kingdom of God—is the focus of this experience, simultaneously its source and presence, gift and fulfillment. . . . [A liturgy is] an action *(ergon)* in which the essence of what is taking place is simultaneously revealed and ful-filled."[34] When liturgists are beckoned to "lift up their hearts" they are not being urged toward lofty disposition or mystical inclination. The Eucharist that the Church is about to do can only be done in heaven, and if it can also be done here on earth it is because Christ has unified heaven and earth. The state of being called "good" by God at the brink of history, and again on Mount Tabor, is revealed and fulfilled at the altar before us. And this is not because we leave earth and ascend to heaven, but because heaven has transfigured earth, and earth has accepted heaven as the ultimate truth about itself.

> Salvation is complete. After the darkness of sin, the fall and death, a man once again offers to God the pure, sinless, free and perfect thanksgiving. A man is returned to the place that God had prepared for him when he created the world. He stands at the heights, before the throne of God; he stands in heaven, before the face of God himself, and freely, in the fulness of love and knowledge, uniting in himself the whole world, all creation, he offers thanksgiving, and in him the whole world affirms and acknowledges this thanksgiving to be "meet and right." This man is Christ.[35]

Because Christ returns the world to the Father, the Church offers thanksgiving of Christ in its sacrificial prayer.

The unity of this prayer, then, is thanksgiving.[36] More than a grateful nod, this thanksgiving is the experience of paradise! It is an experience of the divine "good" that God affirmed. Paradise is our state before the fall (before our "banishment from paradise") and our state upon salvation by Christ. Paradise is the beginning and the end to which the entire life of man and woman is directed as *homo adorans*, and through them all creation. The content of eternal life is revealed as the triunity of knowledge, freedom, and thanksgiving. When these concepts are investigated, we find that the first two are fulfilled in the last. First of all, knowledge of God—not knowledge about God, but knowledge of God—was forfeited in our rebellion. "Adam did not cease to 'know about God' . . . but he ceased to *know God*, and his life ceased to be that meeting with God, that communion with him. . . ."[37] Eucharistic thanksgiving is the joy and fullness of knowing God. Second, freedom was forfeited, and *anthropos* was banished from paradise. With this loss of freedom, God appeared to be the enemy, and was henceforth defined in categories of power, authority, necessity, and law. Since such categories enslave people, for the sake of freedom men and women found it necessary that God should not exist. Until Christ broke sin's categories, *anthropos* overlooked the truth that God is in fact love, and human life is in fact freedom. The Church meets its freedom in its thanksgiving.

Sin is thus revealed. In the highest moment of the liturgy we receive new knowledge of sin because we know the depths only from the heights, the distorted only from the straight ("Let us stand aright"). Christianity is not anthropological minimalism, says Schmemann, but anthropological maximalism. The former normalizes sin and death, and in turn supposes salvation to be supernatural; the latter recognizes the tremendous potential of humankind and knows deification as our natural end. That is why the fall was not due to deficiency and weakness; it was due to overabundance of gifts and power. Pride is the root of this sin, and pride is opposed to thanksgiving. Not giving thanks is the root, driving force, and mark of pride. Giving thanks both reveals and fulfills salvation (and this, it will be remembered, is how Schmemann earlier defined liturgy: an action that both reveals and fulfills). Christ's thanksgiving, his knowledge, and his filial freedom have become ours.

> Because it is of Christ and *from above*, this thanksgiving raises us up to paradise, as anticipation of it, and partaking while still on earth of the kingdom which is to come. And thus, each time it is raised up the *salvation of the world is complete.* . . . Man again stands where God placed him, restored to his vocation: to offer to God a "reasonable service," to know God, to thank and to worship him "in spirit and in truth," and through this knowledge and thanksgiving to transform the world itself into communion in the life that "was in the beginning with God," with God the Father, and was manifested to us.[38]

From this height the Church remembers one event: the Last Supper of Christ with his disciples. This is the *Sacrament of Remembrance.*

Schmemann regrets that the eucharistic prayer has suffered a disjunction from the liturgy as a whole, and dismemberment within. Each portion of the prayer has been studied in isolation, without attention to its connection with the whole, and as a result the anamnesis (remembrance) has suffered two reductions: the first, theological and the second, historical.

As noted elsewhere, Schmemann opposes the practice of dealing with liturgical questions in isolation from the whole liturgical coefficient. He thinks it a rationalistic reduction when the academy views a part instead of the whole in motion, and this is what the term *scholasticism* means in Schmemann's vocabulary. In the case of remembrance, the result is to treat remembrance as mainly "a 'consecratory' *reference* to Christ's establishment, at the last supper, of the sacrament of the eucharist. . . . The remembrance is the 'cause' of the actuality of the sacrament, just as the *institution* of the eucharist at the last supper is the cause of the actuality of the commemoration itself."[39] In other words, Christ's action is remembered in order to primarily, or only, effect consecration. The institution narrative becomes the central point of the prayer in deference to a second order debate about confection. Schmemann thinks all three Christian traditions show an inordinate focus upon the words of Christ at the last supper. a) It exists in its purest form in the Latin tradition where transubstantiation has limited the words of the narrative to their consecratory power; b) although Protestant theology has dismissed any objective change of the gifts, it nevertheless makes these isolated words a proposition that personal faith should hold; and c) although Orthodoxy affirms consecration at the epiclesis and not at the narrative, nevertheless a special isolation of the narrative has occurred in the east as well, observed when the celebrant points his hand to the bread and says the narrative aloud even though the rest of the prayer is read in secret ("to himself"). By the narrowed emphasis upon the institutionary character of the narrative, Schmemann sees the Golgotha sacrifice to be variously reenacted in the Mass (Latin), described verbally for the opportunity of subjective commitment (Protestant), or given symbolic representation (Orthodox). Even though these approaches are quite different otherwise, Schmemann calls all three of them a reduction, Eastern as well as Western, because they have substituted a derivative question for the fundamental question. They ask "how" (how the institution of the Last Supper operates in the Eucharist) instead of "what" (what Christ accomplished through this last act of his earthly ministry before his death). This misplaced question has led to an almost total rupture between eucharistic sacrifice and sacramental communion.

There is a second reduction at work, a historical one. Certainly Schmemann is not against historical scholarship. He is only pointing out that liturgiology is not liturgical theology. Our knowledge about the likely form of Christ's last supper has been greatly advanced by historical research, of course.

> However, this knowledge itself, no matter how useful and necessary, cannot give us the *complete* answer to the question we posed at the beginning of this chapter: of the meaning of the *commemoration* of the last supper. . . . Therefore, unreservedly acknowledging the full indisputable use and, moreover, absolute necessity of historical research into liturgical theology, which I wrote of with—I hope—sufficient clarity in my *Introduction to Liturgical Theology*, I consider the lowering of the liturgy to a history of the worship services, which replaced the earlier imprisonment of theological scholasticism, to be wrong and harmful. . . .[40]

The eucharistic remembrance should be reduced neither to a question about what happens to the consecrated elements, nor to a history of worship services. These may be valuable for their specialized purposes, but the method that lies at the basis of Schmemann's entire understanding of liturgical theology does not follow this path. "We must seek the complete answer to the question of the meaning of this commemoration, of the meaning of the liturgy as the *sacrament of remembrance*, in the Eucharist itself—and this means in the continuity, in the identity of the *experience*, not personal, not subjective, but precisely *ecclesial*, which is incarnated in the eucharistic celebration and is fulfilled each time the eucharist is celebrated."[41] The method of liturgical theology that Schmemann advocates, we might say, seeks to answer the question, what does the Church do? because that is what the ordo of the liturgy reveals. He explained on the first page of the first chapter that "the fundamental task of liturgical theology is uncovering the meaning and essence of the unity between assembly, eucharist, and Church." The meaning of the liturgy as the sacrament of remembrance must also be answered from within the liturgy itself, and this means in continuity with a liturgical, ecclesial experience of the heavenly Christ. The whole liturgy is a sacrament of Christ's presence. That is why the sacrament of remembrance (i.e., the consecrating power of the Words of Institution) should be understood in this context. Since the institutional narrative is part of the thanksgiving, the remembrance is part of the faithful's ascension into heaven. Remembrance is the reality of the kingdom present in our midst. As the earthly Jesus manifested the kingdom to his disciples at the last supper, so the heavenly

Christ is present in love to manifest the kingdom to his Church at the eucharistic supper.

Herein lies the connection between eucharist-sacrifice and eucharist-communion for Schmemann. The sacrament of remembrance is not the power to convert elements, but it is the kingdom in our midst. At the last supper, Christ founded the Church. The Eucharist is not a means to distribute the benefits of the kingdom; it is the kingdom itself manifest. The whole meaning of this commemoration is precisely that it remembers the last supper not as a means but as a manifestation. Jesus said to do something for the remembrance of him. Do what? A transubstantiation? A dramatic reenactment of the supper to assist faith? A mystical representation? No. "The essence of the liturgy and its multifaceted nature consists in the fact that it is all, from beginning to end, a *remembrance,* manifestation, 'epiphany,' the salvation of the world accomplished by Christ."[42]

Schmemann thinks school theology has one-sidedly and thereby falsely linked sacrifice with sin instead of love. The key to understanding the Eucharist as sacrifice is actually to understand it as an act of love, for sacrifice is the self-giving of love. There is no sacrifice without love, but neither is there any love without sacrifice, because love is the giving of one's self to another. If sacrifice is now linked with suffering, it is the consequence of the fall. It was indeed a fallen world into which Christ came, so his sacrifice meant a cross; and it is still a fallen world in which the Church works, so the Christian's sacrifice means carrying a cross; but in fact, sacrifice is love acted out under the condition of sin. Asceticism involves mortification, but asceticism is glad discipleship. At our baptismal *sacramentum,* the believer vows to follow Christ through death in order to receive the gift of new life. "The sacrament of the assembly, the sacrament of offering, the sacrament of anaphora and thanksgiving, and, finally, remembrance, are a single sacrament of the kingdom of God, of a single sacrifice of Christ's love, and therefore they are the sacrament of the manifestation, the gift to us of our life as sacrifice. For Christ took our life in himself and gave it to God."[43] To follow Christ is to be crucified to this world, but it is a sacrifice that love is willing to make.

That a liturgy served on earth could be accomplished in heaven requires God's own spirit. How else could it happen? So the liturgy is also the *Sacrament of the Holy Spirit.* A simplistic account of the difference between Western and Eastern Christianity would have

it that the squabble between them is over timing. This uncritical
reckoning thinks the former says consecration occurs at the institution
narrative, while the latter claims consecration happens at the epiclesis.
If that were the case, it would appear that nothing of consequence was
being debated. Both Eastern Orthodox and Western Catholic confess
the reality of the body of Christ, and the quarrel over institution
narrative or epiclesis would seem to be a very inconsequential debate
about when it happens. Schmemann challenges this simple construal.
If Orthodox theology were to accept the question on these terms,
it would indicate that Orthodox theology had already succumbed to
school theology. Schmemann thinks this has, indeed, already happened
to a degree, and it explains why "in contrast to the passions and emo-
tions attendant to the great dogmatic disputes of the patristic era, the
question of the epiklesis, of the transformation of the holy gifts, and
of the theology of the sacraments in general did not arouse particular
interest in the East."[44] Schmemann does not excuse his own tradition.
In the East, too, eucharistic theology has suffered the reductions he
bemoans, and instead of the Eucharist being seen as a sacrament
of unity, it is thought of as one of the means for sanctifying the faithful.
Instead of being an act of the communal *ekklesia*, the sacrament is
thought of as an act of personal piety. This is a distortion of the *lex
orandi* of the Church.

Such are the stakes of a correct liturgical theology of the Holy
Spirit's role in the Eucharist. We start by recalling that Schmemann
finds all the elements of the Divine Liturgy to be interdependent.

> The liturgy, as a sacrament, begins with the preparation of the holy gifts
> and the *assembly as the Church*. After the gathering follows the *entrance*
> and the proclamation of the word of God, and after that the *offering*,
> the placing of the eucharistic gifts on the alter. After the *kiss of peace* and
> the confession of faith we begin the *anaphora;* the lifting up of the gifts
> in the prayer of thanksgiving and remembrance. The anaphora concludes
> with the *epiklesis,* i.e., the prayer that God will manifest the Holy Spirit,
> will show the bread and wine of our offering to be the body and blood of
> Christ and make us worthy to partake of it.[45]

The entire Divine Liturgy is a single act, a common task. The rites
should therefore not be isolated as separate objects of study and
definition, which is the defining mark of school theology, whether it
afflicts the East or the West. Originally the word *sacrament* referred to

the entire mystery of salvation, not to a list of seven rites. The liturgy celebrates one mystery, sacramentally. Again, this is why he begins each chapter title with the words "Sacrament of. . . ." The assembly is not one act, the offering another, the kiss of peace a socialization that warms people up for the lofty anaphora, and now, at the end of a checklist of activities, comes the epiclesis. A view so discrete cannot see the spiritual reality in the parts of the whole. The Holy Spirit unifies the various symbols into a single, unified sacred reality. He uses a favorite illustration: "The liturgy can be likened to a man going through a building—which, though familiar and beautiful, is hid in darkness—with a flashlight, part by part, and in these parts identifying the entire building in its wholeness, unity and beauty. So it is with our liturgy, which, while being accomplished on earth is accomplished in heaven."[46]

The liturgy does not build the building—this would be cult!—it confesses and experiences and celebrates what Christ has already accomplished. Liturgy remembers. The epicletic act is part of a prayer that is anamnetic. The Church ascends into the mystery of salvation which has already been accomplished, and that is why the epiclesis must not be reduced to the moment of the gifts' supernatural change. This will make it seem like the only purpose of the epiclesis is the creation of an unworldly reality, and that the other liturgical moments are unessential preliminaries that only exist for the sake of this transformation. The liturgy's epicletic character certainly does reveal the Church as a new creation, but this does not mean another, unworldly creation is made. It means that this creation is made new. "Not a temple made by hands, but the opening of the heavens, the world transfigured into a temple, all life into the liturgy—such is the foundation of the Christian lex orandi."[47] In this space, the assembly experiences heaven on earth, and that is a work of the Holy Spirit.

Liturgical theology should speak of this experience. For theology to be what it should be, it must refer us to the single mystery manifest in the liturgy, not to parts of the liturgy in isolation. Earlier, in chapter six, Schmemann defined the essence of theology as "the search for 'words appropriate to God' *[theoprepeislogoi]*," and suggested that such words are only spoken by the power of God. Theology fulfills its mission "not through 'words about words,' but by referring words to that reality . . . that is more primary than the word itself. . . ." *Lex orandi* establishes *lex credendi* because "in Christianity, faith, as experience of an encounter and a gift received in this encounter, precedes words."[48] Liturgical theology deals with the symbols because liturgical theology does not refer us to words about words, or to isolated moments, or to rubrics; instead it refers us to the reality symbolized. This theology is faith language because to perceive the reality in the symbol requires faith. "It is impossible to explain and define the symbol. It is realized or 'actualized' in its *own* reality through its transformation into that to which it points and witnesses, of which it is a *symbol*. But this conversion remains invisible, for it is accomplished by the Holy Spirit, in the new time, and is certified only by *faith*."[49] The person who prays can be called a theologian. Theology is pneumatic speech first of all, whether or not it is also academic.

Sometimes it is said that the East differs from the West merely in a matter of timing: that the former thinks the change happens in the epiclesis, and the latter thinks the change happens at the words of institution. Schmemann does not think this yet goes to the theological heart of what the epiclesis means. He is not interested in simply clocking the appearance of the gift. Instead of being a question about "when," the theology of the epiclesis is an affirmation that the Divine Liturgy cannot be done without the Holy Spirit. As it was by the Spirit that Christ was made present to the world in his Incarnation, so it is by the Spirit that Christ is made present to his Church in the Eucharist. "[T]he liturgy is accomplished in the new time through the Holy Spirit. It is entirely, from beginning to end, an *epiklesis*, an invocation of the Holy Spirit, who transfigures everything done in it, each solemn rite, into that which it manifests and reveals to us."[50] Schmemann thinks that neglecting the Holy Spirit in a theology of consecration will have unfortunate results. The liturgy served on earth is accomplished in heaven, and the epiclesis organically connects the Church's anaphora prayer with the remembrance of Christ's institution. The epiclesis may be said to be the conclusion of the remembrance, for the latter is nothing else than confession of the knowledge of this mystery. The invocation of the Holy Spirit is not a separate act worked upon the bread and wine; it is woven interdependently into the complex of liturgical rites that manifests symbolically the reality already accomplished. Thus, "the *progression* here is not in the accomplishment but in the manifestation. For what is manifested is not something *new*, that did not exist before the manifestation. No—in Christ all is already *accomplished*, all is *real*, all is granted."[51]

This accomplished reality, manifested to faith in earthly symbol, is received by the communicant in the *Sacrament of Communion*. Schmemann thinks it unfortunate that many Orthodox believers do not see communion as the participatory climax of the liturgy, and therefore "the contemporary faithful, churchly person sees no necessity of approaching communion at every liturgy."[52] Of all the changes that have taken place over the centuries, none is judged more significant by Schmemann than the one which distorts communion into an individualistic act. How did this happen? Schmemann sees two causes. The first is the repeated injunction that a communicant needs to be worthy in order to approach the cup frequently. Force was added to the laity's feeling of unworthiness by a sort of clericalization, and that changed the whole atmosphere, Schmemann says. He cites John Chrysostom's words to describe another, earlier atmosphere. While there are differences between cleric and laity, John goes on to say that

> there are cases where the priest does *not* differ from those under him, for instance, *when he must partake of the Holy Mysteries*. We are all equally honored with them, not as in the Old Testament when one food was for the priests and another for the people and when it was not permitted to the people to partake of that which was for the priests. Now it is not so, for the same body and the same cup is offered to all. . . .[53]

A second cause of turning communion into an individualistic act has been the emphasis upon private preparation for communion. While there is a difference in category between catechumen and baptized, nowhere in the liturgy of the faithful "do we find a single reference to the roles of two 'categories' of worshipers: the communicants of the holy mysteries and the noncommunicants."[54] The anaphora is organically linked with reception in Communion; to hang back from the table until one is subjectively satisfied with one's preparation is inconsistent with the ordo. World, Church, and kingdom come together at the table at this holy moment, and no one can claim worthiness to stand at such a juncture. Therefore, the preparation cannot be a calculation of one's preparedness or unpreparedness, it is the answer of love to love. The Church gracefully receives God's invitation to participate in the banquet of the Lamb.

CONCLUSION

In *Introduction to Liturgical Theology* Schmemann complained that the field of liturgics is usually a more or less detailed practical study of ecclesiastical rites—the study of rubrics—which answers the question "how" (how worship is to be carried out according to the rules) but does not answer the question "what" (what is done in worship). He therefore distinguished liturgical theology from liturgics, because the approach he advocates puts questions to the liturgy, which are about the theological what, not the historical how. In the terms of this distinction, it is clear that *The Eucharist* is liturgical theology, not liturgics. In this book he has worked out a concrete example of his definition of liturgical theology whose task it is, he has written, to elucidate the meaning of worship, to give theological basis to the explanation of worship, to explain how the Church expresses and fulfills itself in the liturgical act (all one-line definitions from *Introduction*). This book on the Eucharist fulfills these definitions, and in so doing exemplifies the first mark of my definition of liturgical theology. It is theology.

It exhibits the second mark of my definition as well. The meaning of the Eucharist which liturgical theology bespeaks must derive from the rite. If liturgical theology is fundamentally the community's adjustment to its existential encounter with God, then the only way for someone to write it down is to examine the rite in motion, just as the only way to understand a top is to spin it. Schmemann made this very point 20 years earlier in *Introduction* when he wrote,

> Worship simply cannot be equated either with texts or with forms of worship. It is a whole, within which everything, the words of prayer, lections, chanting, ceremonies, the relationship of all these things in a "sequence" or "order" and, finally, what can be defined as the "liturgical coefficient" of each of these elements (i.e. that significance which, apart from its own immediate content, each acquires as a result of its place in the general sequence or order of worship), only all this together defines the meaning of the whole and is therefore the proper subject of study and theological evaluation.[55]

Schmemann has kept this understanding before his readers' eyes in various ways. The very set-up of the chapters was intended to demonstrate that although the liturgy is multifaceted, it is a single sacrament in which all parts manifest the divine meaning that can only be known by observing their sequence and structure and coordination. He regularly complains about a defect in what he calls "school theology" insofar as it isolates an individual part of worship from its liturgical context. If one wants to know what happens in the Eucharist, one must look at the liturgy and the assembly as well, not merely at questions of how and when the bread is transubstantiated. Scholastic dogmatics, he complains, has been inadequately aware of the integrated ecclesiological meaning of the Eucharist and the eucharistic dimension of ecclesiology. The *lex orandi* of the Church is a single diamond with multiple facets, not a series of beads on a string that can be removed and studied in isolation (even though the book is written as a series of chapters). The subject of liturgical theology is the liturgical coefficient of all the parts, where *theologia* will be found in its womb in language that is primary and symbolic.

Schmemann's language is more amenable to the conventions of the academy, and his book seems more familiar to our mode of publication than was Germanus' style, but each speaks to his own day. If Germanus' commentary reacted to the rise of iconoclasm and the pastoral challenge of witnessing salvation to new converts, Schmemann's book reacts to those cases in which symbol is reduced to mere symbolism, and to times when a disjunction between sacred and profane continues. Taft says the theological craft is exercised at the intersection of tradition and contemporary culture, and if that is so, then these two liturgical commentaries can surely be called theological craft. Neither of them give a history of worship services, or offer personal devotional commentary, or weave private allegories. They each give a commentary that is derived from the primary liturgical theology residing in the liturgical coefficient of ritual words and acts committed by the Church. Then God's kingdom comes on earth, as it is in heaven.

---

1. Alexander Schmemann, *The Eucharist* (Crestwood, NY: St. Vladimir's Seminary Press, 1987) 9.

2. _____, 161.

3. _____, 12.

4. _____, 14.

5. _____, 17.

6. _____, 18.

7. _____, 19.

8. _____, 20.

9. When symbol is thus estranged from reality, the sacrament is taken to be a special, supernatural symbol! That is, the sacrament is treated as *sui generis* reality, having its own form of existence, its own psychology, its own grace. These latter are the very words of Anscar Vonier, whom Schmemann here takes to task.

10. Alexander Schmemann, *The Eucharist*, 43.

11. If liturgical symbolism is illustrative and representative, then liturgy can be no more than illustrative catechism. And there is nothing special enough about worship in this symbolic format to deserve the *statuat* claim. Only if liturgical symbol is epiphany can liturgical ordo be *lex orandi*. Revelatory symbol is not the same as illustrative symbol.

12. Alexander Schmemann, *The Eucharist*, 59.

13. The antiphons originally constituted a separate service, which took place before the Eucharist and outside the church building, but "following that logic of liturgical development in which a kind of law functions according to which the 'peculiarities' become the 'general rule' this antiphon became part of the liturgy—an entrance before the Little Entrance." (Ibid., 52).

14. _____, 53.

15. _____, 68.

16. _____, 71. If the Gospel book is a verbal icon of Christ's presence, then the Little Entrance cannot be a sacred dramatization of Christ going out to preach; it must be a real liturgical act.

17. _____, 78.

18. _____, 82.

19. _____, 89. One sees the misplaced goal of the democratic agenda in this light. If one objects to excessive hierarchy, then of what advance is it to give a few hieratic duties to the laity? The discriminating structure remains. But Schmemann does not think that the clergy and lay distinction is discriminatory.

20. _____, 91.

21. _____, 101.

22. _____, 102. The similarity to Peter Brown's "lower tier" should not go unnoticed.

23. _____, 103.

24. _____, 104.

25. _____, 107.

26. _____, 108.

27. _____, 109.

28. _____, 110.

29. _____, 126. I might add, conversely, that God's amnesia is wrath and human amnesia is sin.

30. _____, 128.

31. _____, 136.

32. _____, 152.

33. But remember—that question can be answered only by looking at the liturgy as a whole (liturgical theology), not by narrowing to one moment of it. What should be an indissoluble link of the sacrament with the liturgy, school theology destroys "through its arbitrary isolation of one 'moment' (act, formula) in the liturgy and the identification of it alone with the sacrament. . . ." (Ibid., 161).

34. _____, 165.

35. _____, 170.

36. Because the people are the ones who lift up the Eucharist, they should, in Schmemann's opinion, know the prayer. "The laity . . . have simply not heard and thus do not know this veritable prayer of prayers. . . . If we add to this the fact that in many Orthodox churches these prayers, being 'secret,' are moreover read behind closed royal doors, and sometimes even behind a drawn altar curtain, then it would be no exaggeration to say that the prayer of thanksgiving has for all practical purposes been dropped from the church service. I repeat, the laymen simply do not know it, theologians are not interested in it, and the priest, who is forced to glance over it while the choir is singing . . . is hardly capable of perceiving it in its fulness, unity and integrity" (Schmemann, 172).

37. _____, 175.

38. _____, 181.

39. _____, 193.

40. _____, 197.

41. _____, 187.

42. _____, 221.

43. _____, 210.

44. _____, 214.

45. _____, 216.

46. _____, 221–22.

47. _____, 200.

48. _____, 149.

49. _____, 222.

50. _____.

51. _____, 225.

52. _____, 230.

53. _____, 232.

54. _____, 233.

55. Alexander Schmemann, *Introduction to Liturgical Theology,* 15–16.

Chapter 8

A Century of Consequences

I said in the preface that this second edition is substantially the same as the first because, although my voice has changed, I have not changed my mind about the fundamental thesis. Yet that thesis has brought in its wake a great number of consequences, and I am desirous to express some of them. The consequences that liturgical theology has upon our understanding of liturgy, theology, and asceticism cannot be treated in their entirety at one sitting, by one person, and so I wish to invite the reader to join the reflection. To do so I am adopting a distinct literary style in this final chapter.

Ascetical texts frequently presented a summary of traditional wisdom in the form of paragraphs, or chapters, strung together, often one hundred in number and hence called a century. Monastic authors did it to make traditional teachings easier to ponder and assimilate. I am making a poor imitation of it so I can invite the reader to connections not foreseen by me, since one of the advantages of centuries is that the format does not exclude complementary angles of thought. A paragraph does not have to lead only to the next sequential paragraph; it can lead many places, and the reader becomes an active participant in making connections. This style is friendly to paradox. Metaphor is the currency of the realm. Instead of merely juxtaposing one thing to another (X is to Y), relationships are compared (as X is to Y, so A is to B).

This style is more suited to antinomy because it does not coordinate two extremes by searching for a golden mean. It leaves each term of the antinomy at full strength. Chesterton once wrote, "It is true that the historic Church has at once emphasised celibacy and emphasised the family; has at once (if one may put it so) been fiercely for having children and fiercely for not having children. It has kept them side by side like two strong colours, red and white, like the red and white upon the shield of St. George. It has always had a healthy hatred of pink."[1] The Century format presents complementary angles of an antinomy by simply placing them side by side, without one diluting the other into pink.

1.   The liturgy is the faith of the Church in motion, like listening is friendship in motion, or studying is scholarship in motion, or sitting down at supper together is family in motion, or comforting a child with a skinned knee is parenting in motion, or making love is marriage in motion.

2.   Imagine finding a big machine on the front lawn, just recently uncrated. It has wheels, dials, levers, switches, buttons, gizmos, throttles, pedals, toggles, cogs, sprockets, steering sticks, gears, pinions, rigging, and other appurtenances. And on the lid of the shipping crate lying on the grass is stenciled the words "Liturgical Rite." Two different kinds of people, seeking two different kinds of knowledge, are revealed by the two different ways they approach this machine. The first person, buckling on a utility belt stocked with the tools of historical method, literary theory, textual study, lower and higher criticism, hermeneutics, archeology, architecture, and comparative religious studies, will raise the hood, rub his or her hands together with anticipation, and exclaim, "Now, let's see how this thing works!" The second will climb into the driver's seat and exclaim, "Now, let's see how to work this thing." Liturgical theology is different from liturgiology.

3.   I mean to imply that knowing how a rite works is not the same kind of knowledge as knowing how to work a rite; that academic knowledge is not the same as practical knowledge, and liturgy is a practical thing; that similarities in architecture, prayer book structure, and musical form do not prove identity in meaning; that theory and praxis are related, but not synonymous; that religious rite cannot be reduced to that which can be taught, neither can one deduce adequate rite from the sum of what is taught; that *lex orandi* requires driver's ed training and is the reason for the manual, *lex credendi*, not vice-versa; that the presence of symbols borrowed from a common inventory does not prove the same liturgy is taking place any more than the serving of food at both a wake and a wedding proves the same social event is taking place; that people who commit liturgy know more

than they can tell; that working a liturgy is the skill possessed by Kavanagh's friend, Mrs. Murphy.[2]

4.   Just as we must listen to the grammar beneath the words in a sentence, so also the meaning of a symbol is in its use, not simply its presence. Wittgenstein can help us avoid an error and clear up a confusion on this point. It is sometimes said it is difficult to effect liturgical reform because the symbols are worn out, threadbare, archaic, and do not speak to us anymore. But symbols should not be thought to hold meaning the way a boxcar holds freight; symbols are used by an agent to mean with, just as Wittgenstein says about words. If oil, for example, lacks meaning it should cause us to look at ourselves, at our failure of nerve, at whether we still believe oil can heal, or make kings and queens, or inscribe charismatic character. The power of our language does not depend upon making up new words, but using words powerfully. The reform of liturgical symbols might begin with the reform of the liturgists' faith which handles them.

5.   Taft said that because liturgies have histories they "can only be understood in motion, just as the only way to understand a top is to spin it."[3] A theology of worship tends to halt the top's revolution in order to get a clearer picture of it. In theologies of worship, the object of study is no longer the rite in motion, and becomes a theology in suspended animation. One should not separate the sacraments from their liturgical life to be kept alive by artificial academic respirators. It is one thing to study a frog in motion, hopping around the banks of a pond; it is another to pith the frog and lay it on a dissection board in biology class. Dissection yields information, that is true; but one learns other, more animated facts by watching the *lex orandi* in motion. Liturgical theology is different from theologies of worship.

6.   What the assembly does in its liturgy does not have to be touched up by academicians in order to become *theologia*. The theology worked out and preserved in ritual logistics does not take the same form as academic theology, that is quite true, but this only means it is not academic, not that it is not theological.

7.   Liturgical theology is inadequately conceived so long as liturgy is treated as a branch of esthetics instead of the root of theology. "Liturgical" does not refer to a certain style of expression, but it refers to our source and summit.

8.   Liturgical theology is unavailable to us if we treat liturgy as an expression of our sentiments instead of the source of our Christian

self. Both priests and laity can be guilty of this: the former when he treats the altar as a personal space at which to exercise his private piety without regard to the community, and the latter when they stray from rubric and tradition in favor of self-expression. Humility is required to commit liturgy, since liturgy is corporate act.[4]

9.   Liturgical theology is not an individual theologian's ruminations on the topic of doxology; it is the meaning rooted in the Church's traditional structures. For example, the fact that liturgy requires an assembly should itself teach us something about the natural unity of the human family which we've long since forgotten; the fact that the structure is hierarchical should be seen as an icon of Trinitarian unity, except we have allowed the concept to petrify into an administrative structure; and the fact that our celebrations require space, time, and matter (in the form of temples, festivals, icons, sacraments, incense, and relics) should convince us that the kingdom will transfigure this world, not nullify it.

10.   If one takes liturgy only in its thin sense, as ritual etiquette, then liturgical theology is not possible, and other prejudices—puritanism, biblicism, pietism, rationalism, moralism—will determine the meaning. Then neither theology nor asceticism will be significantly impacted.

11.   Liturgy's reduction to ritual protocol brings a series of other reductions in its wake: Symbol degenerates to sign, icon to picture, performative speech to didactic explanation, sacrament to souvenir, church to juridical overseer.

12.   The worlds of liturgy and theology and asceticism have been estranged both in the lives of believers and in the systems of *theologia secunda*. The way to overcome this estrangement is not to insinuate so-called "liturgical issues" into secondary theology, but to recognize liturgy itself as theological and ascetical. The approach, which alone should receive the name "liturgical theology," is one that organically connects liturgy and theology—a Chalcedonian, and not a Nestorian definition.

13.   Liturgical asceticism is memory repair. *Anthropos* was created to remember God *(mnesis)*, but has forgotten *(amnesia)*, so men and women must be re-capacitated if they are to make *anamnesis* at the eucharistic table.

14.   Recognizing the difference between liturgy and *leitourgia* dramatically changes what is meant when a worship is accused of

being nonliturgical. Being liturgical decidedly does *not* mean possessing repetitive protocol, doing things in a rigid and overbearing manner, or festooning simple actions with paraphernalia and lush choral accompaniment.

15.   Recognizing the difference between liturgy and *leitourgia* dramatically changes the objective of liturgical reform. It would no longer be shuffling the sanctuary furniture, retranslating a sacramentary, redecorating the nave, permitting the laity a share in the duties that properly belong to the priest, or reprising the liturgical style of whatever era is deemed golden. *Leitourgia* means an action by which a group of people become something corporately that they had not been as a mere collection of individuals. In this case, believers become Christ's body. The objective of liturgical reform would be to make the community into liturgists.

16.   I should like one day to write an article about liturgists — their duties, their training, their significance, their resources — and have it only slowly dawn on the reader that I am talking about Mrs. Murphy, the liturgist, and not about the choir director, the presiding presbyter, or the scholar.

17.   The Church has need of more liturgists. The liturgist's duties at Mass include prayer, acclamation, song, praise, petition, and sacrifice. The liturgist should be a deeply faithful person. We need a renewal and reform of liturgists. Whom have I been talking about?

18.   Liturgy is not the work of a rubricist or a worship committee or a floral arranger or a musician or a scholar or the presider; it is the synergistic work of a deified people, a filial race grafted by the paschal mystery into eighth-day existence. The primary agenda of liturgy is the creation of a new heaven and a new earth, not a new chasuble or a new altar cloth.

19.   If liturgy were only an act of self-expression, then the amount of time and resource we spend on the subject might convict us of a kind of ecclesiastical narcissism: We have fallen in love with our own ritual image. Or perhaps it would convict us of the kind of blasphemy pointed out by the prophets: We think the Lion of Judah can be rendered harmless by the ritual catnip we offer him.

20.   The issue is not high church versus low church; the issue is whether the liturgy is deep or shallow. These are not determined by the same criteria. I have been to shallow high church liturgies, and the only thing worse is a shallow low church liturgy. But I have been

to both high church and low church liturgies that have been deep. The factors that make a liturgy high or low are not the same factors that make it deep or shallow.

21.   Sometimes whole differences hang on a single phrase, a single word, even a single letter. The Church fought down to the iota over *homoousios* and *homoiousios*. A single letter might make the difference here, too: Liturgy should be effective, not merely affective.

22.   The Word of God is never passive, and it is not chiefly didactic. The Word of God is always effective. It is creative. Therefore the adjustment that Kavanagh calls theological is first of all an adjustment to "what did God do?" This means that being a liturgical theologian will involve liturgical asceticism.

23.   Liturgical language is not at all the same as the language of magic. Nevertheless, liturgical language has more in common with "Open Sesame!" than with "Please pass the potatoes." When these former words are spoken, the mountain is expected to split open and reveal the treasure within. When liturgical words are spoken, we should expect the heavens to rend and offer their treasures to us. Regrettably, all too often we are only registering our likes or dislikes.[5]

24.   To agree that liturgy is theological, one must agree that liturgical rite is ruled, shaped, traditional.

25.   When Athanasius defended orthodoxy against the Arians he said, "In accordance with the Apostolic faith delivered to us *by tradition* from the Fathers, I have delivered *the tradition*, without inventing anything extraneous to it."[6] Tradition would therefore seem to be both *how* something is delivered, and *what* is delivered. By an action called tradition (a verb), a content called tradition (a noun) is delivered.

26.   The tradition handed on by tradition is a share in eternal life, inherited from Christ through the Apostles. The epistle 1 John 1:3 provides a definition when it identifies the aim of the apostles: "We declare to you what we have seen and heard so that you also may have fellowship with us; and truly our fellowship is with the Father and with his Son Jesus Christ." The Twelve pass on what they have seen and heard, not so we can know what they saw and listened to, but so that we too may participate in the fellowship they had with the Father through the Son.

27.   This means, Karl Rahner suggests, that the apostolic succession is a living experience. "It is not only propositions about

their experience that the Apostles bequeath, but their Spirit, the Holy Spirit of God, the very reality, then, of what they have experienced in Christ. Their own experience is preserved and present together with their Word."[7]

28.   This thick understanding of tradition can become thin, just like a thick understanding of *leitourgia* can become thin liturgy. A thin sense of tradition is merely precedence. By this definition anything can become traditional if given enough time. Do it more than once and it becomes a tradition. In this thin sense, everything was untraditional the first time it was done.

29.   Under a more complete grammar, the thick meaning for which I am searching, something could be said to be traditional the first time it was done. A sacramentary in Latin, the iconostasis, Gothic architecture, the Great Canon of St. Andrew of Crete, the term *homoousios*—all these were traditional the first time they appeared.

30.   What kind of tradition is this? Liturgical, because the Holy Spirit makes possible our participation in the Son's mysteries. What kind of liturgy is this? Traditional, because the mystery became an event to be handed on to the whole Church, even that part of the Church which extended into the future.

31.   The life of Christ is handed on through the apostles to us. Archimandrite Vasileios points out that in the book of Revelation Saint John the Theologian wrote "all that he saw," and nothing else, because he was unable to write anything more. "In other words, he was flooded with life which overflowed his earthen vessel on all sides. And this superabundance of life was theology." This living experience is the content of the Church's life. "The first Christians lived their theology totally and with the whole of their bodies, just as they were baptized with the whole of their body and soul into the new life. Thus their liturgical gatherings were an initiation into the mystery of theology."[8] Vasileios says each of the faithful is called to become a "theologian soul."

32.   One consequence of *leitourgia* would be to create more theologians—a true empowerment of the laity.

33.   I might say simplistically that theology is the answer to the question, what happened? What happened after God passed through Ur of Chaldees and beckoned Abram out; what happened at the burning bush on Sinai when Moses was commissioned;

what happened at the barn behind the Bethlehem inn? Liturgy is theological because those who are faithful wonder what happened to them.

    34.   Olivier Clement maintains that "All the mysteries of the Gospel are not only performed in the liturgy but take possession of us in the spiritual life. The Word is continually being born in the stable of our heart. . . . To ensure this birth of Christ in us is the true function of liturgical times and seasons, interpreted inwardly by ascesis, prayer and contemplation."[9] This means that the holy days of obligation are not only historical celebrations, they are also celebrations in our Christian life.

    35.   Scripture is the source of theology. The Old Testament is witness to what happened when God disclosed himself to Abraham the father of faith, to Moses the lawgiver, to Isaiah the fire-eater, and the New Testament is witness to what happened when God clothed himself in the flesh. The reason *lex orandi* can be called the ontological condition of theology and not be in competition with scripture, says Schmemann, is because "it is in the Church, of which the *leitourgia* is the expression and the life, that the sources of theology are functioning precisely as sources."[10]

    36.   It is a most awful tragedy to read scripture only historically, instead of also liturgically. Charles Williams writes that "all the events in the life of our Lord, as well as happening in Judea, happen in the soul."[11] What the Father accomplished by incarnation with his right hand in Judea, he does again by sacrament with his left hand in the spiritual assembly known as Church.

    37.   Christ is the premiere liturgist, and baptismal regeneration is a sacramental sign that he summons apprentices to his work. Christ is the firstborn of many little liturgists swimming in the font like Tertullian's tadpoles.

    38.   Columba Marmion insists that "The mysteries of Jesus have this characteristic that they are ours as much as they are His. . . . To each of His mysteries, he attaches a grace which is to help us to reproduce within ourselves His divine features in order to make us like unto Him."[12] In liturgy's sacramental axis, what happened by Jesus happens to us. Any explanation of this by us *(lex credendi)*, depends upon it first happening to us *(lex orandi)*.

    39.   This mystery comes again in the liturgy. It beckons faith and provokes a theological struggle to adjust to what happened.

What happens after God passes sacramentally through a life with regenerating grace, or charismatic grace, or the grace of immortality, or absolving grace?

40.   If nothing happens, one cannot ask the theological question of the rite. There is no liturgical theology. This should be of concern to the liturgical reform.

41.   Lay people might assume that theology is beyond their ken because Sunday after Sunday they sit through liturgies so anemic that no one is provoked to furrow their brow and wonder what has happened. The liturgical reform should not be content with their assumption.

42.   The *lex orandi* yields a doctrine of creation that asserts matter was made to be sacrament; it yields an eschatology that asserts everything is destined for glory; it yields an anthropology that asserts the image of God can attain the likeness of God (deification); it yields a christology that asserts the reign of God brings with it obligations to the poor, imprisoned, and outcast; and it yields an ecclesiology that asserts the Church manifests the potency of the world. We should expect Mrs. Murphy to know all this. It is required of her as a Christian.

43.   Adding the suffix *ize* turns a noun or adjective into a verb, in the sense of "causing it to be or become." To verbalize is to make verbal, to sanitize is to make sanitary, to jeopardize is to put into jeopardy. The liturgy actual-izes, visual-izes, symbol-izes the kingdom of God, like a kiss conveys the love it symbolizes. If it doesn't, then its *lex orandi* cannot establish any *lex credendi*, that is true.

44.   Liturgy is participation in the life of God. If religion brings one to stand before God, then liturgy brings one to stand within the Trinity. Liturgical life consists of living God's life: deification. And deification is the goal of asceticism.

45.   Christ did not found a new religion, he founded the Church. Olivier Clement says, "In its deepest understanding the Church is nothing other than the world in the course of transfiguration. . . ."[13]

46.   Andrew Louth calls prayer, as seen by the Fathers, "the amniotic fluid in which our knowledge of God takes form." That is why participation in the tradition of the Church "implies participation in a life of love, of loving devotion to God and loving care of our neighbor. Participation in the tradition is indeed a moral activity: It implies a growing attentiveness to Our Lord, and a growing likeness

to him." [14] What is handed on by liturgical tradition is not some
pile of propositions about Jesus, or a collection of rubrics about the Mass;
it is our very deification. Participation in the tradition of the Church
is not by the intellectual faculty alone. The cost is greater than that.

47.   The mystery communicated by the mysteries makes a new
people *(laos)*, called into existence for the very purpose of continuing
the work *(ergeia)* of Christ. Christian liturgy is not a species of human
religious ritual; *leitourgia* is Christ's work that has become ours.
Marmion writes, "Christ does not separate Himself from His Mystical
Body. Before ascending into Heaven, He bequeaths His riches and
mission to His Church. Christ, in uniting Himself to the Church, gives
her His power of adoring and praising the Father; this is the liturgy.
It is the praise of the Church united to Jesus, supported by Jesus;
or rather it is the praise of Christ, the Incarnate Word, passing through
the lips of the Church." [15] Liturgy is grounded in the filial union of the
Son with the Father in the Holy Spirit, and is communicated to us
through the hypostatic union.

48.   Christ was human nature assumed by the Logos; therefore
Christ made perfect human religion. Liturgy is a continuation of
his religion, not a manifestation of ours. The Son's sacred humanity
and perfect religion is the foundation of every ecclesial act.

49.   The kingdom's coming was prepared for by patriarchs,
prophets, psalmists, and priests, and when the time had fully come
God sent forth his Son who in words and deeds proclaimed that the
kingdom was at hand. Liturgy is the product of the reign of God.
Liturgy is the restoration of humanity by resurrection power every
eighth day.

50.   Then the Church asks itself the theological question:
What happened to us as a result of our encounter with the paschal
mystery? to the world? to God?

51.   There are reasons for formal, doctrinal precision. It can
ask more questions than Mrs. Murphy can. But it cannot ask questions more fundamental than these which she asks.

52.   The dilation of our understanding of liturgy brings with
it an enlargement of our understanding of theology. Theology is a
genus larger than the academic species. It should touch every enterprise
in which every Christian engages, and not be thought of confined
to the jargon of a special guild. To be Christian involves the capacity

to theologize, to speak of God and to God, even if one's professional occupation isn't talking about God.

53.   Liturgy's theology is a form, shape, or grammar which should become the form, shape, or grammar of each liturgist's life.

54.   If theology is like a grammar, then learning theology is not an end in itself. One learns a grammar in order to say something, and Christians learn kingdom grammar in the liturgy in order to tell the world the truth about itself. Only using theology to speak about church business is the rational version of cultism. The reason for liturgists to become godly is not so they can talk among themselves. Asceticism's purpose is to draw life back to its source.

55.   Ouspensky says, "What the Church accepts from the world is determined not by the needs of the Church but by those of the world, for in this participation of the world in building the Kingdom of God (depending, of course, on its free will) lies the principal meaning of its existence. And inversely, the principal meaning of the existence in this world of the Church itself is the work of drawing this world into the fullness of the revelation—its salvation." [16]

56.   Like a needle pulling thread through fabric to stitch up a rent cloth, the liturgist moves in and out, in and out, between heaven and earth, eternity and time, the sacred and the profane, plunging into one and then the other and drawing them together by the thread of his or her life. We have stumbled across the ascetical dimension to liturgical theology again.

57.   By the enfeebled definition, liturgy in its thin sense appears to be an exchange between the priest and laity inside the club-house. Liturgy in its thick sense involves an exchange between Church and world. Maximus the Confessor drives this point home when he regards the whole Church (sanctuary and nave) as an image of the world.[17] The Church is a mystical image of the whole creation, not just the sacred part of it. Liturgical space is a microcosm.

58.   Microcosm does not mean a fragment of the whole (a kitchen is not the microcosm of a house); it means everything that can be found in the whole can be found here on a smaller order (a doll house with kitchen, bedroom, and bathroom is the microcosm of a house). The Church is not called microcosm because it is the sacred fragment of the cosmos surrounded by a sea of profanity. The Church is called microcosm because here is found everything that is in the

entire cosmos: earth and heaven, matter and spirit, the visible and invisible, creature and creator.

59.   The very division of this microcosm into sanctuary and nave means for Maximus that the Church is an image of the whole world, not an image of just a part of the world. The Church is divided into sanctuary (which symbolizes the invisible, spiritual world) and nave (which symbolizes the visible, sensible world) because the Church, just like the cosmos, "is one in its basic reality without being divided into its parts by reason of the differences between them, but rather by their relationship to the unity it frees these parts from the difference arising from their names." [18]

60.   Sanctuary is different from nave, and nave is different from sanctuary, but this difference does not divide them into pieces. Instead, they each have their own way of relating to the unity. "It shows to each other that they are both the same thing, and reveals that one is to the other in turn what each one is for itself." [19]

61.   What does the sanctuary reveal about the nave, and the nave about the sanctuary? "The nave is the sanctuary *in potency* by being consecrated by the relationship of the sacrament toward its end, and in turn the sanctuary is the nave *in act* by possessing the principle of its own sacrament." [20] There is a potency in the world that can be realized in act.

62.   There is potency in *anthropos* to be deified, and in matter to be transfigured. Christianity is an attitude toward the totality of creation, and liturgy acts upon the world in its totality. When the fathers worked out the typology of the priestly tribe of Levi in the Old Testament, they did *not* say Levites are to the 11 tribes of Israel what priests are to the laity; they said Levites are to the 11 tribes of Israel what the Church is to the world.

63.   The end of a watch is to tell time, the end of a knife is to cut, the end of creation is sacrament, the end of *anthropos* is perfect liturgist. Paul Evdokimov says "that everything is destined for a liturgical fulfillment. . . . The final destiny of water is to participate in the mystery of the Epiphany; of wood, to become a cross; of the earth, to receive the body of the Lord during his rest on the Sabbath. . . . Olive oil and water attain their fullness as conductor elements for grace on regenerated man. Wheat and wine achieve their ultimate *raison d'etre* in the eucharistic chalice. . . . A piece of being becomes a hierophany, an epiphany of the sacred. . . ." [21]

64.   An ancient philosopher said that beauty requires a perception of the whole, because integrity is one of the constituents of beauty. No one could know if a creature measuring a thousand miles long was beautiful, because no one could see the whole creature in its entirety. Similarly, no one can know whether a creation extending a thousand millennia is beautiful, because no human life span is long enough to see history in its entirety. But the liturgy is a microcosm of time, as well as space. It is the historical span from creation to parousia writ small enough to see whole. And it turns out to be beautiful.

65.   The Church does not exist as a replacement to the world. The Church is sign and instrument of the transformation let loose upon the world by Christ having assumed a human nature and material flesh. A world in despair needs a sign of hope; a world in death needs to be touched by an instrument of resurrection.

66.   The created world could be our means of material worship if we had not been spiritually corrupted. "Carnal sin is essentially the sin of the spirit against the flesh."[22]

67.   No thing is evil. But neither has any thing been unaffected by the injury caused when *anthropos* failed his liturgical vocation. That spirit can have such an effect on matter is a sign of their original union.

68.   Plato was close to the truth when he noticed a tension between spirit and matter, but he got misled by a dualism that attributed the problem to matter. Because the Desert Fathers use this vocabulary, they sometimes sound dualistic, or Manichean, or Platonic, but in fact they are using the words in a different grammar.

69.   Plato was wrong when he said the body is a prison for the soul, but he did notice a truth even in being wrong. His detractors have not even noticed this much. One party says there is no tension between soul and body because there is no soul; another party says there is no tension because the soul should make itself hedonistically at home in the body and not seek anything loftier. Both of these parties err by overlooking the tension that Plato noticed. Christianity says neither the body nor the spirit fell; rather, *anthropos* fell, putting body and spirit in tension. And if many forward-thinking moderns have overlooked this tension, Plato did not, and that is why Christian ascetics may continue to find his vocabulary more useful than the

dismissive language of those who think ascetical discipline of the body is altogether primitive and unnecessary.

70.   For us to receive the world as showing forth the power and beauty and love of God requires more than a gnostic watchfulness. The problem affects *anthropos'* intellectual faculty, but it is not rooted in the intellectual faculty. It is rooted in the spirit, and its correction requires a spiritual healing.

71.   Water could be a sign of God's love if I gave a cup of it to someone who is thirsty, but not if I use up on my golf course the water he needs for his vegetable patch. To receive the world as sacrament now requires the discipline of *anthropos'* appetites (asceticism). To do the world the way it was meant to be done (Kavanagh's definition of liturgy) demands ascetical mortification. How can I look at food rightly if I am gluttonous, or at my neighbor's property if I am covetous, or at my neighbor herself if I am lustful?

72.   Let the angels do an ideal liturgy; it would be enough if *anthropos* could do a sensible one.[23]

73.   C. S. Lewis has the devil Screwtape give this advice in his letters to his nephew Wormwood: "Never forget that when we are dealing with any pleasure in its healthy and normal and satisfying form, we are, in a sense, on the Enemy's ground [i.e. God's]. I know we have won many a soul through pleasure. All the same, it is His invention, not ours. He made the pleasures: all our research so far has not enabled us to produce one. . . . God is a hedonist at heart. All those fasts and vigils and stakes and crosses are only a facade. Or only like foam on the seashore. Out at sea, out in His seas, there is pleasure, and more pleasure. . . . He's vulgar, Wormwood. He has a bourgeois mind. He has filled His world full of pleasures. . . . Everything has to be twisted before it's any use to us. We fight under cruel disadvantages."[24]

74.   Though ignorance is a sizable part of the problem, the passions are now what stand between us and our cosmological priesthood, so not until the passions are overcome can we share the work of the *eskata Adam*. A prerequisite for committing liturgy is the asceticism that is vowed at baptismal *sacramentum*.

75.   Liturgical asceticism — Evagrius of Pontus said the ascetical battle *(praktike)* that leads toward control of the passions enables one to see the world correctly *(physike)* and attain union with God *(theologia)* by prayer of the heart. It would appear that in the middle stage one becomes a physician. I don't mean the medical kind;

I don't mean the scientific kind, either. This is the kind of physic that heals (like the former) by means of accurate knowledge of the world (like the latter). A true physician knows the true science, and the world is seen to be a temple. "In the final analysis, we are talking of the ascetical rehabilitation of matter as the substratum of the resurrection and the medium in which all epiphanies take place."[25]

76.   Liturgical priesthood—we cannot raise our hands in true *orans* until we discipline our proclivity to twist all things egocentrically.

77.   Liturgical theology—coming to rest in the Trinity.

78.   One consequence of *leitourgia* would be to create more ascetics—a true empowerment of the *laos*. If asceticism was brought to perfection in the sands of the desert, it is born in the waters of the font. The specialized identities of theologian, priest, and monk are simply colors refracted from the brilliant light coming from Mt. Tabor.

79.   In the final step of *The Ladder of Divine Ascent*, John Climacus advises, "It is risky to swim in one's clothes. A slave of passion should not dabble in theology."[26] There is an enterprise practiced in the academy which goes by the name of "theology," and which some think is immune from John's words of warning. This intellectual coordination of information is thought to be an exercise so rational that the passions do not impact it. Whether this is really the case, I will not consider here. Might it be possible, as claimed, to remove the passions from the working of memory, imagination, intellect, insight, reason, speculation, and wit? I am not interested in exploring the question because I have other theologians in mind—ones who would not be interested in separating mind from heart even if it were possible.[27]

80.   To do liturgical asceticism one must become an ascetic, even if not of the monastic variety. To do liturgical theology, one must become a theologian, even if not of the academic variety.

81.   John Climacus also recommends, "Control your appetites before they control you."[28] If liturgy is doing the world the way it was meant to be done, then I must keep control of my appetites. In order to be a liturgist, I must be an ascetic.

82.   Christian asceticism, then, is not masochism, not hatred of the world, not just for monks or priests, not just expressed by celibacy, and not beating one's head against the wall because it feels good when one stops. Christian asceticism is keeping control of the appetites. That is what Evagrius of Pontus understood by *apatheia:* controlling your appetite, keeping custody of the heart's passions.[29]

And Cassian translated it as *puritas cordis* (purity of heart), which philosophers from Augustine to Petrarch to Kierkegaard have known means to will one thing.

83.   The cause of Christian asceticism — the motive and reason and goal of Christian asceticism — is told by the good and humble Mare, Hwin, in C. S. Lewis's Narnia Chronicle, *The Horse and His Boy*. When Hwin met Aslan for the first time, she shook all over as she trotted up to the Lion. " 'Please,' she said, 'you're so beautiful. You may eat me if you like. I'd sooner be eaten by you than fed by anyone else.' "[30]

84.   Augustine pictures Christ saying to the communicant: "I am your food, but instead of my being changed into you, it is you who shall be transformed into me." In the normal digestive system of the human body, a piece of bread is changed into me, my energy, my muscle and bone. In the sacramental digestive system of the body of Christ, the bread we eat turns us into his body. Our mother is right when she says you are what you eat.

85.   Thomas Aquinas said our divine filiation is a resemblance of the eternal filiation because in its substance it is the same grace that fills the created soul of Jesus and deifies us. Ascetical discipline proposes to conform our lives to Christ, so the one we are to imitate is the Son of God. "The Father will only recognise us as His children if we bear in us the features of his Son Jesus."[31] Does this seem too audacious? Would we draw back in feigned humility? But "to desire to reproduce this ideal is neither pride nor presumption, but a response to God's own desire."[32]

86.   Liturgical asceticism is everything that capacitates a liturgist.

87.   The ascetical exercises are an apprenticeship to the Suffering Servant.

88.   The baptized person is taken up into Christ's liturgical activity of eucharistic self-sacrifice to the Father and redemptive self-sacrifice for the world. Liturgical asceticism refers to every aspect of how we are conformed to Christ, the premiere liturgist. Its starting point is catechumenal mortification, which leads to liquid regeneration and unguentary perfection and the food of immortality, all effected by an epiclesis of the Holy Spirit.

89.   If liturgy means sharing the life of Christ (washed in his resurrection, chrismated with his anointing, eating his body), and

if *askesis* means discipline (in the sense of forming), then liturgical asceticism is the discipline required to become an icon of Christ. His image is made visible in our faces.

90.   Gennadios Limouris defines icon as face. "The icon, then, is the Christ, the God who became a face. Then it is also the faces of all the friends of God who are our friends and who insist on including us in their circle. And already, the icon represents the Kingdom of God; anticipating the Kingdom of God, starting from the one place where we see this already anticipated: here on earth in the human face! The Kingdom of God is anticipated . . . starting from certain faces, certain old faces, fashioned by a long life, faces which have not been plunged into resentment or bitterness or the fear of death, faces of those who do not flinch as they approach death, faces that know precisely where they are, and have found again the mind of a child."[33] Ascetical faces.

91.   Plato called beauty the splendor of truth, but Evdokimov adds that truth's splendor cannot exist in the abstract. "In its fullness, truth requires a personalization and seeks to be 'enhypostazied,' that is, rooted and grounded in a person."[34] The splendor of God's truth is the beauty of Jesus, and the Church is an icon of Jesus' splendor repeated in each glorified face.

92.   The Church is called forth to stand before the world as an icon of the resurrection.

93.   Paul Claudel said it seems as if the acorn knows its destiny and carries within itself an active idea of the oak required of it, and in the same way it seems as if memory and foresight join together in the hearts of Adam's sons to deny the immediate the right to prevail. Asceticism is the cost of breaking the enchantment of the immediate.

94.   Already, one can participate in the eternal dimension.[35] There is an entity, called the Church, which God has brought into existence and is bringing to completion. Its charter is the incarnation of Jesus, in whom the divine and human mingled, and who is the firstborn of many brothers and sisters with whom he shares his life. Liturgical life is participation in Christ's life in the Father. It is enjoying by means of Holy Spirit the relationship Christ has with God.

95.   Liturgical life unravels death's shroud.

96.   Christian liturgists are born from a font that stood in a baptistry decorated like the Garden of Eden where death had no dominion. Christian liturgists are fed at an altar with an antidote to death that the fathers called the "medicine of immortality." And Christian liturgists are disciplined in an asceticism which is a sort of preemptive mortification and resurrection.

97.   Asceticism turns our allegiance away from the fading goods of the flesh to eternal goods of the spirit, not because the former are not good but because they fade. Liturgical asceticism consists of nothing but overcoming death by death, and being capacitated to contain the glory of God.

98.   To realize that we were made for eternity radically reorientates priorities, as the saints have always witnessed. Gregory of Nyssa says, "If you realize this you will not allow your eye to rest on anything of this world. Indeed, you will no longer marvel even at the heavens. For how can you admire the heavens, my [child], when you see that you are more permanent than they? For the heavens pass away, but you will abide for all eternity with Him who is forever."[36]

99.   Liturgical asceticism is an attitude toward the world which results from seeing the world in an eschatological light. That is the light that shines forth from the Divine Liturgy, as it did on Mt. Tabor. Liturgical theology is seeing with the eye of the dove the cosmos bathed in Taboric light.

100.   Though space, time, and matter will evanesce; they are capable of being made into a three-sided liturgical loom on which eternal life is woven, one day to be gently lifted off by the master weaver, without dropping a stitch, and fitted into his own radiant garment. The sepulcher becomes a birth canal.

---

1. Gilbert Chesterton, *Orthodoxy,* Ignatius Press in *The Collected Works,* vol. I (San Francisco: Ignatius Press, 1986) 301–2.

2. David Fagerberg, "Pseudo Academic Ecumenism," *Antiphon,* vol. 4:2, October 1999, 8–9.

3. Robert Taft, "The Structural Analysis of Liturgical Units," 317.

4. See Romano Guardini's *The Spirit of the Liturgy* (New York: Sheed & Ward, 1953) who contrasts a series of "personality types" who will have difficulty entering into the liturgy: individualist v. socialist, those who sharply define v. those who amalgamate body-soul, esthete v. grave and earnest person, public ritual v. private piety.

5. C. S. Lewis says he finds in the Eucharist "a hand from the hidden country [that] touches not only my soul but my body. . . . Here is big medicine and

strong magic. *Favete linguis.* When I say 'magic' I am not thinking of the paltry and pathetic techniques by which fools attempt and quacks pretend to control nature. I mean rather what is suggested by fairy-tale sentences like 'This is a magic flower, and if you carry it the seven gates will open to you of their own accord,' or 'This is a magic cave and those who enter it will renew their youth.' I should define magic in this sense as 'objective efficacy which cannot be further analysed.' " *Letters to Malcolm: Chiefly on Prayer* (New York: Harcourt, Brace, Jovanovich, 1964) 103.

6. See Fagerberg, "Traditional Liturgy and Liturgical Tradition," *Worship*, 72:6, Nov. 1998, 482–500.

7. Karl Rahner, "The Development of Dogma," *Theological Investigations*, vol. 1 (New York: Seabury, 1974) 68.

8. Archimandrite Vasileios, *Hymn of Entry*, 27 and 29.

9. Olivier Clement, *The Roots of Christian Mysticism* (Hyde Park, NY: New City Press, 1996) 251.

10. Alexander Schmemann, "Theology and Liturgical Tradition," 175.

11. Charles Williams, *Essential Writings in Spirituality and Theology*, ed. Charles Hefling (Boston: Cowly Publications, 1993) 13.

12. Columba Marmion, *Christ in His Mysteries*, (St. Louis: B. Herder Book Co., 1931) 233. See Fagerberg, "Theosis in a Roman Key? The Conferences of Columba Marmion," *Antiphon*, vol. 7:1, 2002, 30–39.

13. Oliver Clement, *Origins of Christian Mysticism*, 95. Rahner remarks somewhere that the Church is the uniformed part of the parade.

14. Andrew Louth, *Discerning the Mystery: An Essay on the Nature of Theology* (Oxford: Clarendon Press, 1983) 65.

15. Columba Marmion, *Christ, the Ideal of the Monk*, (London & Edinburgh: Sands, and St. Louis: Herder, 1922) 297.

16. Leonid Ouspensky, "The Meaning and Language of Icons," in *The Meaning of Icons*, eds. Ouspensky & Lossky (Crestwood, NY: St. Vladimir's Seminary Press, 1983) 28.

17. Maximus, "The Church's Mystagogy," *Maximus Confessor: Selected Writings* (New York: Paulist Press, 1985).

18. _____, 188

19. _____.

20. _____, emphasis added.

21. Paul Evdokimov, *The Art of the Icon*, 117.

22. _____, *The Art of the Icon*, 104.

23. See Fagerberg, "Cosmological Liturgy and a Sensible Priesthood," *New Blackfriars,* vol. 82:960, February 2001, 76–87.

24. C. S. Lewis, *The Screwtape Letters* (New York: MacMillan Co., 1944) 102.

25. Paul Evdokimov, *The Art of the Icon,* 28.

26. John Climacus, *The Ladder of Divine Ascent* (New York: Paulist Press, The Classics of Western Spirituality, 1982) 262.

27. David Fagerberg, "A Century on Liturgical Asceticism," *Diakonia,* vol. 31:1, 1998, 31–60

28. Step 14.

29. See Aidan Kavanagh, "Eastern Influences on the Rule of Saint Benedict," *Monasticism and the Arts* (Syracuse University Press, 1984) 58. Evagrius Ponticus, *The Praktikos & Chapters on Prayer* (Kalamazoo: Cistercian Publications, 1981) 33–39.

30. C. S. Lewis, *The Horse and His Boy,* (New York: Collier, 1970) 193.

31. Columba Marmion, *Christ in His Mysteries,* 50.

32. _____, *Life of the Soul,* (London & Edinburgh: Sands, and St. Louis: Herder, 1926) 45.

33. Gennadios Limouris, "The Microcosm and Macrocosm of the Icon: Theology, Spirituality and Worship in Colour," in *Icons, Windows on Eternity,* comp. Gennadios Limouris (Geneva: WCC Publications, Faith and Order Paper 147, 1990) 119.

34. Paul Evdokimov, 24.

35. For what follows, see Fagerberg, *The Cresset,* vol. 60:8, Michaelmas 1997, 15–17.

36. Gregory of Nyssa, *From Glory to Glory: Texts from Gregory of Nyssa's Mystical Writings,* Selected and Introduced by Jean Danielou, trans. Herbert Musurillo, (Crestwood, NY: St. Vladimir's Seminary Press, 1979) 163.

Index

Msgr. Reynold Hillenbrand
1904-1979

Monsignor Reynold Hillenbrand, ordained a priest by Cardinal George Mundelein in 1929, was Rector of St. Mary of the Lake Seminary from 1936 to 1944.

He was a leading figure in the liturgical and social action movement in the United States during the 1930s and worked to promote active, intelligent, and informed participation in the Church's liturgy.

He believed that a reconstruction of society would occur as a result of the renewal of the Christian spirit, whose source and center is the liturgy.

Hillenbrand taught that, since the ultimate purpose of Catholic action is to Christianize society, the renewal of the liturgy must undoubtedly play the key role in achieving this goal.

Hillenbrand Books® strives to reflect the spirit of Monsignor Reynold Hillenbrand's pioneering work by asking available innovative and scholarly resource that advance the liturgical and sacramental life of the Church.

About the Author

David W. Fagerberg is an Associate Professor of Liturgy at the University of Notre Dame and Senior Advisor, Notre Dame Center for Liturgy. He was the former acting director and professor of liturgical studies at the Liturgical Institute, University of St. Mary of the Lake, Mundelein Seminary. He holds an MDIV from Luther Northwestern Seminary; an MA in Liturgical Studies from St. John's University, Collegeville; an STM from Yale Divinity School and a PHD in liturgical theology from Yale University. Publications include *What Is Liturgical Theology?* (Liturgical Press, 1992); *The Size of Chesterton's Catholicism* (University of Notre Dame Press, 1998), *On Liturgical Asceticism* (Catholic University Press, 2012); *Chesterton is Everywhere*, (Emmaus Press, 2012) as well as journal articles in *Worship, America, New Blackfriars, Pro Ecclesia, Diakonia, Antiphon, Louvain Studies, Letter and Spirit, St. Vladimir's Theological Quarterly,* and *Logos.*